I0889229

New Politics in the Old South

New Politics in the Old South

Ernest F. Hollings in the Civil Rights Era

★ ★ ★

David T. Ballantyne

THE UNIVERSITY OF SOUTH CAROLINA PRESS

© 2016 University of South Carolina

Published by the University of South Carolina Press
Columbia, South Carolina 29208

www.sc.edu/uscpress

Manufactured in the United States of America

25 24 23 22 21 20 19 18 17 16
10 9 8 7 6 5 4 3 2 1

Library of Congress Cataloging-in-Publication Data
can be found at http://catalog.loc.gov/.

ISBN 978-1-61117-703-9 (cloth)
ISBN 978-1-61117-704-6 (ebook)

This book was printed on recycled paper with
30 percent postconsumer waste content.

For Kate

Contents

Illustrations

Acknowledgments

I am indebted to countless individuals and organizations who helped me during the course of this project. Tony Badger's patience and expertise greatly improved the quality of my work. Adam Fairclough, too, has been extremely generous with his time in offering me advice on research, teaching, and academic employment. I am also grateful to the conveners and participants of the American History Graduate Workshop at the University of Cambridge who reviewed preliminary versions of several chapter drafts. I owe thanks as well to the editorial staff at the University of South Carolina Press, especially Alex Moore, Linda Fogle, and Bill Adams, for their repeated assistance in bringing this project to fruition.

I have been fortunate to receive extraordinary levels of assistance from many archivists and librarians at the Hollings and South Caroliniana Libraries at the University of South Carolina, the Citadel Archives, the South Carolina Department of Archives and History, the South Carolina State Library, the U.S. Senate Historical Office, and the Johnson and Nixon Presidential Libraries. Patrick Scott, alongside the staff from the Hollings and South Caroliniana Libraries, made me feel welcome in Columbia throughout my stay there. In particular I must thank Herb Hartsook, who graciously responded to my constant questioning and put me in touch with many of the people I later interviewed.

My thanks go to Bob Ellis from the University of South Carolina's Institute for Southern Studies for his encouragement and assistance throughout my work in the state. The visiting fellowship provided by the institute enabled my prolonged study in South Carolina during the 2011–12 academic year. I am also the recipient of a Richard A. Baker Graduate Student Research Travel Grant from the Association of Centers for the Study of Congress and several funding grants from the Cambridge History Trust Funds and Gonville and Caius College, Cambridge.

For the images reproduced in this book, my thanks go to the Hollings Library's Kate Moore, Heather Moore of the U.S. Senate Historical Office, and Bill Barley. I am also indebted to the interviewees and correspondents themselves. Their willingness to engage with me added significantly to my understanding of the topic and the richness of my research. Beyond those cited in the endnotes, I am grateful to John Mark Dean and Joe Riley for talking with me;

and Michael Hollings, Hayes Mizell, and Nic Butler, who kindly corresponded with me about my project. Various historians, including Jim Cobb, Walter Edgar, David Farber, Philip Grose, Laura Kalman, Felicia Kornbluh, Thomas Lekan, Don Ritchie, Ellie Shermer, Bryant Simon, Pat Sullivan, and Kerry Taylor, took the time to discuss my work with me. Their suggestions have much improved this book.

Without the repeated encouragement and support of my whole family, especially my parents, this project would not have been possible. Finally I must thank my wife, Kate, whose proofreading, emotional support, and endless tolerance for all things South Carolina–related made my research vastly more manageable and enjoyable than it otherwise could have been.

Introduction

Ernest F. "Fritz" Hollings was a key figure in South Carolina and national political developments in the second half of the twentieth century. He was arguably the state's most influential Democrat in that period, serving more than fifty years in elective politics. By the time he retired in 2005, he was also the last Democrat to hold high-level statewide office in South Carolina, a remarkable turnaround in the partisan landscape of the formerly one-party Democratic state. First elected as a state representative from Charleston in 1948, Hollings won the state's governorship in 1958 and a U.S. Senate seat in 1966, which he held until his retirement thirty-eight years later. Having served alongside the party-switching Republican Strom Thurmond for thirty-six years, Hollings was the longest-serving junior senator in U.S. history.

Throughout his career Hollings was renowned for his willingness to voice what he perceived to be unpleasant truths. According to John West, who was elected governor himself in 1970, Hollings's closing speech to the General Assembly as governor in January 1963, in which he urged legislators to accept the desegregation of Clemson College peacefully, "simply deflated the strong, pro-segregation sentiment" in the state.[1] A racial moderate by South Carolina standards in the late 1950s and early 1960s, Hollings influenced his state in its grudging but peaceful move away from total defiance of the Supreme Court's *Brown v. Board of Education* ruling. When the national Democratic Party forthrightly embraced civil rights concerns, Hollings remained a Democrat, unlike Thurmond, and made a gradual but tangible shift away from segregationist politics in the late 1960s. By the early 1970s, he had embraced a degree of racial moderation. In contrast older southern Democrats such as Georgia senator Richard Russell or North Carolina's Sam Ervin continued to reject the legitimacy of black political participation and civil rights advances.

Known as the "bull-headed Dutchman" while studying at the Citadel, Hollings was renowned as an energetic and confident, sometimes abrasive, politician with an acid wit.[2] During his reelection campaign in 1986, he silenced his Republican opponent by agreeing take a drug test "if [he would] take an IQ test."[3] Meanwhile on *This Week with David Brinkley* in 1990, ABC's Sam Donaldson

★ *Hollings as a cadet at the Citadel.*
SOURCE: South Carolina Political Collections, University of South Carolina, Columbia.

discovered Hollings's harsh humor in a segment discussing textile protectionism. After Donaldson questioned Hollings on the origins of his suit (allegedly from Korea), Hollings replied, "Sam, if you want to personalize it, I got it right down the street from where you got that wig."[4]

Despite the occasionally blustery exterior, Hollings was a policy-oriented politician. From his championing as a state legislator of a sales tax to improve school facilities to his promotion of a technical training program as governor and his advocacy as a U.S. senator for expanded federal antihunger programs and ocean preservation measures, Hollings was concerned to make substantive policy gains. Vice President Joe Biden was sufficiently impressed by his Senate desk partner of thirty-two years that he proclaimed during a speech in 2010 that Hollings had "contributed more over the course of his life to the state of South Carolina than any man in all of political history in this state."[5]

Hollings's comparatively early shift away from supporting "massive resistance" in South Carolina and his advocacy of several progressive policy causes marked him as a moderate "New South" politician. His outlook was similar to the group of New South Democratic governors such as Jimmy Carter, Dale Bumpers, Reubin Askew, and John West, elected in 1970 in Georgia, Arkansas, Florida, and South Carolina, respectively. Yet unlike that group of moderate southern politicians, Hollings, elected to the Senate in 1966, needed to make negotiations around race in the late 1960s, at a moment when anger over the national Democratic Party's racial and social policies temporarily boosted the newly emergent state Republican parties across the South. The adaptation of South Carolina Democrats to large-scale African American voting took place against the backdrop of significant Republican gains. During the decade African Americans also began to register to vote in significant numbers and cast their ballots overwhelmingly for Democratic candidates.

South Carolina Democrats, almost all of whom had previously promoted racial segregation and courted the votes of segregationist whites, faced the challenge of making sufficient accommodation to the interests of the state's newly enfranchised blacks without alienating their historic white support base. Like Thurmond, Ervin, and numerous other southern senators, Hollings voted against civil rights measures in the late 1960s and opposed the confirmation of the first African American Supreme Court nominee, Thurgood Marshall. Hollings, however, made small but tangible accommodations with African Americans in South Carolina at this time. Meanwhile the justifications he offered for his voting behavior demonstrated the balancing act he played in responding sufficiently to black demands while not alienating conservative white voters, many of whom voted for the hardline presidential candidate George Wallace in 1968. The examination of this small-scale accommodation provides great insight into both the fluidity of southern politics in the 1960s and the dimensions of southern political "moderation" at this time.

Before now there has been no sustained scholarly study of Hollings's career. Previous scholars have examined his role in the white South Carolinian response to civil rights pressures in the 1950s and early 1960s and his efforts to limit foreign textile imports throughout his career, while Hollings published a memoir himself in 2008.[6] There have been numerous scholarly accounts of Hollings's Senate counterpart Thurmond, yet the adaptation of South Carolina Democrats, the flip side of the success of Thurmond's conservative Republicanism, has remained understudied.[7]

This book is not a traditional cradle-to-retirement biography. Although Hollings was one of five children, little personal correspondence between him and his siblings or wider family is available in the major archival collection documenting his career. The present book addresses Hollings's prepolitical life and life outside of politics, but these are not its main focuses. Rather it uses Hollings's career as a lens for examining the upheaval in southern politics and society between the 1940s and 1970s, dates that span his earliest campaign for elective office to his successful reelection to a second full Senate term. By 1975 he became truly electorally entrenched and voted for an extension of the Voting Rights Act for the first time. Beyond offering an account of Hollings's career, this hybrid of biography and political history offers insight into the major social and political changes affecting life in the American South since 1945.

Hollings was a key figure in the movement of southern Democrats away from openly endorsing white supremacy and toward acknowledging the interests of racial minorities, however halting and reluctant that change was. His career path demonstrated how a relative racial moderate could negotiate the period of massive resistance in the 1950s, and furthers the understanding of the interplay between civil rights pressures and the actions of white South Carolinian politicians. Moreover Hollings negotiated the politically troublesome issues of civil rights and voting rights legislation, school busing, and divisive Supreme Court nomination battles in the 1960s and early 1970s, while remaining acceptable to both his conservative white constituents and the typically more liberal black electorate, issues that derailed the careers of several moderate southern Democrats at that time. This element of Hollings's career offers a great case study of the route he took toward embracing racial change at a time when there remained substantial opposition to civil rights initiatives from his white constituents and when the Republican Party was gaining popularity in his state. Hollings also negotiated an emerging cultural politics, especially over religious issues, which often joined the cluster of concerns held by conservative Americans.

South Carolina underwent profound demographic change during Hollings's career. In 1940 more than 75 percent of the state's 1.9 million citizens lived in rural areas. The state's population was 57 percent white and 43 percent black, although rural farm areas of the state had a majority-black population.[8] The largest portion of the state electorate comprised whites who lived in rural, majority-black settings.[9] By 1980 the state's population had increased to 3.1 million, of whom 69 percent were white, 30 percent black, and 1 percent of Spanish-speaking origin.[10] Fifty-four percent of the state's residents lived in urban areas, up from 48 percent in 1970.[11] South Carolina enjoyed a great increase in per capita income relative to the national average: residents earned 80 percent of the national average income in 1980, compared with less than 60 percent in 1950.[12]

Of the manufacturing jobs in the state in 1940, the textile industry, which almost entirely excluded blacks, was dominant.[13] The widespread involvement of politicians in industrial boosterism was beginning, alongside the ongoing militarization of the landscape in the early 1940s. Fort Jackson in Columbia was reactivated in 1939, air bases were opened in Lexington and Sumter Counties, while Charleston's Navy Yard increased its production.[14] Federal military spending became increasingly important to the state's economy after World War II, with the location of a hydrogen bomb production plant near Aiken in 1950 and numerous other facilities over the next two decades.[15] Charleston's Democratic congressman Mendel Rivers was essential in bringing military facilities to his district. A colleague joked that if Rivers "puts anything else in Charleston, the whole place will sink completely from sight from the sheer weight of the military installations."[16] Rivers's relentless acquisition of defense spending was part of a region-wide trend. Across the South in 1973, employees in defense-related industries outnumbered the combined total of those in apparel, textiles, and synthetics.[17]

Beyond South Carolinian and southern politics, Hollings's career impacted American politics more generally, especially in the evolution of the U.S. Senate and the emergence of a national political consensus on civil rights issues by the mid-1970s. Hollings became a senator when the identity of the institution was in considerable flux. In the 1960s the Senate as a whole became less conservative, and senators became more publicly prominent in the proposal and shaping of policy solutions thanks to the increase in the number of liberal senators and the greater institutional clout they carried as they accumulated seniority.[18] Ira Shapiro, a staff member for various Democratic senators in the 1970s and 1980s, dubbed the institution between 1963 and 1980 the "Great Senate."[19] In contrast historian Lewis Gould claimed that "the capacity of the Senate to play a constructive role in national politics had significantly slipped during the 1970s," while the crafting of legislation often took a backseat to reelection concerns owing to "the increasing effect of outside money on campaigns and the resulting emphasis on the 'money chase.'"[20] Hollings viewed the increased cost of campaigns as a corrosive influence on politics, supported the passage of laws requiring contributions disclosure and contribution and expenditure limits in federal elections, and especially after the Supreme Court's 1976 *Buckley v. Valeo* decision, criticized the influence of money in the political process.[21] Though no liberal by national standards, Hollings was an active participant in the movement of senators toward publicly advocating policy solutions.[22] His record was often surprising for a southern senator, especially in his advocacy for expanding federal antihunger programs and ocean preservation and his qualified opposition to the Vietnam War in the early 1970s.

Hollings's career provides a counternarrative to historiographical interpretations that privilege conservative and reactionary trends in southern politics after World War II. The emergence of a conservative Republican Party that capitalized on the disillusionment of many conservative white voters toward the social, economic, and foreign policies of the national Democratic Party was undeniably a central development in southern politics in the second half of the twentieth century, especially after the passage of the Civil Rights Act and Voting Rights Act in 1964 and 1965, respectively. Some disaffected Democratic politicians, such as Strom Thurmond, made an early switch to the GOP, while many other politically entrenched southern Democrats continued to pursue economically and racially conservative courses until they could no longer win nomination from an increasingly black Democratic primary electorate. Hollings, however, represented a separate trend, that of Democrats who adapted to the changed politics of the 1960s while pursuing a relatively progressive political course. Politicians such as

Hollings, the New South group of Democratic governors elected in 1970, and Terry Sanford of North Carolina represented the more liberal group of southern politicians who enjoyed state-level success. While Hollings was at times an atypical southern senator, his behavior in the 1960s and 1970s provided a model for adaptation and survival as a politically moderate southern Democrat. His approach to voting rights, military spending, and social and cultural issues was mirrored by numerous southern Democrats in the Senate in the 1980s and 1990s.[23] Hollings's career demonstrated an alternative to hard-edged conservatism, one that was conspicuously successful throughout his Senate tenure. As a politician Hollings had a great impact on his state's trajectory in economic and racial affairs. His legislative legacy is evident at both the local and national level.

★ ★ ★ CHAPTER 1 ★ ★ ★

From Charleston to Columbia

The fourth of five children, Ernest F. "Fritz" Hollings was born on January 1, 1922, in Charleston, South Carolina. The grandson of German immigrants and a Lutheran, he was not a member of the "patrician" class of Charlestonians, who typically resided south of Broad Street. He lived farther up the peninsula in the middle-class Hampton Park Terrace section, at 338 President Street. His father, Adolph, ran A. G. Hollings Paper Company, a business that sold brown paper bags to grocery stores and schools, while his mother, Wilhelmine, was a housewife. Hollings's uncle J. D. Ernest "Major" Meyer, whose law practice Fritz later joined, also lived with the family. Growing up in the 1920s and 1930s, Hollings was one of the generation of politicians whose value system was shaped by the experiences of the Great Depression. After his paper business failed, Hollings's father worked as a salesman for the Charleston Paper Company.[1] In his unsuccessful run for the 1984 Democratic presidential nomination, Hollings's biographical material recalled how the collapse of his father's business during the Depression taught Hollings "the value of hard work and responsibility at a young age."[2]

Although Hollings played down its importance, he had an unusual entry into South Carolina Democratic politics, in that he attended the Republican National Convention in Philadelphia in 1940 as part of the state party's racially integrated delegation.[3] He attended the convention as an eighteen-year-old page for the "Tieless Joe" Tolbert faction of the state party. At the time Hollings's uncle was a member of the tiny state GOP, nicknamed the "Post Office" Republican Party, since its only apparent purpose was for its members to receive patronage appointments when there was a Republican in the White House. Major Meyer served as the Republican appointee for U.S. district attorney for the eastern district of South Carolina from 1922 to 1930.[4] Hollings later emphasized that he never held a close affiliation with the state GOP: "That was it [attending the 1940 Republican National Convention]. . . . I never have been to a Republican Party meeting in South Carolina, period."[5] Despite getting an early taste of Republican politics, he could have had no illusions that the Democratic Party was the only viable avenue to political success in South Carolina in the 1940s. Although the Republican

★ *Hollings (right) during service in World War II, 1943.*
SOURCE: South Carolina Political Collections, University of South Carolina, Columbia.

Party was competitive in presidential elections in South Carolina in the 1950s, it did not elect its first member of the state legislature in the twentieth century until 1961.[6]

Financed by his uncle, Hollings went to college at the Citadel, a military institute in Charleston, in 1938 at the age of sixteen.[7] He graduated in the class of 1942 alongside several others who went on to figure prominently in South Carolina politics, including future governor John West and future congressmen Jim Mann and Hugo Sims. Upon leaving the Citadel, Hollings served in World War II in North Africa, Corsica, France, and Germany, where he commanded a searchlight and antiaircraft artillery unit for the 353rd Coast Artillery Battalion of the Seventh Army. He was honorably relieved from active duty in February 1946 as a captain, after he had received five bronze service stars, the Bronze Star Medal, and the American Campaign Medal.[8] Hollings's Citadel class was remarkable for the number of graduates who went on to hold elective office, a fact attributed by West to the "special but demanding kind" of public service required during World War II.[9]

Once he had returned from Europe, Hollings enrolled at the University of South Carolina (USC) law school, where he graduated in August 1947. After a brief period working as a lawyer at his uncle's firm, Meyer, Goldberg and Hollings, he ran for election to the South Carolina House in 1948. Here Hollings was an "accidental politician," as he later described himself.[10] At the time in South Carolina, it was illegal for lawyers to advertise for business, given the state's barratry law. As a consequence many lawyers seeking clients would run for political office and let their profession be known in their campaign literature.[11] The Jewish partner in the law firm, David S. "Rocky" Goldberg, had run twice for the South Carolina House already and lost on both occasions, so Hollings was pressured into entering the race.[12] He won election to the Charleston House delegation and actually led the ticket in the 1948 election. In his memoir he attributed his success to the good relations his late father had built with local businesses as a result of his efforts to continue repaying debts after his company ceased to function.[13]

During his first House campaign, Hollings marked himself out as somewhat enlightened on racial matters compared with the prevailing political climate in the state. The 1948 Democratic primary, effectively the general election in South Carolina politics at the time, took place against the backdrop of the *Brown v. Baskin* district court decision. *Brown v. Baskin* ruled that South Carolina had to open its Democratic primary to black voters. South Carolina's political class had taken some time to acquiesce to the abolition of the white primary. The *Smith v. Allwright* Supreme Court decision of 1944 established the precedent that suffrage restrictions based on race in primary elections were unconstitutional. Upon the issuing of the *Smith* ruling, Gov. Olin Johnston called South Carolina's legislators to an emergency session, where they eliminated all state laws mentioning the Democratic Party. The party thus operated as a private club and would not be subject to *Smith*. After the *Elmore v. Rice* decision of 1947 outlawed this attempt to circumvent *Smith* in South Carolina, the state Democratic Party then adopted a lengthy loyalty oath that required voters to swear that they supported the principles of the Democratic Party, racial segregation in social, religious, and educational spheres, and states' rights and opposed the "proposed federal so-called FEPC law." This oath too was thrown out in federal court by Judge Waties Waring in *Brown v. Baskin* as "a clear and flagrant evasion of the law."[14] In protest against *Brown v. Baskin*, several Democrats pulled out of the Democratic primary and chose to run only in the general election. The *Charleston News and Courier*, described by one embittered observer as "conservative, if not downright reactionary, not only on the race issue but in all political, economic and social questions,"[15] sent a questionnaire to each candidate that asked, "Do you or do you not solicit the Negro vote?" In an early example of his acid wit, which later caused him some political difficulty as a senator, Hollings responded simply, "Do you or do you not solicit Negro subscribers and advertisers to your newspaper?"[16]

Nineteen forty-eight was also the year that South Carolina governor Strom Thurmond ran for president as a States' Rights Democrat or "Dixiecrat." The Dixiecrat movement was dominated by economically and racially conservative black belt whites as well as industrial and agricultural elites, groups for whom grassroots civil rights activism and President Truman's embrace of civil rights legislation in 1948 constituted the "last straw" for their support of the national Democratic presidential candidate.[17] The Dixiecrat ticket carried four Deep South states: Alabama, Louisiana, Mississippi, and South Carolina. In each case that the Dixiecrats were successful, their candidates were listed as the official Democratic nominees. This was the case in South Carolina, where Hollings voted for Thurmond as the state's official Democratic presidential candidate.[18]

There were many other World War II veterans elected to serve in South Carolina's state government alongside Hollings in 1948. Of the House's 124 members elected in 1948, 59 were veterans, of whom only 4 had served before the war.[19] Hollings viewed the war as having had a formative effect on him and other returning veterans: in an oral history interview in 2008, he claimed that "it shaped my life and all of us veterans in public office." Moreover the experiences veterans had endured made them more aware of the shortcomings of their home states. Hollings recalled that once elected to the legislature, "we immediately went to work playing catch-up ball."[20] Historian Jennifer Brooks observed a similar trend in her study of the impact of returning World War II veterans on Georgia politics. Military service directly impacted veterans' political views "because it had exposed them to a more modernized world. The paved highways, efficient sanitation systems, advanced educational facilities, and public health services encountered in the course of their wartime journeys often revealed glaring deficiencies at home." The war had a more complex impact on the state's racial politics, though, as both progressive and reactionary white Georgian veterans used the legacy of the war as a justification for their own racial views: they disagreed whether World War II had been fought to ensure freedom at home and abroad or to maintain the southern system of race relations. Even the progressive veterans generally offered a racially limited political vision: in Georgia "it was the rare white southerner who had the moral conviction and courage to risk community censure, opprobrium, and personal safety for the cause of black political freedom."[21] Hollings was not one of those rare white southerners. Although unwilling to challenge the racial status quo at this stage in his career, once in office, like many other veterans turned politicians, he began to push for ameliorations of his state's long-neglected system of public services, particularly its schools.

As a state representative, Hollings immediately became involved in efforts to improve the state's school system through the implementation of a sales tax. In November 1948, the day after being sworn in, he traveled with the Charleston County superintendent for education, Creighton Frampton, to a single-story black elementary school on Johns Island ironically named the Promised Land.[22] Inside there was one stove in the middle of the classroom to keep the building warm. One teacher was conducting two classes simultaneously, one consisting of forty-two pupils and the other of forty-seven, with three children sharing each desk. Frampton told Hollings that "the white schools are not much better."[23] Hollings later recounted details of his visit in talks to civic clubs, telling one such Charleston group: "On the walls were the U.S. and South Carolina Constitutions guaranteeing every child, white or black, an equal chance. I don't think you are proud of things like that. I know I am not."[24]

To address the sorry state of public schooling in the state, in his first term Hollings advocated for a sales tax to fund a program of school improvement, modeled on the tax already in place in North Carolina. Lacking support in the state senate, he introduced and had passed a resolution to appoint a six-member House committee, which he chaired, to study the implementation of a possible sales tax in June 1950. Although not as egregious as it had once been, in 1950 there remained a startling disparity in educational funding for black and white pupils. In that year white schools received 2.4 times as much in per-pupil expenditures as their black counterparts.[25] With the help of the hugely prestigious incoming governor, James F. Byrnes, the bill providing for a 3 percent sales tax to fund a projected $75 million school construction program was passed during the 1951 legislative session. Historian Numan Bartley described the passage of the tax as "a tribute to the governor's prestige."[26] Hollings offered a similar analysis: "We couldn't get it [sales tax] by the Senate, and Byrnes helped us get those folks. He publicly embarrassed the senators, and passed a three percent sales tax."[27]

Of course the main reason for the passage of the sales tax was not simply to improve the quality of black schooling in the state: rather it was central to the state's defense of racially segregated schools. As Steve Griffith, a state representative in the early 1960s, noted, Byrnes persuaded the legislature to pass the sales tax "on a segregation mode."[28] In March 1948 black parents in Clarendon County, a majority-black county in the state's lowcountry, filed *Levi Pearson v. Clarendon County and School District No. 26*, which called for the local school district to provide a school bus system for black children to use to travel to school. Clarendon County provided one of the starkest examples of racially separate but unequal school facilities in America, where blacks made up about 70 percent of the county's population, yet the county spent three times as much on the education of each white child as on black children, and $112,000 more overall on white schooling than black. While the county provided thirty buses to transport its white children, it would not extend this service to black children, who often had to walk for miles to and from school along roads that were frequently flooded owing to the overflow from the nearby Pinopolis Dam.[29] After it was discovered that the plaintiff, Levi Pearson, paid taxes in nearby District 5, the case was dropped.

Urged on by National Association for the Advancement of Colored People (NAACP) attorney Thurgood Marshall, a group of African Americans in Clarendon County subsequently filed the *Briggs v. Elliot* case in May 1950, which demanded the equalization of the obviously unequal school facilities in the county.[30] This suit was dropped in December 1950 in favor of a frontal attack on the constitutionality of racial segregation in public schooling, which contended that it was a violation of the equal protection clause of the Fourteenth Amendment. A three-judge federal court heard the new case in May 1951. The legal defense for the Clarendon County officials rested on the contention that school segregation did not violate the Fourteenth Amendment and hence all the plaintiffs could demand was the equalization of school facilities. Pointing to the school equalization program recently passed by the state legislature, attorney Robert McCormick Figg Jr., a close confidant of Byrnes, argued for "reasonable" time to equalize school facilities. It is in this context that Byrnes's call in his inaugural address for "substantial equality in school facilities" and the passage of the 3 percent sales tax should be understood. In May 1951 the district court ruled 2–1 in favor of the defendants in the *Briggs* case but demanded that equality of educational facilities and opportunities for black students be provided "promptly" and "in good faith."[31]

The school construction program was one of several "preparedness measures" passed during Byrnes's governorship in case the constitutionality of racial segregation in public schooling was invalidated. These measures included the empowering of local school authorities to sell or lease public property to private individuals and the implementation of a local pupil assignment law that required students who wished to transfer schools to receive written permission from the school superintendents of both schools.[32]

More importantly, at Byrnes's behest a fifteen-man committee consisting of legislators and gubernatorial appointees was established to study threats to school segregation in 1951.[33] This group soon became known as the Gressette Committee after its chairman, Calhoun County senator L. Marion Gressette. Gressette later claimed in an oral history interview that the committee's purpose was "to provide the best means to prepare [the state] for integration."[34] The characterization offered by Judge Matthew Perry, one of the key NAACP attorneys to argue civil rights cases in South Carolina, is more accurate, however: "The role of that committee was to seek, through the introduction of legislation, and through other means, ways to stymie and thwart the efforts of blacks to desegregate state-supported institutions and practices."[35] Likewise in a statewide television and radio address given in November 1955, Gov. George Bell Timmerman provided a valuable description of the committee's purpose: "[the committee] has worked untiringly to secure information and to formulate plans for the preservation of our separate but equal public school system, within the framework of the law."[36] From its creation in 1951, the Gressette Committee monitored all proposed legislation on racial matters and recommended other legislation it deemed necessary to ward off racial integration.

One historian has argued that Hollings was "part of the inner circle masterminding South Carolina's strategy of defiance" in the 1950s.[37] Hollings was close enough to Byrnes to be appointed by him to travel to Washington as part of the state's legal defense for *Briggs*, which was incorporated into the *Brown v. Board of Education* case, when it was initially argued before the Supreme Court in 1952.[38] It seems unlikely, however, that Byrnes and Hollings shared much more than a professional relationship. If they had, it is doubtful that Byrnes's protégé Donald Russell, his old law partner and assistant secretary of state, would have run against Hollings for the South Carolina governorship in 1958. In an oral history, Hollings recalled that "Byrnes really raised Donald Russell" and "was giving him very sound political advice."[39] Neither Byrnes in his memoir, nor David Robertson in his biography of Byrnes, mention Hollings at all.[40] While cordial, Hollings's relationship with Byrnes does not seem to have extended beyond a professional capacity.

Hollings also developed an easy rapport with powerbrokers in the state legislature. At the beginning of the 1951 legislative session, he was affirmed unanimously as the Speaker pro tempore of the House. The powerful Speaker of the House and a member of the so-called Barnwell Ring, Sol Blatt, was a political ally. Thurmond coined the term "Barnwell Ring" when running for governor in 1946 to describe the small group of Barnwell legislators, whom he alleged to be an unaccountable clique with excessive influence over the legislative process. According to a biography of the longtime House Speaker, Hollings became a "close personal, as well as official," friend of Blatt and graduated from his "School of the Gavel" in the House.[41] When he ran for the governorship in 1958, Hollings received Blatt's backing as well as the endorsement of Senate Finance Committee chairman Edgar Brown, another influential Barnwell-based politician. In his study of southern politics, V. O. Key described Brown as a virtual "prime minister" in the South Carolina legislative process.[42] At the outset of the 1959 legislative session, Blatt gave the newly inaugurated Governor Hollings a full-throated endorsement. Hollings was "a young, able, vigorous and experienced man who has pledged himself to the further development of the state. He got his start and learned the right ways as a member of this House."[43] Hollings's easy relationship with the state's political elite was essential for the implementation of his legislative agenda once he became governor.

Despite Hollings's closeness to the state's most important politicians, his racial views were somewhat more moderate than those of many of his peers. Although undoubtedly a segregationist through the 1950s and early 1960s, he did not advocate the same degree of defiance suggested by the state's other leading politicians. Governor Byrnes announced in 1951 that South Carolina would "reluctantly" abandon its public school system rather than integrate it. He also promoted a referendum on the repeal of the state constitution's provision that required a state-supported public school system, an early measure employed to stave off school desegregation in South Carolina. The bill passed the legislature in February 1952 and was approved by the voting public by a 68–32 margin in November of that year. Speaker Blatt gained notoriety in 1966, once some public school desegregation had taken place, for his racially tinged plea against the reinstatement of the compulsory school attendance law. He asked rhetorically: "Do you want some 16-year-old so-and-so holding the hand of your little granddaughter in the classroom?"[44] There is little doubt as to the skin color of the "so-and-so" in question.

Although Hollings voted for the referendum on the state's requirement to provide public education in 1952 as a member of the House, he later opposed the abolition of public schooling.[45] As lieutenant governor he claimed that "it's foolish to even consider for a moment that abolishing public education is the solution. . . . We can never abandon our public school system." Rather Hollings suggested an alternative pupil placement system premised on local control, which he thought would pass constitutional muster. Trustees would be able to assign pupils to schools on nonracial bases such as "sex, aptitude, proximity of school to home and available classroom space."[46] Similar pupil placement schemes were enacted in Mississippi, North Carolina, Alabama, and Florida.[47] In his study of the "moderate" southern governors James P. Coleman of Mississippi, Luther H. Hodges of North Carolina, and LeRoy Collins of Florida, historian Anders Walker argued that ostensibly nonracial pupil placement plans formed "the foundations for a new legal idiom through which racial inequality could be maintained in the post-*Brown* era."[48] While Hollings's opposition to school closures differentiated him from some massive resisters in South Carolina, such "moderation" was far removed from supporting racially integrated schooling.

Several other episodes from his early career hinted at Hollings's relative moderation on racial issues, at least by contemporary standards. In 1950 he authored an antilynching bill, signed into law by Governor Thurmond, which classified lynching as a capital offense and made mob violence not resulting in death a second-degree crime.[49] The antilynching bill was viewed, at least by Thurmond, as a response to the nationally prominent lynching of the epileptic African American Willie Earle in Pickens County in 1947, for which all twenty-eight suspects were acquitted in a jury trial.[50] Meanwhile, as a member of the Charleston delegation, in 1952 Hollings nominated an African American to serve on the Charleston school board. Although the nomination was defeated, Hollings received a letter from the Charleston branch of the NAACP thanking him for his action.[51] He later stated that this was a simple matter of representation, as the board already had a Jew, a Catholic, a Lutheran, and a Greek member: "Everybody had a slot on the board, but the blacks."[52]

In 1954 Hollings announced his candidacy for the lieutenant governorship, a decision that angered his law partners in Charleston, who instead wanted him to return to practice law.[53] By the time of Hollings's inauguration in January 1955, he had been locked out of his former law practice, after a professional and personal break from his uncle.[54] By then the "accidental politician" had acquired a taste for the uses of political power. However he faced a major political obstacle. The son of U.S. senator Burnet Maybank, Burnet Maybank Jr., a fellow war veteran and Citadel man, was interested in entering the race as well. In a race generating low levels of public exposure, as was likely with a lieutenant governor's contest, the younger Maybank would win on account of his name recognition alone. Recognizing this problem, Hollings requested a meeting with Maybank Sr., at which he told the bemused senator that he planned to run against him.[55] If Hollings was going to lose, he "might as well get beat first class, not waste all that time and effort."[56] A few days later, Maybank assured Hollings that his son, in fact, had decided not to enter politics that year.[57] Hollings's brinkmanship had worked.

As a sign of the limited scope for dissent from the state's racial orthodoxy at this time, Hollings's eventual primary opponent for the lieutenant governorship in 1954, the first-time state senator Clator Arrants, used the nomination of the black board member for the Charleston schools as proof of Hollings's integrationist proclivities.[58] This issue followed him into his run for the governorship four years later, where one anti-Hollings advertisement reminded readers that he had "voted for a negro [*sic*] to govern the public schools. . . . Integration of school boards means mixing the races in the schools."[59]

The race for the lieutenant governorship was largely fought over local issues. The major areas of disagreement between the two candidates were the state's recently passed sales tax, which Hollings had championed and Arrants had opposed, and the local option (whether a county could choose for itself whether to sell liquor or not).[60] As Hollings remarked in his memoir, "nobody paid much attention to the Lieutenant Governor's race."[61] Despite support for integration being "pure fire and brimstone" in 1954, Hollings won the Democratic nomination for the lieutenant governorship with two-thirds of the vote and, facing no Republican opposition in the general election, was duly elected.[62]

Hollings served alongside Timmerman, who beat Columbia mayor Lester Bates in a bruising Democratic primary in June 1954. In both Georgia and South Carolina, historian Bartley concluded, *Brown v. Board of Education* "was *the* issue, inundating all others, as politicians maneuvered frantically to occupy the extreme segregationist position."[63] Bates criticized Timmerman's triple school system plan (one for whites, one for blacks, and one for those who wanted racial integration) as allowing some racial integration, while Timmerman charged that Bates was the NAACP's favored candidate.[64] Timmerman won easily. Dolly Hamby, a member of the advertising firm that worked for Timmerman in the campaign, recalled that *Ebony* magazine's decision to endorse Bates "was all we needed. We never used it; we just passed the word around."[65] Timmerman, a lawyer from then-rural Lexington County and a World War II veteran, had served as lieutenant governor for the previous eight years. Like other conservative and reactionary veterans, his primary concern was to maintain the state's racial customs.[66] Described as "a humorless and fanatical segregationist" by Howard Quint, who before leaving South Carolina wrote a monograph on the state's race relations in 1958, Timmerman followed an inflexible approach to the perceived threats of segregation and communism throughout his governorship.[67]

Timmerman's equation of communism with racial integration was apparent in his demand in 1957 for the resignation of three prointegration members of Allen University's faculty, two of them white, who had been cited in House Un-American Activities reports. The state board of education suspended Allen's teacher training accreditation when the private university's board of trustees refused to dismiss the faculty members in question. Simultaneous with the dispute over the objectionable faculty members, five white Hungarian refugees had enrolled at Allen, marking the first modern breakdown of racial segregation in education in South Carolina, albeit in a private, religious institution. Timmerman explained the removal of Allen's accreditation: he and the chairman of Allen's board of trustees had sought to protect the student body from "atheism" and "communism."[68] As one historian asserted, by 1958 the threats of communism and integration were "almost interchangeable" in Timmerman's thought.[69] Likewise when Timmerman forced Clemson College to return a grant from the Atomic Energy Commission that carried with it a nondiscrimination clause, he claimed publicly that the inclusion of the word *creed* in the grant's conditions meant that the college could be compelled to admit a communist onto the atomic energy program.[70] As Timmerman's private correspondence with Clemson trustees reveals, however, his central concern was to preserve segregation.[71]

Timmerman's tenure as governor was a grim one for advocates of racial integration. Legislators promoted de facto "interposition" against the Supreme Court's *Brown* ruling, a constitutional doctrine that contended that states could interpose their own sovereignty in the place of the federal government to prevent apparently obnoxious laws from taking effect. Such legislative defiance formed part of a wider pattern of "massive resistance" to the decision across the Deep South and several Outer South states. Under the guidance of the Gressette Committee, the General Assembly passed a huge volume of prosegregation measures during Timmerman's governorship, especially during the 1956 legislative session, which Quint described as passing anti-integration and anti-NAACP laws at "almost a mass production rate."[72]

A common feature of South Carolina's legislative reaction to the *Brown* decision was the harassment of the state's NAACP. South Carolina was one of five states to pass a law requiring the organization to register and provide complete lists of its members and financial contributors, a law that was later invalidated by the Supreme Court in 1958.[73] In the 1956 session, South Carolina's legislature passed a law rendering NAACP members ineligible for state employment. The continued harassment was particularly apparent in the dismissal of twenty-four black teachers from Orangeburg who refused to sign an oath of nonmembership in the NAACP in 1956. After a suit contesting the state law that prohibited NAACP members from public employment reached the Supreme Court, the General Assembly replaced it with an ostensibly nonracial alternative that left NAACP members open to reprisal: it required state employees to provide complete disclosure "as to active or honorary membership in or affiliation with all membership associations and organizations."[74]

As lieutenant governor Hollings was well versed in racial demagoguery, particularly toward the NAACP. In October 1955 he described the group as "against our way of life in the South." He continued: "If the U.S. Supreme Court can declare certain organizations as subversive, I believe South Carolina can declare the NAACP both subversive and illegal."[75] Hollings capitalized on the potency of the race issue in the aftermath of the *Brown* decision and continued to do so in his campaign for governor in 1958. Resistance to *Brown* was, as historian Tony Badger has argued, "a top-down phenomenon."[76]

In addition to the legislative resistance espoused by lawmakers, White Citizens' Councils also emerged to enforce racial conformity. Originating in Indianola, Mississippi, in 1954, the Citizens' Councils had spread across the South by the next year. In South Carolina the first council was organized in August 1955 at Elloree, in Orangeburg County, in response to a school desegregation petition by black parents. By the summer of 1956, the councils had as many as forty thousand members in South Carolina, concentrated in the lowcountry areas of the state, where African Americans were most numerous.[77] They promoted supposedly respectable forms of resistance to racial desegregation. Although the councils soon moved away from openly endorsing the economic coercion of black activists, the organized boycott became "the trademark of the councils." In July 1955 Robert Patterson, executive secretary of the Mississippi Association of Citizens' Councils, remarked that "we do not recommend economic pressure. . . . But of course we don't denounce 'freedom of choice' in business arrangements. If employers fire their help, that's their business."[78]

As whites were economically dominant in many rural areas, they could exercise considerable coercive force against African Americans seeking desegregated schools. The reaction in Orangeburg was typical. Following the filing of a desegregation petition in July 1955, economic retaliation soon followed, led by the mayor and the head of the local Citizens' Council. After the *Orangeburg Times Democrat* printed the names of the petitioners, many were fired from their jobs, evicted from rented homes, and denied new insurance policies and credit and had their mortgages recalled. By November 1955 only twenty-six of the original fifty-seven petitioners remained listed on the petition.[79] African Americans led by the NAACP soon organized a counterboycott against twenty-three white businesses owned by council members or council sympathizers in the town.[80] Similar white economic reprisals against black petitioners took place in Clarendon County as well.[81] The various legislative and more informal forms of harassment against black activists depressed NAACP membership in the mid-1950s. Mirroring a regional trend, South Carolina's NAACP membership numbers declined from 8,226 to 2,202 between 1955 and 1957.[82]

"Respectable" methods of enforcing racial conformity were accompanied by violence directed against both black activists and whites deemed insufficiently vehement in their support of segregation. Rev. Joseph A. Delaine, an African American leader of an organization that sponsored the Clarendon County school case, was the subject of violent reprisals. First his church in Lake City was burned down. Later he returned fire against two assailants who had fired shots into his house from a car. For this retaliation Delaine was indicted for assault with intent to kill. He fled South Carolina and never returned.[83] In 1954 the white editor of the *Florence Morning News*, Jack O'Dowd, editorialized that the *Brown* decision was the law of the land and ought to be obeyed. After two years of physical harassment, which included being chased by Ku Klux Klan members on one occasion, O'Dowd left the state in 1956.[84] In his final editorial for the paper, he described himself not as a "pro-integrationist" but rather as an "anti-pro-segregationist."[85]

The bombing of the house of Claudia Sanders and subsequent acquittal of the assailants in November 1957 highlights the pressure exercised on white South Carolinians to conform socially in the 1950s. Sanders, a member of a prominent family in Gaffney, had contributed an article to *South Carolinians Speak: A Moderate Approach to Race Relations*, a publication that countenanced the possibility of racial integration in the future. After the book's publication, several local Ku Klux Klan members dynamited the Sanders home, although none of the inhabitants were injured. After one of the bombers, who had signed a full confession, mysteriously suffered a violent death at his workplace, an all-white jury acquitted the other defendants after two and a half hours of discussion. The trial took place amid a total absence of condemnation of the bombing from any prominent public official. As historian Timothy Tyson observed, "The silence was louder than the dynamite."[86]

Alongside defending racial segregation, governors across the South became active in the pursuit of outside industrial investment in the post–World War II era. Speaking in June 1958, Hollings captured the rationale of many southern boosters in their pursuit of new industry: "new industry means new jobs, and new jobs means new payrolls."[87] By 1964 southern governors had become "the *de facto* executive directors of the state chambers of commerce."[88]

South Carolina governors took on a greater role as industrial boosters from about 1939, when Gov. Burnet R. Maybank proposed the creation of a state board of development.[89] Coordinated economic development efforts became more aggressive after World War II, as southern communities competed among themselves for industries that sought to move away from the higher wages and more heavily unionized areas of the industrial Northeast. Several outside factors aided this southern industrial transformation, such as the May 1947 Supreme Court decision in *ICC v. Mechling Barge Lines* that demanded for the freight rates set by the Interstate Commerce Commission to be equalized. Additionally the Taft-Hartley Act of 1947 allowed southern states to enact right-to-work laws and thus burnish their probusiness (and antilabor) credentials.[90] The main types of industry that located in South Carolina in the 1950s produced paper and pulp, woolen textiles, and chemicals.[91] During the Hollings administration, the state began to attract metalworking and electronics industries as well.[92]

Byrnes, generationally removed from other postwar South Carolina governors, noted his surprise upon taking office at finding state officials demanding his involvement in enticing new industry to the state.[93] Although South Carolina's postwar governors did become more involved in economic development, the success of governors pursuing outside industry for South Carolina before the 1960s was limited. While a recent biographer labeled Thurmond "one of the most energetic and effective advocates of industrial development" during his time as governor (1947 to 1951), outside investment in South Carolina was small by the standards of later governorships.[94] Hollings later remarked of Thurmond's term: "We did get DuPont . . . but that was it, period."[95] The overall value of new and expanded industries locating in South Carolina reflected the growth of outside investment in the state through the 1950s and 1960s: between 1951 and 1954, new investment averaged $71 million annually; from 1955 to 1958, the figure was $132 million; between 1959 and 1962, investment averaged $211 million a year.[96]

Hollings's predecessor, George Bell Timmerman, made strides in bringing in outside industry to South Carolina, although he was far from an energetic governor. Marshall Parker, then a state senator from Oconee, recalled that Timmerman "didn't do a lot. Fritz [Hollings] was more the activist. No question about that."[97] Although unwilling to pursue prospects actively, Timmerman was cooperative with industries that sought to locate in the state, as the activities surrounding the Bowater Paper Corporation's relocation in 1956 demonstrated. The legislature convened a special session in June, at a cost of three hundred thousand dollars to the taxpayer, to rewrite South Carolina's alien land ownership law to allow the British company to set up in the state. Failure to act, Timmerman warned, would lose the "best industrial prospect" in South Carolina's history. In addition to the legislature's alteration of the alien land ownership law, the state's Water Pollution Authority granted the company an exemption from recently passed pollution standards.[98] Hollings had attended meetings with Timmerman and a few other senior lawmakers to devise a strategy for the special session and would later use the "Bowaters [*sic*] case" in talks to industrial executives to demonstrate the state government's friendliness to prospective industries.[99]

By the mid-1950s it was becoming much more common for southern governors to travel to northern states to persuade businessmen to relocate their industries, to the point that even the following satirical exchange was not considered that far-fetched:

SECRETARY: There's a salesman here to see you.
MANAGER: Does he have an appointment?
SECRETARY: No.
MANAGER: What's he selling?
SECRETARY: A state.
MANAGER: A what? Who is he?
SECRETARY: He claims he's the governor.[100]

Despite conducting a three-day business trip to New York with the South Carolinian construction magnate Charlie Daniel early in 1955, Timmerman was generally unwilling to travel out of state to meet industrial prospects. Hollings later recalled of Timmerman's laissez-faire approach to industrial development: "He thought if the president of the company wanted to come and ask about the tax structure, he'd bring over the tax man and they'd answer the questions. . . . But it was unbecoming for a governor or a head of a state to run around after an industry."[101] Hollings deputized for the governor on several occasions, at the behest of the chairman of the State Development Board, Bob Cooper. He later claimed that Cooper "was always making appointments for the governor that I was filling in on. So I got every opportunity in the world to fill in a lot of that."[102]

Hollings exploited his experiences of selling South Carolina in his successful 1958 gubernatorial campaign. Contesting the Democratic primary was Bill Johnston, the brother of U.S. senator Olin Johnston, and Donald Russell, the former president of the USC and close confidant of former governor Byrnes. Hollings made his experience in industrial development and a pledge to maintain racial segregation key planks of his campaign. A campaign pamphlet touted his record of working "long and hard to change our tax laws to place South Carolina in a better position to get much needed new industries and to encourage existing industries to expand," his "vigor to press hard to secure new industries," and his "energy to work long and hard to advance our state." On segregation it noted Hollings's appointment by Governor Byrnes to argue the *Briggs* case before the

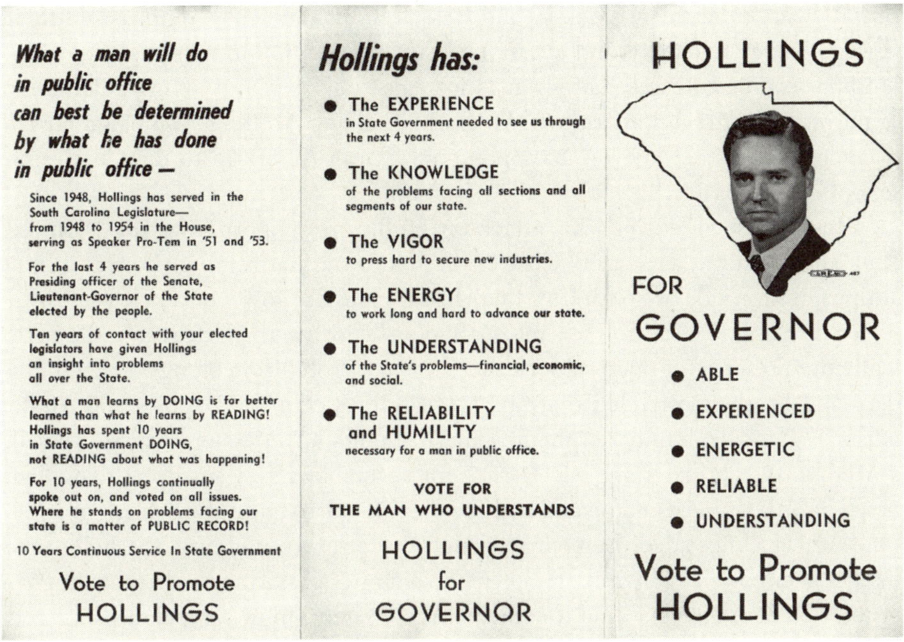

★ *"Hollings for Governor," campaign pamphlet, 1958.*
SOURCE: South Carolina Political Collections, University of South Carolina, Columbia.

Supreme Court and his coauthorship of bills "to prevent forced integration." The same pamphlet needled Russell's academic background and his lack of experience as a legislator: "What a man learns by DOING is far better learned than what he learns by READING! Hollings has spent 10 years in State Government DOING, not READING about what was happening!"[103] This line of attack was ironic given Hollings's simultaneous advocacy of improved educational standards throughout the campaign and during his governorship.[104]

All the major candidates for governor supported racial segregation. In a speech at the state capitol in January 1958, Hollings declared that "our greatest problem is segregation. . . . During my time in public office absolute segregation has been maintained in the schools, and let me state now that, as long as I am Governor, they will continue to remain segregated."[105] The *Greer Citizen*, one of the few newspapers to support Hollings, highlighted his racial bona fides in its endorsement before the first Democratic primary, calling him "one of South Carolina's most ardent supporters of segregation and the ideals of a way of life in our state."[106]

Hollings led the first June 10 primary with 42 percent of the vote to Russell's 35 percent. Johnston trailed far behind with 23 percent of the vote. During the runoff election between Hollings and Russell, both candidates emphasized their segregationist credentials and questioned the other's commitment to segregation. Hollings claimed Russell had given "a lot fancy talk" without taking a definitive stand on the segregation issue.[107] Meanwhile an anti-Hollings campaign advertisement resurrected his vote to appoint an African American to the Charleston school board in 1952.[108]

Russell also intensified his attack on Hollings's support from the Barnwell Ring and his status as a "wet" Charleston politician, that is, one who was on the antiprohibition side of South Carolina's historic upstate-lowcountry cleavage over liquor drinking. Charleston was more religiously diverse than the rest of the state, while the presence of open saloons there during Prohibition alongside gambling dens and brothels offended the moral sensibilities of many Baptists and Methodists.[109] Baptists dominated the upstate. Although a Mississippi native, Russell, a Methodist, worked alongside Byrnes for several years in an upstate law firm based in Spartanburg and owned a house there from 1947 until his death in 1998. One anti-Hollings advertisement reproduced a letter from Henry Mitchell of the Schlitz beer company inviting recipients to a dinner honoring the lieutenant governor.[110] These attacks came together in the contention in campaign pamphlets that Hollings was "the bottle baby of the Barnwell Ring."[111]

To counter these allegations, Hollings's campaign circulated an endorsement from state senator Robert Wasson, a "dry" leader in South Carolina. According to Wasson, Hollings had promised that as governor he would sign into law a local option bill pertaining to "all acts passed by the General Assembly for the moral welfare of our great State."[112] As a demonstration of the continued importance of liquor to the state's politics, Steve Griffith, who served in the 1961–62 legislative session, remembered House Speaker Blatt's advice: "Don't you vote wet one time, because if you do you're going to get defeated."[113] Liquor politics died hard in South Carolina.

In the runoff primary, Hollings won 57 percent of the vote and carried every major demographic category in the state.[114] He later attributed his victory to television advertising to counteract Russell's support from print media in the state and to Russell's inexperience in politicking.[115] Hollings also guessed he made about five times as many mill shift visits as Russell, the typical venue for shaking hands with millworkers and soliciting their votes. When Russell did meet with voters, "it was more like getting a handshake from the banker wanting to know when you're going to pay your note."[116]

Having won the Democratic primary, Hollings faced no Republican opposition in the general election—the next to last time a Democratic gubernatorial nominee ran unopposed in South Carolina. At thirty-seven years old, he became the youngest South Carolina governor in the twentieth century. He was also only the second Charleston native to be elected governor since the Civil War. Entering office, Hollings continued the courtship of outside industries and the related improvement of the state's educational system. However, the increasing number of antisegregation lawsuits and the advent of a more activist civil rights movement threatened to disrupt his efforts: given South Carolina's tense racial atmosphere, it seemed likely that there would be more violent racially motivated crimes across the state, thereby possibly sullying the state in the eyes of potential industrial investors.

★ ★ ★ CHAPTER 2 ★ ★ ★

Segregation with "Dignity"?

Upon becoming governor of South Carolina in 1959, Fritz Hollings oversaw the final stages of his state's total opposition to the *Brown v. Board of Education* decision. In his inaugural address, he adopted a familiar defiant approach to the validity of *Brown* and claimed that "the Constitution of the United States has been amended illegally by the Supreme Court and today we struggle to recognize the original."[1] Yet by the end of his term, Hollings was counseling peaceful compliance with the federal court order to admit the black student Harvey Gantt to Clemson College. In a stirring closing address to the state's General Assembly, he urged South Carolinians to "realize the lesson of 100 years ago and move on for the good of South Carolina and our United States."[2] His words contrasted with the rhetoric of other Deep South governors at the time, such as Mississippi's Ross Barnett or Alabama's George Wallace, who pledged in the same month to preserve "segregation forever."

The address, credited with preparing the way for the peaceful integration of Clemson College later that month, received widespread acclaim.[3] While the drive for pursuing new business prospects to the state did not necessarily motivate Hollings's move away from the more extreme racial stances adopted by other Deep South governors, his emphasis on industrial development did allow for a more moderate racial policy and for some small changes in racial employment opportunities. The Hollings administration's careful policing of civil rights protest ensured the absence of deadly violence in the state, yet the simultaneous refusal to negotiate with the demands of protestors pointed to the continued tenacity of South Carolina's political leadership in defending Jim Crow until all legal remedies had been exhausted.

The notion that South Carolina was a moderate state in its race relations was popularized almost immediately after the peaceful integration of Clemson, with the publication of John McMillan's feature "Integration with Dignity" in the March 16, 1963, issue of the *Saturday Evening Post.* In it McMillan described a two-year-long "conspiracy for peace" orchestrated by six key politicians and economic magnates.[4] Views of scholars of civil rights in South Carolina follow three broad interpretations: one that emphasizes the peaceful nature of racial change in the state (with the exception of the Orangeburg Massacre of 1968); one that focuses on the perceived cynicism of the state's white politicians and characterizes the concessions made to blacks as "tokenism"; and a third that takes a sympathetic but skeptical approach to the conduct of white elites and the changes made in race relations.[5]

Hollings's "moderation" marked a perceptible break from the policies of previous South Carolina governors yet in the early 1960s was sharply limited: it extended to ensuring the physical safety of antisegregation dissidents and marginally expanding employment opportunities for blacks, but it did not countenance the desegregation of public education facilities until all legal obstacles had been overcome.

The "moderate" label itself is problematic. Hollings never described himself as a moderate: rather he presented himself as "constructively conservative," as in his Senate campaign against Olin Johnston in 1962.[6] His campaign literature presented "Hollings for U.S. Senate: *conservative on record.*"[7] A better way of understanding his ideology can be gained by viewing him as a "modernizer," that is, a politician who sought economic diversification, supported government activism (and taxation) to improve state infrastructure, and was somewhat responsive to the demands of minority groups "in the interests of social stability and economic gain."[8] Hollings never espoused an integrationist platform while governor, but his maintenance of public order in South Carolina throughout his term in office marked him out as more racially moderate than his gubernatorial predecessors in South Carolina and his contemporaries across the Deep South states. Hence the use of the term *moderate.*

John West, elected governor himself in 1970, described Hollings's governorship as "a watershed in terms of economics."[9] The South Carolinian journalist and historian Jack Bass also viewed Hollings as a "transformative" figure for both racial and economic affairs.[10] While previous governors had made efforts to bring new industry to the state, the scale and success of the industry hunting during Hollings's governorship set it apart. Once he won the Democratic nomination in 1958, his correspondence with journalist William Workman of the *State* discussing the possible contents of an inaugural address made it apparent that he saw bringing new industry to the state as a central goal of his governorship: "My work will be cut out for me in securing new industry, and we can't be diverted into every luncheon group, beauty contest, and state convention. I want to tell these last groups to go to hell diplomatically so we can work with the General Assembly on the industrial problem."[11]

Once governor, Hollings oversaw important structural and personnel changes to the mechanisms for attracting industry to South Carolina. He persuaded the legislature to correct the state's chronic budget deficit, which required the implementation of a tax increase. Hollings saw the tax increase as a prerequisite to the successful courtship of outside industry. It passed despite the opposition of several powerful groups, including the chambers of commerce, textiles, and tobacco.[12] The resulting balanced budget brought about the upgrading of the state's bond rating to AAA status by both Moody's and Standard and Poor's, a point that was repeatedly highlighted in outgoing industrial correspondence.[13]

At Hollings's urging the membership of State Development Board, created in 1945 (and originally named the Department of Research, Planning and Development), was increased from five to fifteen. To counter accusations that the board was favoring one part of the state over another in its development efforts, under the new system one representative was selected from each judicial district with a chairman serving at large. The development board's budget was greatly enlarged as well: in 1959 five hundred thousand dollars was spent on salaries and recruitment efforts, whereas the figure for 1958 was just below three hundred thousand dollars.[14] Hollings considered his dealings as lieutenant governor with the chairman of the development board, Bob Cooper, to be pivotal in bringing about this reorganization. In Hollings's opinion the development board was really a "one-man operation" before 1959.[15]

In addition to expanding the state's committee for attracting industrial investment, Hollings also drew key figures from the regional pacesetter in industrialization, North Carolina. Hollings's industrial assistant, S. Ernie Wright, was brought in from the Tar Heel State, and Wright persuaded the new director of the State Development Board, Walter W. Harper, to switch from North to South Carolina as well.[16] Wade Martin also came from North Carolina to head the state's new Technical Training Program. Hollings's imitation of the North Carolina industrialization model was not restricted to personnel. He recalled even mumbling his name as "Governor Hollings from Carolina" when trying to secure meetings with industrial executives in an effort to be mistaken for his gubernatorial counterpart Luther Hodges, the self-professed "businessman in the statehouse."[17]

Rivalry with North Carolina was a recurring theme in Hollings's industry hunting. There was a widespread concern among South Carolina officials over the industrializing maneuvers enacted by their northern neighbor: Cotesworth Means, a member of South Carolina's Ports Authority, informed Hollings of a trip undertaken by Hodges to Europe alongside some fifty North Carolina businessmen, during which Sir Eric Bowater held "a special luncheon in London" for the North Carolina governor. Bowater was the head of a British paper company that had recently located in South Carolina. "I hope that next year," Means wrote, "someone on the Authority won't tell me that we are losing business to Wilmington and Morehead City because of North Carolina's foresight."[18] The industrialist Charles Daniel was also wary of the competition posed by North Carolina to South Carolina's development prospects.[19] In following the North Carolina blueprint for economic expansion, Hollings even imitated Hodges's international

★ *Hollings as an industrializing governor, c. 1959–62.*
SOURCE: South Carolina Political Collections, University of South Carolina, Columbia.

industrial missions, a first for a South Carolina governor. Beyond numerous visits to northern states, Hollings traveled to Latin America and Europe on business-attracting trips. In his memoir he claimed that by the end of his term in office, the state had crossed a "threshold of respectability" in the eyes of potential industrial investors.[20]

As South Carolina's governor had limited powers in comparison to the state legislature, the chief executive had to use all of his persuasive skills in order to have his legislative agenda implemented.[21] Steve Griffith, a House member from Newberry County in the 1961–62 legislative session, remembered Hollings as "extremely popular." "He mingled with the legislators, schmoozed them. We went to the governor's mansion at night, would have a drink and have a good time. . . . Fritz could talk to anybody."[22] Hollings recalled having several allies in both houses of the legislature: "I had a House team of Bob McNair, Floyd Spence, and Rex Carter, and I had John West with Marshall Parker and Billy Goldberg [in the state senate]."[23] He used his existing relationship with members of the legislature to get his pet schemes, such as the State Organization for Associated Research (SOAR) and the technical education program (TEC), passed.

Viewed as a mechanism for keeping pace with the state's regional rivals Georgia and North Carolina, TEC was recommended as a means of providing the state with a more sophisticated workforce, considered a prerequisite for industrialization. Under the scheme, described by historian James Cobb as "pioneering," the state would pay for the training of an industrial workforce in necessary technical skills. The prospective business could then "start up in the black," a tagline that become synonymous with the program. Despite only starting up with a quarter of the recommended appropriation for the scheme (which even then took an evening of Hollings's persuading Senate Finance Committee chairman Edgar Brown over a bottle of bourbon), imitations of TEC were soon to be found across the South.[24]

SOAR marked an effort to create in South Carolina something akin to North Carolina's Research Triangle. SOAR, the State Development Board claimed, would "help to create the climate and atmosphere most attractive to the type [of] industry being sought by the state," in other words, industries that required more highly skilled workers.[25] The program provided state funds for research projects relevant to economic growth in the state, with funds distributed between Clemson and USC on a competitive basis. However the scheme fell flat. After bickering over the allocation of grant funds, the appropriation for the scheme the next year divided the monies equally between Clemson and USC, which destroyed the competitiveness of the program and, with it, its effectiveness.[26] The director of the development board, Walter Harper, also bemoaned the general irrelevance of the proposed research projects to the board's development goals. "Out of a hundred [project proposals]," he recalled, "there were about eight to twelve that would be useful to us."[27]

Despite the implementation of schemes like these across the South to lure industry to their communities, there was a widespread fear among southern economic boosters during the 1950s and 1960s that the region's perceived racial troubles would prevent industry from relocating there. The chairman of Arkansas's Industrial Development Commission, Winthrop Rockefeller, captured this concern when he warned that industry would stay away if a state or community developed an "unhealthy reputation" in race relations.[28] As lieutenant governor Hollings also speculated that "industries with labor trouble in New England are not going to re-locate in South Carolina or the South where school racial problems exist."[29]

The moderate Southern Regional Council (SRC) and its South Carolina offshoot, the South Carolina Council on Human Relations (SCCHR), sought to cultivate any apparent connection between racial unrest and economic stagnation to encourage businessmen to lead desegregation efforts in their communities. This was evident in the SRC's Southern Leadership Project, which sent "L Reports" to business leaders. These reports couched desegregation in terms of both moral and economic leadership.[30] The industrial fate of Little Rock after its school desegregation crisis in 1957 was a favored example. Former SRC executive director Leslie Dunbar said the group would use "any little scrap of evidence we could put our hands on that Little Rock was suffering economically."[31] The Arkansas capital attracted eight new industrial plants in 1957, yet it failed to attract another industry for the next four years. Across Arkansas new industrial investment created 1,400 fewer jobs in 1958 than it had in 1957.[32]

As far as businessmen accepted this claimed relationship between racial unrest and economic stagnation, they generally only promoted measures to prevent violent racial incidents and school closures, not the desegregation of local public accommodations. Arkansas booster Rockefeller counseled that "the industrial prospect doesn't give a hoot whether your schools are segregated or not, but he wants no part of disorder and violence."[33] A study of the racial views of southern businessmen published in 1963 concluded similarly that economic concerns promoted "only enough 'moderation' as is necessary to oppose extreme measures such as violence and the closing of schools to avoid integration. It is these extreme measures that would constitute the public controversy from which prospective new industries might shy."[34] A parallel can be drawn to the economic motivations of Atlanta's business elite in presenting their city as "too busy to hate" in the early 1960s. Opie Shelton, an Atlanta Chamber of Commerce member (an organization led at the time by future mayor Ivan Allen Jr.), claimed that his fellow members "weren't a bunch of do-gooders." Rather "they were hard-headed businessmen who realized that you can't sell peanuts at a funeral."[35] Although it is hard to demonstrate statistically the negative impact of segregation or racial strife on industrial development, it is apparent, as historian Joe Crespino has asserted, that whether or not industrialists avoided strictly segregated areas, "they certainly wanted to maintain a public impression that they did."[36]

The supposed relationship between a desire to attract new industry and an opposition to extreme racial policies was far from perfect. Even Barnett, arguably the most demagogic southern governor in the early 1960s, argued that his administration's greatest achievements were in industrial development and not in the state's defense against breaches of the color line. Shortly after he left office, at a speech at Harvard Law School in February 1963, he claimed credit for bringing 555 new industries and forty thousand new jobs to Mississippi during his governorship. Barnett even argued at a White Citizens' Council meeting that the decision of Standard Oil to locate in Mississippi demonstrated nationwide support for the state's stand against racial integration, although he backed down after being publicly rebuked by the company's president.[37]

One of the most notorious instances of southern racial strife took place during Barnett's governorship, when riots erupted over the court-ordered admission of the black student James Meredith to the University of Mississippi in September and October 1962. Encouraged by Barnett's vocal opposition to the integration order, the subsequent disorder left two people dead, twenty-eight federal marshals with gunshot wounds, and hundreds injured.[38] As with the Little Rock desegregation crisis of 1957, the SRC again sought to connect racial violence in Mississippi with a bleak economic future for the state. The L-Report "What Price Violence?" reproduced newspaper articles quoting businessmen from across the South who saw the violence as bad for business. *Atlanta Constitution* business editor Jim Montgomery contended that the violent resistance in Mississippi amounted to "economic suicide."[39]

The violence at Ole Miss is certainly thought to have affected the response of South Carolina's white politicians to the court order to admit Harvey Gantt to Clemson. The importance of economic factors in bringing peaceful compliance with the desegregation order was played up by John McMillan in his "Integration with Dignity" article. In a reported conversation between Clemson president Bob Edwards and Marion Gressette, the chairman of the state's school committee (tasked with maintaining racial separation in public schools), Edwards swayed Gressette by reminding him of the potential economic repercussions violence at Clemson could have for his home county, Calhoun, which had been courting industrial investment. Edwards allegedly remarked: "Senator, if there's a ruckus at Clemson, those people won't even plant scrub oak in Calhoun County."[40] Historian Orville Vernon Burton, too, maintained that the violence in Mississippi was centrally important in shaping South Carolina's response to its own integration problem and preventing a violent reaction: "If it is true that the passage of time brought a change in attitude, it was only because Ole Miss happened in the meantime. . . . The situation in Mississippi was a major influence on the thinking of South Carolina at the time."[41]

While the violence in Mississippi may have persuaded some of the state's more recalcitrant politicians, Gressette included, to accept the desegregation of Clemson, Hollings had moved toward this acceptance earlier. Throughout his governorship he pursued a racial policy that sought to prevent violent incidents and instead promoted the appearance of a "stable," businesslike state, aims that were consonant with his efforts to attract outside industry to South Carolina. In his memoir Hollings made this connection explicitly, with the contention that "my main goal [as governor] was to keep the lid on everything. All my efforts to bring prosperity to the state would have been for naught if businesses were constantly worried that racial strife was right around the corner."[42]

Hollings was familiar with the economic arguments for racial moderation. His office received numerous letters from other southern politicians counseling moderation to help in the pursuit of industry.[43] Hollings put this advice into practice, as his recollection of his efforts to bring the Owens Corning Corporation to Aiken illustrated. Hollings knew that the publisher of the local newspaper opposed continuing public education if it meant acceding to racial integration, a viewpoint that would likely be fatal to Aiken's chance of attracting Owens Corning if it was noticed, since the corporation's chairman was himself a school board chairman in Toledo, Ohio. As a result Hollings instructed his State Law Enforcement Division (SLED) officers to "run around to all the stands at the hotels and down the street" to buy every copy of the *Aiken Standard and Review* they could find.[44] His concern to maintain public education, or at least offer the impression that South Carolinians were in favor of public education, distinguished him from many stridently segregationist contemporaries. Not all of his colleagues agreed that public education should be prioritized over preserving racially separate schools. For instance in the lead-up to the admission of Gantt to Clemson, state senator John D. Long claimed he would "prefer that [his] children be raised in ignorance . . . than to see them cringing and bowing before tyranny."[45] Sol Blatt, the Speaker of the South Carolina House, remained opposed to compulsory public education as well. As late as March 1966, when the legislature was debating the reinstatement of the compulsory school attendance law, repealed in 1952 to prevent white parents from being forced to send their children to racially integrated schools, Blatt argued passionately (and unsuccessfully) against the measure.[46]

Although Hollings made no secret of his opposition to school desegregation in public pronouncements, he maintained a rhetorical stand against violence. In his testimony in Washington before the Senate Subcommittee on Constitutional Rights and the House Judiciary Committee in April 1959, he contended that the "thinking leaders of both races in the South realize that integration is unwise, impractical and will never be accomplished," yet he also declared: "we will maintain law and order in South Carolina. We don't need further federal authority." In an interesting example of the contours of southern racial "moderation" at this time, Hollings spoke of a general "revulsion" in the state against the supposedly equivalent Ku Klux Klan and the NAACP, extremist "pressure groups."[47] Hollings has noted proudly the decline of Klan membership during his gubernatorial term. By the time he left office, he claimed there were only three hundred members of the Klan in the state, of whom about half were police informants.[48] Informants were spying on both the NAACP and the Klan throughout Hollings's governorship, although SLED files suggest that the NAACP was the more heavily monitored.[49] Hollings's calls for sound law enforcement mark a contrast with the rhetoric of Alabama governor John Patterson, who exclaimed in December 1960: "You'll have a riot on your hands if they [the federal government] try forced integration . . . I'll be one of the first ones stirring up trouble, any way I can."[50]

Hollings supported legislation aimed at preventing or at least punishing violence. Before entering office he had discussed in correspondence with Marion Gressette passing a "clear-cut and strong law against the use of explosives," legislation that was later introduced in the General Assembly's 1959 session.[51] The concern to avoid violent incidents occupied Hollings throughout his governorship, a tenure that coincided with a phase of increasingly militant civil rights protest across the region, apparent in widespread antisegregation marches, sit-ins, and Freedom Rides.

Hollings's concern for preserving the peace was clear in his handling of the sit-in protests that came to South Carolina in February 1960. I. DeQuincey Newman, the NAACP field secretary for South Carolina, recorded eighty "protest demonstrations" in the state that year involving some four thousand college and high school students.[52] There was one serious attack on a sit-in participant: Lonnie Glover, an African American Benedict College student, was stabbed during a sit-in in downtown Columbia in March 1961.[53] However there were no fatalities in South Carolina during this period, unlike in several other Deep South states. In addition to ensuring a strong SLED presence at protests (which was doubtless helped by the network of informants used to infiltrate pro–civil rights groups), Hollings was in contact with the prosegregation Citizens' Council in order to promote public order. After a demonstration in Rock Hill, Hollings wrote to Farley Smith, the head of the South Carolina councils, and congratulated him for his "leadership and cooperation in promoting law and order in the Rock Hill area."[54]

Hollings's later comments on civil rights protests indicate that preventing any racial "incident" that could place South Carolina in the national media spotlight was paramount, a goal that required close control of the state's police force. Speaking about possible SCLC demonstrations in South Carolina, Hollings remarked:

> They [SCLC] could stay in the Barringer Hotel in North Carolina and come right across the line into Rock Hill and be in the Deep South and get the TV and the pictures. I found out they [Rock Hill] had a lousy city police force, and I had to pull them over, they'd get us into trouble. I didn't know that they wouldn't knock them in the head and every other thing of that kind, so I pulled them out of the way and called my SLED people in. When there were big demonstrations I got as many blacks out there as I could. I took the blacks off the force in Charleston, Columbia, State College security in Orangeburg, and I had black police officers on the streets so when they came in, there would be a black officer apprehending a black, and so they threw the cameras away. They didn't want to find law enforcement like that, and that's when they went down to Montgomery and Birmingham. . . . They couldn't get the picture they wanted here, and I knew what they wanted. I needed a real professional reliable kind of police force that I could rely on where nobody would get hurt.[55]

Hollings's strategy was one of avoiding newsworthy confrontations. Without photograph opportunities for white-on-black violence, protestors struggled to achieve their goals.

Civil rights activists agreed that law enforcement officials helped minimize altercations between civil rights protestors and hecklers. Cecil A. Ivory, the president of the Rock Hill branch of the South Carolina NAACP, provided a summary of the sit-down demonstrations in the town in February 1960. In the first demonstration, involving some 150 students from Friendship Junior College and held on February 12 at McCrory's Variety Store and Woolworth's Variety Store, despite one female student being kicked and one male student being pushed out of his seat, state officials were on hand to prevent escalating violence. "We received very adequate police protection through a mob of white teenagers and a few white adults on our march back to the school," Ivory wrote. Moreover "a close police surveillance was placed over the school for several days following this demonstration."[56]

Hollings's concern to avoid violent confrontation was also apparent in his handling of an Emancipation Day pilgrimage to Greenville Municipal Airport in January 1960. State Congress of Racial Equality (CORE) and NAACP leaders organized the event to protest segregated waiting rooms at the airport, where the black baseball star Jackie Robinson had been ordered to leave a whites-only waiting area the previous October. Alice Spearman, the executive director of SCCHR, attended the protest and noted that Hollings sent highway patrolmen to protect the marchers, a first for a southern governor.[57] Hollings's legal assistant, Harry Walker, had met up with SLED chief Pete Strom, city administration leaders, and the city chief of police a few days earlier. As Walker recalled, following the meeting "the city fathers knew that the Governor's office and SLED were available to them for assistance. . . . Once they became of one mind, the city police officers knew that they were backed by the city administration, and consequently when the officers were called on to police the sit-ins they . . . were top-notch."[58]

Police handling of protests was not always restrained, as at the Orangeburg protest of March 15, 1960, where one thousand student protestors from Claflin and South Carolina State marched. The protestors were teargassed by police and fire-hosed by the fire department before 388 students were arrested and left in a yard outside the county jail. Some students suffered from exposure, while several others were left with external injuries.[59] However this case served as an exception to the generally peaceful, but unyielding, treatment of protestors by law enforcement in the state. According to Walker the Hollings administration did not get notice of the Orangeburg protest until it had already occurred and had been handled poorly by local police forces.[60]

Because of the general concern of law enforcement to avoid violent altercations at protests, when Freedom Riders came through the state they were generally afforded adequate police protection: although John Lewis and Albert Bigelow were beaten up outside a "whites only" waiting room in Rock Hill on May 9, 1961, this act paled into insignificance next to the state-condoned (and FBI-witnessed) terrorism experienced by the riders in Alabama.[61] After the initial ride in May 1961, Freedom Riders were studiously protected when they entered South Carolina. In an article for *Newsday* on a group of cleric Freedom Riders traveling in June 1961, one participant, a Rev. Mr. Smith, said that state officials "definitely kept violence from occurring." The article also highlighted the importance of state officials, particularly SLED and Walker, in diffusing racially charged situations. Walker's official comments are revealing with respect to the Hollings administration's effort to preserve law and order. Walker consciously distinguished South Carolina from the Alabama experience of civil rights protest by noting that Sumter "will be no Montgomery," while he later offered the administration's public line that "we do not enforce segregation or integration. Our job is to maintain good order and enforce the law."[62]

Coupled with a concern for preserving law and order was a refusal to negotiate with protestors' demands, a strategy that paralleled police chief Laurie Pritchett's approach in Albany, Georgia, in 1961 and 1962.[63] Customarily protests were supervised by police forces, which would then break up the demonstration and charge the participants with "breach of the peace." The arbitrary nature of the arrests angered black leaders, as was obvious in a wireless exchange between Hollings and the NAACP executive secretary, Roy Wilkins. In response to Wilkins's complaint that students who had been peacefully demonstrating in Columbia at the statehouse were arrested "on a technicality that demonstrators were making illegal use of statehouse grounds," Hollings gave his stock justification for the arrests: "When clear and present danger of riot, disorder . . . or other immediate threats to public safety, peace or order, appears, the power of the state to punish is obvious. *Salus populi suprema lex* [the safety of the people is the supreme law]."[64] The state's policy of charging peaceful demonstrators with breach of the peace was later ruled unconstitutional by the Supreme Court in the *Edwards* decision of February 25, 1963, which overturned the convictions made in the Columbia statehouse demonstration case.[65] Hollings's approach shifted the focus away from the merits of black demands and toward the imperative of preserving public order. As a result while serious violence was averted during Hollings's governorship, scant regard was given to black grievances.

Hollings remained committed to preserving segregated public education in South Carolina, as his reaction to efforts to integrate the schools in Charleston's School District 20 in 1961 illustrated. The District 20 example also demonstrated the varied attitude of local African Americans toward integrating public schooling: while NAACP members pursued integration efforts, other black Charlestonians, led by the local parent-teacher association (PTA), were concerned primarily with improving the quality of existing school facilities for African Americans. The district was later the first in the state to desegregate, when Judge Robert Martin ordered the admission of black plaintiffs to white schools in August 1963.[66] In her

Ph.D. dissertation, Millicent Brown, the daughter of the local NAACP president and the named plaintiff in the case (*Millicent F. Brown, et al. v. School Board District No. 20*), contended that Charleston's African Americans "were not philosophically or emotionally interested in being with whites, but they were determined to gain improvements." After numerous complaints, dating back to 1959, about overcrowding in the district's black schools and a PTA-led school boycott, an integration petition was filed to admit black children to the white schools. An earlier open letter from the PTA to the *Charleston News and Courier* demanded improvements in black school conditions; failure to reduce overcrowding would lead to aggressive efforts to integrate the local white schools.[67]

The white school board of District 20 faced a quandary in acceding to the PTA demands. It would exceed its debt limit of 8 percent if it borrowed the necessary four hundred thousand dollars from the state's Sinking Funds Commission to continue working on the "equalization" of black schools. After discussing the issue with the Gressette Committee and the director of the Sinking Funds Commission, the participants decided that the district's debt limit could be sidestepped if Charleston County borrowed the four hundred thousand dollars and then lent it to School District 20.[68] After this solution had been reached, Hollings wrote to the school district chairman and congratulated him and his board "on the approach you have used toward avoiding any 'incident' in your district."[69] In this case the "incident" would have been a unified local black commitment to desegregated schooling in the city. The Charleston schools case revealed how, while the legal case for integrating schools progressed slowly, local African Americans worked within the existing Jim Crow system to secure improvements to segregated school facilities. Discussing the year and a half of "agreeable interaction" between the white school board and the black PTA, Millicent Brown concluded that while PTA representatives recognized the motivation of white school officials "to avoid desegregation at all costs," they still welcomed the new school construction programs as progress, as they had done previously with the increase in black teacher salaries.[70]

The actions of PTA members in Charleston paralleled the negotiations of the Jim Crow system by the state's black university presidents. Dr. Benner C. Turner, first as dean of the South Carolina State Law School and then as college president, cooperated with the white political establishment and opposed the actions of black student protestors in order to procure greater funding for his college. In return Governor Byrnes secured a five-hundred-thousand-dollar grant for South Carolina State from John D. Rockefeller III to finance a building program, as well as a 40 percent increase in the college's appropriation for maintenance and operations. Although Turner's cooperation ensured greater funding for his college, Byrnes used this system of "rewards" to strengthen black conservatives in the state and weaken those he perceived as militants.[71]

Hollings's own concern to preserve stability was further apparent in his relationship with South Carolina's Citizens' Councils. Although the classic monograph on Citizens' Councils viewed South Carolina's councils as "comparatively small and inactive by Deep South standards," the group maintained substantial economic clout.[72] Throughout Hollings's term there remained numerous cases of coordinated economic reprisals directed at black civil rights activists, a favored tactic of the Citizens' Councils. Such economic coercion was particularly apparent in Clarendon County, home to the *Briggs v. Elliot* case, after local blacks filed a school integration petition. There the Clarendon County Improvement Association, an organization of some eighty black farmers whose affairs were administered by local undertaker Billy Fleming, was unable to find any state or local source of credit at the start of 1959 to allow for the planting of crops. Fleming was subjected to Klan harassment, with Klan caravans often being parked outside his business, as well as economic pressures. He also used his hearse as a makeshift ambulance, but patients taken to the local hospital by him were either refused admittance or subjected to lengthy delays. Fleming continued to be subject to economic reprisals later in 1959. Two days after he returned to the county from giving testimony in Washington on civil rights legislation, the local bank called in a property note held by his brother. It was even difficult for black petition signers in Clarendon County to receive medical care: lacking any black physician in the area, those who signed the school integration petition had "great difficulty in persuading local white doctors to visit them."[73]

Although publicly affirming his support of the Citizens' Councils, Hollings refused membership to the group (as did his gubernatorial predecessor, Timmerman), turned down invitations to attend meetings, and repeatedly overlooked the more militant council suggestions in dealing with civil rights crises. Hollings's hands-off approach toward the Citizens' Councils, in contrast with Mississippi governor Barnett's extraordinarily close identification with them, and his keenness to avoid inciting racial violence are captured well by his response to the desegregation of the New Orleans school system in December 1960.[74] Ralph Kolb, chairman of the Sumter Citizens' Council, considered the New Orleans situation "our Rubicon" and urged Hollings to "[strengthen] the position of the Governor of Louisiana in the crisis he faces." In response Hollings offered only his "sympathy and support." Kolb replied that the council did not "believe that a routine expression of sympathy and support generally, under conditions now existing in Louisiana, is sufficient," before recommending that the governors of South Carolina, Mississippi, Alabama, Georgia, and Louisiana "issue a joint statement proclaiming it to be the duty and sole responsibility of Governors, each within his own state, to maintain order and that these five Governors intend to perform their duty in meeting this responsibility and will not be deterred by federal courts or federal marshals in doing so." The Louisiana governor should then "use state police personnel to remove the Negro children from the [New Orleans] schools," despite the possible "unpleasant consequences which may follow." Unsurprisingly given his studious evasion of actions likely to damage public order, Hollings did not act on this advice.[75]

Hollings exhibited his quiet segregationism during the University of Mississippi's integration crisis in September and October 1962, where rioting over the admission of James Meredith left two dead and hundreds injured. Hollings called the situation "Mississippi's problem," a statement that drew an angry editorial response from South Carolina's more fervently segregationist news outlets.[76] Unlike Hollings, Donald Russell, the state's Democratic gubernatorial nominee, praised the Mississippi governor's "courage and resolution" and argued that "Barnett's conduct may be invaluable to us in demonstrating the strength of Southern conviction." Hollings also refused Barnett's suggestion that he lead a motorcade down to Mississippi alongside the governors of Alabama and Georgia in opposition to the court-ordered desegregation. The executive secretary of the Citizens' Councils of South Carolina, Farley Smith, decried Hollings's refusal to join Barnett. It was "inconceivable . . . that South Carolina, of all southern states, has not, through its governor made its position crystal clear."[77] In a 1980 oral history, Hollings prioritized the evasion of violence in his decision making. Recalling a telephone conversation with Barnett, Hollings remarked: "I can't think of anybody following me in a motorcade, for a showdown to Oxford, Mississippi, that wouldn't include every kook, red-neck, crack-pot, Ku Klux Klanner, and everything else that you could find and they'd all follow me out and expect me to do something when I got there. And what am I supposed to do? I said [to Barnett], you, talking wild talk, we get a lot of people killed that way."[78]

Hollings instead sent his legal counsel Walker alongside SLED chief Pete Strom to Oxford to observe the Meredith integration and to come up with a plan to avoid violence if a similar court-ordered desegregation occurred in South Carolina. The result of their Mississippi visit was a seven-page blueprint on preserving order without the need for federal intervention, used when Gantt was admitted to Clemson. The plan set up procedures for law enforcement, the maintenance of student discipline on campus, and the management of the media throughout the day.[79]

As his comments about Barnett suggested, Hollings viewed some of his gubernatorial counterparts, particularly Barnett and Jimmie Davis of Louisiana, as liable to act intemperately on racial matters. In a revealing March 1960 letter to Ted Riley, the chairman of the state Democratic Party, Hollings apologized for his nonappearance at a conference where the governors of Tennessee, Mississippi, Louisiana, and Georgia were scheduled to meet. Knowing that Buford Ellington of Tennessee and Ernest Vandiver of Georgia were not going, Hollings argued that he would not be able to control the actions of Barnett and Davis: "I didn't want to take the responsibility of swaying Davis and Barnett. I figured without Vandiver present that Davis and Barnett would be wanting to make statements that would be a little strong for the particular time. I am personally of the opinion that this same strong talk will be necessary later on. However, I could be wrong and Barnett is the type who would want to talk now rather than trying to get everybody together now. With Ernie [Vandiver] present, we could have controlled it."[80]

Hollings, a Kennedy supporter, was also critical of Barnett's attempt to use the fourteen uncommitted southern delegates in the 1960 presidential election to force president-elect John Kennedy to make civil rights concessions. "The American people are not going to stand for politicking after the election," Hollings claimed.[81]

Hollings viewed his racial policies as a "dignified" yet firm response to attacks on segregation well before his closing address to the state General Assembly, where he argued that the racial integration of Clemson "should be done with dignity" and with "law and order."[82] A memorandum from late 1961 discussing his prospective 1962 Senate candidacy against Olin Johnston provides insight into how Hollings sought to be perceived by the state's electorate. "Maintain segregation—Dignity" is typed, while next to this point, in Hollings's handwriting, are the words "law enforcement."[83]

At the close of his governorship, the SCCHR contended that Hollings had begun "soft-pedalling the race issue" in order to secure greater industrial investment for the state, while "neither businessmen nor workers wanted any racial violence to interfere with this progress."[84] Compared with his predecessor, Hollings muted racial themes in his courtship of outside industry. His public comments rarely referred to racial issues explicitly. Instead these issues became an implicit part of a discourse that emphasized stability. This theme is obvious in Hollings's remarks to the associate editor of *South* magazine at the end of 1959. His forecast was bullish. "Blessed by splendid natural advantages; dynamic, hardworking people; stable, conservative government; and superb business climate, South Carolina looks forward confidently to continued economic growth and development in 1960," he claimed.[85]

Handwritten notes (presumably those of Ernie Wright, Hollings's industrial assistant) from a briefing session with Hollings before a luncheon with New York guests summarized his industrial pitch, which involved evading mentions of race. In order to demonstrate the business-oriented nature of state government, three points were listed: the state's "fiscal integrity," its "stability," and its "attitude toward business," displayed in its corporate tax formula, its right-to-work law, and the "Bowaters [*sic*] case." In the Bowater case, then-governor Timmerman called a special session of the state legislature in order to change the state's alien land ownership law, a change that allowed the British-owned Bowater Paper Company to locate in South Carolina.[86] The central point was written in red (the rest were in blue ink): "Why would you locate in S.C.—To make greater profit."[87]

Timmerman's speech in New York in 1955 before a group of business and industrial leaders contrasted Hollings's race-neutral business pitch. Timmerman was more willing to acknowledge the racial dimensions of South Carolina life with nonsouthern businessmen, apparent in his assertion that "our schools for Negroes are superior to any in the nation." Timmerman left no illusions as to the differences in job prospects between whites and blacks in the state: although "some five thousand of our Negro youth are currently enrolled in institutions of higher education in South Carolina," he claimed that South Carolina "has the highest percentage of white college graduates of any State in the nation. This means a continuing supply of educated personnel for management."[88] An address from Hollings's first year as governor, to New York industrialists, treated race more implicitly. Despite touting South Carolina's school equalization program as evidence of the state's commitment to educational improvement and referring to "the separate but equal pattern" of public education, the words *white* and *colored* were absent from Hollings's remarks.[89] The soft-pedaling of racial issues in economic development efforts during the Hollings administration, in contrast with the Timmerman official line, was also apparent in the materials produced by the State Development Board. While the annual reports from Hollings's time as governor avoided explicit mentions of race, the report for the years 1956–57 (during Timmerman's term) touted the quality of "colored" technical education in the state.[90]

Alongside muting racial issues when pursuing industrialization, when economic necessities clashed with racial mores, Hollings was not entirely wedded to racial segregation. The technical education program, for example, was never segregated according to race, while its governing documents discussed the necessity of providing equal opportunity to all South Carolina citizens.[91] In an oral history recorded in 1980, Hollings noted that "technical training in Greenville had been integrated" before the integration of Clemson, which he again related to maintaining public stability: "We didn't publicize it. But as long as it didn't get to the hotheads . . . nobody said anything."[92] Publicly, however, Hollings did not express support for integrating workforces in the state's industries. When pressed on the issue in 1961, he told reporters that "we will not have a policy of integrating any industry."[93]

Hollings's willingness to break the color line when economic investment was involved contrasted with the rigidity of his predecessor. At Timmerman's insistence Clemson College refused a grant of $350,000 from the Atomic Energy Commission (AEC) in August 1957, even after trustees had accepted an initial payment of $99,050. Timmerman objected to the attachment of a nondiscrimination clause to the grant that barred "unfavorable discrimination on the basis of race, color, creed, or religion."[94] Before they voted to accept the grant, Clemson's trustees received clarification from the AEC's general counsel that the clause could not be used to force Clemson into admitting nonwhite students.[95] Some thirty-three other colleges nationally, including the southern colleges North Carolina State, Georgia Tech, and Auburn, had already accepted grants that carried the same nondiscrimination clause.[96] Timmerman, however, was unsatisfied with the AEC general counsel's assurance and demanded that Clemson's trustees return the grant.[97] The lifetime trustee Charles Daniel, a Greenville-based construction magnate whose company had contracted on several Clemson building projects, opposed Timmerman's demand.[98] Following the state attorney general's conveniently timed July 1957 legal opinion that a member of a college's board of trustees could not hold a contract with that board and benefit financially from it, Daniel offered his resignation.[99] Daniel, according to Timmerman, was "the only Board member . . . who seems to favor a breakdown in our fight to preserve segregation."[100] Clemson's trustees subsequently canceled the contract with the AEC and returned the funds in August 1957.[101]

In his 1958 address to the General Assembly, Timmerman stressed his objection to the grant's nondiscrimination clause: "A grant has been refused until Clemson first agrees to accept a mixing clause, based on race, color, creed, or religion. The word 'creed,' being unqualified, is broad enough to embrace the communist creed."[102] Timmerman had made the pursuit of investment in atomic energy the central theme of his previous annual address to the legislature, which closed with the claim that "the potential of the infinite atom almost defies mere statement of a future policy."[103] The threat of mixing with blacks and/or communists, however, was too high a price to pay for atomic investment.

In a rare instance in which racial issues were discussed alongside industrial matters in correspondence, Hollings denied that there was any racial hiring policy imposed on new industries brought to the state. He wrote: "In our development program, we do not attract industries solely on the basis of those that will hire Negroes or those that will not hire Negroes. We bring them for the employment of all citizens, and to my personal knowledge many Negroes have been employed by the new industries. What the actual number is I do not know, and I would rather think that the Negroes would want a job on their capacity and willingness to work rather than simply because they were Negroes. I am sure this is the dignity and equal treatment that they seek."[104] Hollings's approach again indicates a case of a businessman's priorities trumping racial customs. The SCCHR's reports on merit employment, however, highlight the sluggish pace of black acceptance into previously "white" jobs, despite SRC field reporter Benjamin Muse's 1962 observation of "increasing sentiment in South Carolina in favor of opening more job opportunities to Negroes."[105] In its 1961 report, the SCCHR newsletter noted the employment of one former Benedict College professor as a chemist at the atomic plant near Aiken, two black nurses at the Columbia Veterans Hospital, black professionals at the Veterans Administration in Columbia, and "at least one Negro professional" at the Irmo General Electric plant, while textile companies and other firms with government contracts were "opening non-traditional jobs to Negroes"—slow progress indeed.[106] Moreover employment practices in textiles, the dominant industry in South Carolina, did not change quickly before the implementation of the Civil Rights Act of 1964. According to South Carolina Department of Labor data, blacks made up 6 percent of the textile workforce in 1925 and only 5.5 percent in 1965. The figure increased to 8 percent in 1966 as a result of the nondiscrimination stipulations of Title VII of the 1964 Civil Rights Act.[107]

While it is evident that Hollings's concern to keep the lid on racial tensions was congruent with his efforts to present state government as stable and businesslike, it is uncertain whether his more moderate racial policies were guided by economic concerns or whether he used a program of economic expansion to promote a degree of racial openness that would have been otherwise unacceptable. Given the occasionally violent enforcement of white conformity with respect to segregation during the 1950s, a candidly conciliatory approach to racial issues would likely have been unworkable during Hollings's term.[108] The 1960 publication of *The Case for the South*, written by William Workman, a South Carolina newspaper reporter and later a Republican U.S. Senate candidate, revealed the continued stridency of some of the state's whites on racial issues. Alongside attacking the supposed moral laxity of blacks, Workman denounced southern whites who supported integration as "submissionists" and justified lynching black men to prevent miscegenation.[109]

The most compelling argument for Hollings's having experienced a change of heart came in his off-the-record call to newspaper reporters in January 1962 to prepare their readers for desegregation, since he believed the state's "legal defenses will fall like a house of cards," and his subsequent call for the state to accept the desegregation of Clemson peacefully in his closing gubernatorial address in January 1963.[110] His expressed hope once leaving office in 1963 that southerners would no longer decide their partisan affiliations based on the national parties' racial policies further suggests an evolution in Hollings's views on race.[111] In the twilight of Hollings's Senate career in 2004, Congressman James Clyburn, who had participated in protests at Orangeburg in 1960, recalled a meeting with Hollings where the governor "made it very clear that while he was protecting [segregation], he did not necessarily agree that it was the best system."[112] Clyburn's comments, again, suggested that Hollings was questioning the worth of preserving segregation before he publicly broke with the bitter-end defense of the policy. However there remained a disjuncture between the convictions of white and black South Carolinians over this issue: whites generally thought Hollings had undergone a genuine change of heart, while blacks tended to view his altered behavior as pragmatic accommodation to changed political circumstances, much like Strom Thurmond's after the 1970 elections.[113]

It is possible that Hollings was shocked by the fervency of racial convictions held by some opponents of integration.[114] He received an impressive volume of supportive letters from across the South in the aftermath of his inaugural speech in 1959, some of which were strongly racist, anti-Semitic, or both.[115] While letters in this mold may have shaken Hollings in his attachment to the segregated system, it can only be speculated how much his own moral concerns shaped his moderate racial policies as governor.

Above all Hollings promoted the maintenance of public safety. Although he communicated with local African American political leaders such as I. DeQuincey Newman, it is likely that his distance from the wider population of South Carolina blacks insulated Hollings from the full extent of African American discontent with the segregated system.[116] While his policies helped to prevent violent racial incidents in the state, Hollings firmly defended white privilege while governor, as his unwillingness to negotiate with civil rights protestors indicates. He later acknowledged that, while he took care to prevent violence from occurring at protests, "we weren't for the demonstrators."[117] Neither was he entirely averse to defiant racial gestures, as his successful filibuster against a civil rights' resolution at the National Governors' Conference in April 1962 illustrated.[118]

Despite Hollings's change in behavior in the early 1960s, his governorship did not bring a major sea change in the actions of the state's white politicians. The admission of Gantt to Clemson was no more than token integration. Even then Clemson filed another petition to the Supreme Court to review the class action status of the *Gantt* case, which was argued until the fall of 1963, in an effort to prevent further desegregation of the state's educational facilities.[119] Indicative of this consistent opposition to black gains was the decision of the state forestry commission to close the state's parks rather than operate them on an integrated basis in April 1963. South Carolina was the only state to close its recreational facilities in response to a court order to desegregate.[120] The parks were only reopened on a full basis in July 1966. The redistricting plans passed by the state legislature after the passage of powerful federal civil rights legislation changed single-member districts to multimember ones, a tactic that diluted the impact of the black vote. Redistricting in the state senate in 1967 created five single-member districts and fifteen multimember districts, all of which had white majorities, despite the considerable African American population in the state.[121] It was not until the 1980 *Simkins v. Gressette* case that multimember districts were abolished in South Carolina.[122] While Hollings and his Democratic successors Robert McNair and John West started to move away from white supremacist politics, the transition was slow in the 1960s.

As with the state's white political class as a whole, Hollings's tenure as governor leaves an ambiguous legacy. In a departure from his predecessors, he played down racial issues in his efforts to attract outside industry to South Carolina. When economic necessities demanded it, he quietly broke from traditional southern racial customs. His emphasis on preserving public order helped to prevent violent confrontations, no mean feat considering the violence that wracked other Deep South states in this period and that belatedly occurred in South Carolina with the Orangeburg Massacre in 1968. Hollings's focus on preserving law and order provided the justification for the arbitrary breakup of demonstrations without the consideration of protestors' demands. While Hollings opposed the goals of civil rights groups throughout his governorship, he regarded his racial policies as a responsible, dignified response to the attacks made on the color line in the state. Given the racial turmoil of the early 1960s, the peaceful desegregation of Clemson was a significant achievement. As Benjamin Mays, a lifelong civil rights activist, acknowledged shortly after Gantt's admission: "The white people of South Carolina are perhaps just as much segregationists as the white people of Mississippi. But in Mississippi we had a Barnett; in South Carolina we had Hollings and Russell."[123] Despite Hollings's call for accepting desegregation at Clemson, the movement toward a more racially inclusive politics by South Carolina Democrats, Hollings included, remained a slow process through the 1960s. This remained the case even as African Americans registered to vote in greater numbers and spokesmen for the newly emergent state Republican Party began articulating a forceful anti–civil rights message.

★★★ CHAPTER 3 ★★★

Hollings, the Kennedys, and Democratic Decline in South Carolina

Hollings found himself a frequent candidate and political surrogate in the early 1960s. He served as a lieutenant for Democratic presidential nominee John Kennedy in 1960 and then as a candidate himself for the U.S. Senate in 1962 (when he lost in the Democratic primary) and 1966 (when he narrowly won the general election). These three elections demonstrated the growing relevance of the Republican Party in South Carolina, which until 1961 had not held a seat in the state legislature in the twentieth century. Hollings's justification for supporting Kennedy in 1960 illuminated the increased difficulty faced by South Carolina Democrats in reconciling their own opposition to civil rights measures with the growing liberalism of the national party on the issue. Following the passage of legislation enforcing civil rights and voting rights for African Americans in 1964 and 1965, anger at the national Democratic Party in South Carolina over federal civil rights measures and Great Society programs in general peaked, as Hollings's narrow defeat of his Republican opponent, Marshall Parker, in 1966 aptly illustrated.

These elections provide further evidence of the complementary importance of ostensibly nonracial disillusionment with the New Deal state and anger at the national Democratic Party's racial policies in explaining the collapse of the Solid Democratic South. As Joseph Crespino has argued, historiographical disagreements over the relative importance of economic and racial motivations to partisan change in the postwar South have led to "a both/and issue [getting] framed as an either/or debate."[1] In the case of many South Carolinians who defected from the Democratic Party in the early 1960s, disaffection over the supposedly "socialistic" tendencies of national Democrats and their racial policies were often closely interlinked and prove difficult to untangle. In South Carolina those who fled the Democratic Party were moved by both economic and racial concerns, often simultaneously.

By 1960 many South Carolinians were disillusioned at the perceived liberalism of the national Democratic Party, particularly on civil rights. Although the

★ *Hollings campaigning with John F. Kennedy (left) and Olin D. Johnston (center) in 1960.*
SOURCE: South Carolina Political Collections, University of South Carolina, Columbia.

Democratic nominee had carried the state in every presidential election in the twentieth century aside from Strom Thurmond's Dixiecrat candidacy in 1948, Democrats encountered difficulty in the 1952 and 1956 elections. Adlai Stevenson, the nominee in both races, won only 51 percent of the vote in 1952 and a plurality of the vote in 1956.

By endorsing and campaigning for the nominee of the national Democratic Party in the 1960 election, Hollings broke with the precedent set by the previous three South Carolina governors. In 1948 Thurmond had campaigned for the presidency as a Dixiecrat, as the movement became known in the national press. In 1952 James F. Byrnes, estranged from the national party after his removal as secretary of state by President Truman, chose to endorse the Independents for Eisenhower movement rather than endorse Stevenson. In 1956 George Bell Timmerman put himself forward as a "favorite son" candidate for the presidency at the Democratic National Convention and launched an abortive attempt to revive the Dixiecrat movement.[2] Once this effort fizzled, Timmerman spoke in favor of party unity at South Carolina's Democratic Party reconvention (the only state to reconvene after the national convention), and the delegates narrowly endorsed the Stevenson-Kefauver ticket.[3] By 1960 Byrnes completed his break from the Democratic Party when he appeared alongside Vice President Richard Nixon at a political rally at the state capitol in Columbia under the banner "Dixie Is No Longer in the Bag."[4] Among the state's U.S. senators, Olin Johnston, a New Deal–style economic liberal, remained a national party loyalist at this time, while Thurmond, elected to the Senate in 1954, continued his disengagement from the national party until his switch to the GOP in 1964.

Hollings became acquainted with the Kennedys in 1955 after he and Robert Kennedy were selected as two of the Junior Chamber of Commerce's Ten Outstanding Young Men of 1954. Hollings connected with the Kennedys on a personal level, a key element of his decision to support John F. Kennedy enthusiastically in the 1960 presidential election. Recalling his first meeting with Robert, Hollings wrote in his memoir: "Bob had qualities that I saw time and again in the extended Kennedy family: a seemingly boundless energy and devotion to public service. . . . I rate President Kennedy as one of our country's finest leaders. He inspired people—attracted the best and brightest to government, Republican and Democrat." In 1956 Hollings sought to persuade southern delegates to support Kennedy's nomination as Stevenson's running mate at the Democratic National Convention. Although he had some success in gathering support for Kennedy, Tennessee senator Estes Kefauver won the vice presidential nomination on the third ballot.[5]

As governor Hollings served as the chairman of the South Carolina delegation in 1960, which stayed uncommitted going into the national convention.[6] Though a segregationist, Hollings was far from the most vocal southern critic of the national party in 1960. At the national convention in July, he pleaded for the platform committee not to issue a civil rights plank that would "segregate" the South from the Democratic Party. Rather, in line with the four southerners on the committee (out of a total of twenty), he urged the creation of a moderate civil rights plank, given that a majority favored a more specific civil rights platform than those offered in 1952 and 1956.[7] Hollings also spoke on the convention floor during the unsuccessful southern effort to block the enactment of a strong civil rights plank. Defending the effort to dilute the plank, he claimed that southern officials were actually seeking to protect the rights of African Americans. His state, he asserted, had not interrupted sit-in demonstrations until "radical groups" from outside the state had captured the protesting students. Hollings was not, however, the most vociferous in condemning the plank. Georgia governor Ernest Vandiver, for instance, said that "these [civil rights] proposals are ridiculous and we repudiate them and will not be bound by them."[8] Later in July, Hollings speculated that newspaper coverage of the civil rights platforms adopted by both parties had been responsible for the outbreaks of fighting at lunch-counter demonstrations in Spartanburg, South Carolina: this coverage supposedly had "misguided colored youths into thinking that party platforms are the law of the land."[9]

Despite Hollings's support for Kennedy, the South Carolina delegation cast its votes for fellow southerner Lyndon Johnson. The delegation used the unit rule, whereby all of its votes would be given to the majority candidate. The state party chairman, Ted Riley, offered the unit rule motion, which Hollings claimed made him "useless," as the majority of the state's delegates supported Johnson over Kennedy.[10] Hollings subsequently announced his vote for Johnson, alongside the rest of the delegation.[11]

Although Hollings remained uncommitted leaving the convention, he endorsed the national ticket in early August 1960.[12] Having initially dabbled with the idea of allowing a slate of free electors to be placed on the ballot alongside the Democratic and Republican tickets, he urged party loyalty among other delegates at South Carolina's Democratic reconvention on August 15, 1960.[13] Despite the concerns about the Democratic platform, Hollings contended in a speech to the reconvention that "there is no choice between Democratic and Republican platforms. . . . One is as socialistic as the other, and, if anything, the civil rights plank of the Republican platform is far worse to us here in the South than the Democratic platform." Throughout his speech he maintained his opposition to the Democratic Party's civil rights plank and defended his handling of the sit-ins in South Carolina. Nevertheless Hollings asserted that moving outside of the two-party framework would be futile and urged support for the national ticket: "The only place where we [southerners] can build effectively is in the Democratic Party."[14]

Hollings played a key role in Kennedy's narrow victory in South Carolina. He faced difficulty, however, in carrying South Carolina for the Democrats while maintaining his credibility with his own supporters, many of whom were vehemently opposed to Kennedy's supposed racial and economic liberalism as well as his Catholic faith. Kennedy's Catholicism was a major stumbling block for support in the Baptist-dominated upcountry of South Carolina.[15] Thomas Chadwick, the campaign manager for the Baptist, teetotal, upstate Democrat Olin Johnston, later spoke of the conflict inherent in Johnston's support for Kennedy, a "wet" Catholic.[16] As a Lutheran and a native of Charleston, a city notorious for its flouting of South Carolina's liquor laws, Hollings presumably had no such qualms about Kennedy. In speeches he claimed that accusations that the election of Kennedy would lead to socialist government were a screen for religious intolerance: "The average person won't say that 'look, on account of this religious issue, I'm not going to vote for Kennedy and Johnson' but will say openly 'I'm against socialism and I don't know what I'm going to do but I'm not going to vote for Kennedy and Johnson.'"[17]

State Democrats were split over the election: although Hollings and Johnston endorsed Kennedy, former governor Byrnes openly campaigned for the Republican ticket, while Senator Thurmond claimed he was not "in the bag."[18] (Thurmond later framed the election as "a choice of whether to have a labor government or a government of free enterprise," a thinly veiled reference to his preference for the Republican ticket.)[19] Meanwhile only one South Carolina congressman was willing to give speeches on Kennedy's behalf.[20] Remembering campaigning in 1960, Hollings remarked: "I couldn't get anybody much [to help]. I had Tom Pope and Dick, up there, Richards, the Congressman in the fifth district [Bob Hemphill]. . . . We worked together, just about four or five of us, Ted Riley, we worked together and we carried the state."[21]

Hollings was largely dismissive of the efforts of Johnston, who "made a few talks without giving me a heads-up on his plans."[22] By 1960 it was already rumored that Hollings was going to run against Johnston for his Senate seat in 1962, which undoubtedly strained relations between the two men. The Hollings-Johnston rivalry was well known to the Kennedy White House by 1961.[23] Thomas Chadwick recalled that "the state was so split up" over the prospective Hollings-Johnston race that the Kennedy campaign in South Carolina was run out of two different offices, the state Democratic office and the governor's office, filled with Johnston and Hollings supporters, respectively.[24]

It was hard to be a Kennedy booster in South Carolina. Many businessmen supported Nixon on account of his apparently more conservative economic policies, in addition to their concerns about the growing racial liberalism of the national Democratic Party. Charles Daniel, the construction magnate who had cooperated closely with Hollings and his gubernatorial predecessors in industrial recruitment efforts, voted Republican. Hollings's support for Kennedy heralded a terminal decline in his relationship with Daniel.[25] Riley, the state Democratic chairman, recalled the underwhelming reaction to a speech he gave to the Columbia Chamber of Commerce once Kennedy had been nominated. Most of the audience refused to shake his hand, and he later started receiving threatening telephone calls, which he attributed to the presence of a black Kennedy supporter at the speech. Young people "got the idea that it was the thing to be a Republican. . . . I went to a party at the country club and had a Kennedy button on and somebody asked what I was doing at the party."[26] Similarly, John West remembered having a Kennedy/Johnson bumper sticker on his car that would be torn off each Saturday when he went to the country club to play golf.[27]

Most of the state's newspaper reporters supported the Republican ticket, a practice Hollings railed against in his speeches. A recent study by Sid Bedingfield lends credence to Hollings's claim of journalistic partiality. Bedingfield contends that in the years 1959–62, William Workman of the *News and Courier* and his editor "violated [the] code of professional journalism and used their positions at the newspaper to help build the Republican Party in South Carolina." They conferred with Republican leaders over potential news stories, reworded press releases, withheld from the public certain political news stories, and devised campaign strategies to assist GOP candidates.[28] In one address attacking South Carolina's print media, Hollings told his audience: "All they have been willing to tell you is how horrible the Democratic Party is and how socialistic the Democratic Party is. It wouldn't surprise me to see a daily announcement reporting the growth of Kennedy's horns just like they report the number of shopping days til Christmas."[29] Meanwhile reporters and political analysts predicted that the state would go Republican in November.[30]

A major component of Hollings's effort to secure support for Kennedy was to persuade textile industry leaders that the candidate would protect their industry from foreign competition. Textile production dominated the South Carolina economy: by 1960 the state was the nation's largest textile producer, while the industry accounted for more than 54 percent of all manufacturing jobs in the state. But in the 1950s the textile industry began to shed jobs, which many mill owners blamed on the influx of cheaper imports.[31] The first Japanese cotton imports entered the United States in July 1955, which led to South Carolinian protests against "unfair competition" and "slave labor." Remedial legislation was soon passed at the state level in 1956: the Hart-Arthur Act required all places selling Japanese fabrics to hang a sign reading "Foreign Textiles Sold Here."[32] South Carolina politicians also sought a federal-level solution to preserve the state's textile industry, an ultimately futile task. Despite the efforts of Hollings and several other southern politicians to secure presidential intervention to limit foreign imports during his governorship and later as a senator, the industry continued to decline across the United States. Employment in the textile and apparel industry in South Carolina contracted from 160,000 jobs in 1973 to only 60,000 in 2001.[33]

Earlier in 1960 Hollings had testified before the International Tariff Commission alongside Daniel and spoken with President Eisenhower about securing a remedy for the textile industry's problems, with minimal success on both counts.[34] Once Kennedy won the presidential nomination, Hollings spoke and corresponded with him about Kennedy's commitment to protecting textile manufacturers.[35] In a letter to Hollings, the Massachusetts senator declared the need for "a comprehensive industry-wide remedy" to stem the loss of U.S. textile jobs. He further reassured Hollings that as president he would treat the discovery of a solution to the textile problem as a "high priority objective."[36]

Kennedy's letter on textiles was widely circulated among South Carolina's industry leaders, with positive results. John K. Cauthen, the executive vice president of the Textile Manufacturers Association, wrote to Hollings's administrative assistant that "the Kennedy letter went out to the entire industry. The Governor's efforts in [*sic*] our behalf are deeply appreciated and we look forward to additional assistance from him as being most important in helping to solve our troubles."[37] Using Kennedy's letter in a television broadcast aired on November 3 on Greenville's WFBC, Hollings contrasted the Democrat's cooperation with the lack of assistance he received from the Eisenhower administration. He even attacked the former Republican presidential candidate Thomas Dewey for his role in defending the Japanese side of a textile dispute before the International Tariff Commission, a point he also emphasized in campaign speeches for Kennedy.[38] The contrast between Kennedy and the Republicans on the textile problem was central to Hollings's sale of the Democratic nominee to South Carolina's voters.

Alongside his emphasis on Kennedy's commitment to protect South Carolina's main industry, Hollings sought to repudiate the impression of the candidate as a racial and economic liberal. In remarks before the Charleston Civic Clubs, Hollings assailed the Republican Party for the presence of liberals, civil rights activists, and labor unionists in its ranks. "When you join the Republican club," he argued, "you will be sitting with Jimmy Hoffa and Harry Bridges, Jacob Javits, William Rogers, Roy Wilkins and Martin Luther King." Hollings contended that Kennedy not only opposed the objectionable parts of the Democratic platform but also was antagonistic to the liberal elements in his party, as demonstrated by his choice of Johnson as his ticket-mate. Meanwhile Nixon clashed with the conservative elements of his party when he picked Henry Cabot Lodge. "There's our choice," Hollings claimed. "Nixon who wrote his platform and fought his conservatives—or Kennedy who found his platform and fought the liberals. . . . Anyone who fights liberals is a friend of mine."[39]

Despite the commitment of many of the state's most ardent segregationists to the Republican ticket, among them Farley Smith, Hollings was unwilling to cede the segregationist label to the GOP.[40] If anything, he contended, it was the Republican Party that held the anti-South bias. Hollings described Eisenhower's attorney general, William Rogers, as "a professional South hater" who sought "to crucify the South on a cross of ebony." He asked listeners to "remember what Supreme Court ruled that our laws were illegal, just what Attorney General is enforcing that ruling, and just which administration is giving encouragement to demonstrations, and even riots" the next time they witnessed a protest calling for racial integration.[41]

Hollings was not alone among state Democrats in reminding voters of the Republican administration's role in the push for racial integration in southern public schools. The Little Rock crisis was a prominent motif in this attempt. Much as Hollings decried the Eisenhower administration as one "that can send troops to Little Rock—but not to Cuba," Olin Johnston employed similar rhetoric in his speeches.[42] At a rally in Chesterfield, Johnston claimed that "anyone who votes Republican endorses Republican plans to 'Little Rock' South Carolina schools with federal bayonets . . . [and] endorses Nixon's plans to put a negro in the Cabinet."[43]

On Election Day Kennedy eked out a narrow win nationally and in South Carolina, where he won by 9,800 votes. Party chairman Ted Riley recalled Robert Kennedy's disbelief on the night of the general election when he told him that South Carolina had gone Democratic. Kennedy apparently replied, "Don't pull my leg. We know South Carolina's going Republican."[44] Yet in spite of the Democratic success in the state, Hollings's support of Kennedy became a severe liability for his future political career.

Hollings's joking around with John Kennedy between his election and inauguration offers further insight into the perceived salience of racial politics in South Carolina at the time, as well as the president-elect's tone-deafness on racial issues. After Kennedy told Hollings that he was going to send the liberal Michigan governor "Soapy" Williams to Africa as a special ambassador, Hollings claimed that "we would have carried South Carolina by a landslide" if he had known that during the campaign. Later on Kennedy quipped that "a poll of the African chieftains" on "how they liked [Williams]" came back "medium rare."[45] Historian Dan T. Carter has excoriated Ronald Reagan, a president with questionable interest in minority rights, for joking at a 1965 luncheon with the African American Edward Brooke, then the Massachusetts attorney general, that in some African countries, "when they have a man for lunch, they really have him for lunch." For Carter, Reagan's cannibalism gag was one of the occasions when he "veered over the line of good taste on racial issues."[46]

Hollings had needed to finesse the issue of race in order to support Kennedy enthusiastically in 1960 while still claiming to be "conservative" himself. A campaign document from October 1961 discussing the upcoming Senate primary captured his attempted balancing act. "Continue to play the middle," it read, "anti-Kennedy on civil rights, pro-Kennedy on textiles—until April 15."[47] The fence-straddling attempt failed in 1962, when Hollings lost heavily to the entrenched Democratic senator Johnston. He later claimed his support of Kennedy in 1960 gave people the impression that he was "too smart for his britches."[48]

Shortly after the November presidential election, Hollings and Johnston clashed over patronage appointments as they prepared to run against each other in the 1962 Democratic Senate primary.[49] In one particular case, when they each preferred different appointees to be made collector of customs in Charleston, Johnston brought his aide Tom Chadwick in to speak with President Kennedy. Kennedy subsequently appointed Johnston's preferred candidate. As Chadwick emphasized, the fight over appointments was really about prestige: "If he [Johnston] had not gotten his nomination, in Charleston, which was Fritz's hometown and mine, it would have looked like the Senator had lost his patronage power."[50]

When Hollings ran for the U.S. Senate in 1962, he sought to present himself as the conservative candidate, in contrast with Johnston's New Deal liberalism. A Hollings campaign letter to potential supporters in Aiken County demonstrated this well. The headline read "It's Fritz: Hollings for U.S. Senate. *Conservative on record.*" In the letter Hollings asserted that "I know that a liberal, rubber stamp voting record does not reflect the beliefs of our people or our way of life."[51] On economic issues Johnston was indeed liberal. During his 1935–39 gubernatorial term, he launched his own "Little New Deal" and persisted in pursuing liberal economic policies once elected senator in 1944.[52]

Notably Johnston voted against the Taft-Hartley Act in 1947, which permitted the passage of state-level right-to-work laws. These laws prohibited the "closed shop" and weakened the bargaining power of labor: under the law a union could not require employees to become a member or pay dues to it as a condition of employment. In the effort to present a probusiness image, numerous states in the South and Southwest established right-to-work laws after Taft-Hartley became law. South Carolina passed its own right-to-work law in 1954, which Hollings voted for while he was a state representative. Hollings criticized Johnston's implied opposition to the law and claimed that his opponent was "a tool of the Northern labor goons who are trying to stop the flow of industry into South Carolina."[53] Labor unions were a typical punching bag in South Carolina and southern politics from the 1950s onward: with the region's low unionization rates, politicians often attacked organized labor's alleged pernicious influence in hindering the relocation of industry southward. During his time as lieutenant governor, Hollings alleged that labor unions and New England politicians were contributing to the NAACP so they could present a poor picture of the region's race relations, thereby discouraging industries from leaving the union-heavy Northeast.[54]

Despite his success in pushing through his legislative program and overseeing unprecedented industrial expansion in South Carolina as governor, Hollings was ill placed to challenge Johnston. Johnston was not truly threatened by the right-to-work issue. He was secure politically, especially in the textile-dominated upcountry part of the state. Daily newspapers in the upstate city of Anderson, a Johnston stronghold, charged that Hollings had actually missed several key votes in 1954 during the debate over the right-to-work law.[55] Johnston had himself worked on the floor of a textile mill as a boy and emphasized his rags-to-riches upbringing and support of policies to benefit the working man when campaigning.[56] Concentrated heavily in the upcountry part of the state, mill hands accounted for some 20 percent of white voters when Johnston first ran for governor in 1930; by 1960 a majority of South Carolina's manufacturing jobs were still in the textile industry.[57] Rather than being a question of conservative versus liberal economic philosophies, Johnston offered a class appeal: the Democratic primary was "a contest between those who have and those who do not."[58] Throughout the contest he portrayed Hollings as the politician with the support of the rich. As a former staffer for Johnston and later Hollings, Bubba Meng recalled that if Johnston was late for an event, his daughter, Liz Patterson, would note: "Well, we don't have a plane to fly us around." Meanwhile if Hollings was running late, the Johnston campaign would say something like "Oh well, he'll be here in a little bit, as soon as he finishes over at the country club."[59]

Moreover by 1962 Johnston was deeply entrenched in the Senate. Johnston was the only politician to have defeated Thurmond in a statewide election, no small task given Thurmond's record of relentless politicking and attentive constituent service.[60] Also he used his seniority on the Post Office and Civil Service Committee to great effect in terms of patronage appointments, a simple means of ensuring political loyalty. The result, as Crawford Cook, Hollings's 1966 campaign manager, remarked, was that "anybody that he [Johnston] wanted to have a job in and around government had a job in and around government."[61]

Besides the strength of the Johnston machine, Hollings was significantly weakened by the memory of his support for Kennedy in 1960. Immediately after the election, he criticized the investigations made by Attorney General Robert Kennedy's Justice Department into voter registration practices in the black belt counties of Williamsburg, Dorchester, and Clarendon.[62] In May 1961 Hollings condemned the administration's intervention in the Prince Edward County, Virginia, school suit as "most deplorable." (From 1959 to 1964, Prince Edward County had closed its public schools rather operate them on an integrated basis.) He further announced that he would never "compromise our feelings or our belief" on racial segregation.[63] Hollings repeated his criticism of the attorney general in October 1961, after FBI agents had been sent to Clarendon County, where the *Briggs v. Elliott* school case had been filed. Hollings later remarked: "I said . . . we'll photostat them [voting records] and send them to you. . . . If they're not registering blacks properly, then bring your case. Don't go door-to-door intimidating people."[64] While Hollings may have sincerely believed that the Justice Department was unreasonably investigating South Carolinians without sufficient evidence, his actions also played into an effort to distance himself from the Kennedy family, who were deeply unpopular in South Carolina.

A key problem for Hollings was the apparent contradiction between his professed conservatism and his efforts to elect Kennedy. One Aiken constituent told him that "your claim to conservatism seems to be incompatible with your ardent support of Mr. John F. Kennedy in 1960, support which necessarily implies endorsement of Mr. Kennedy's socialist platform."[65] Hollings received countless other reminders that he had infuriated his former supporters. For instance John Holliday of the Pee Dee Farms Corporation reported to him in December 1961 on the issues raised during a meeting of farmers in Marion County. "They asked you, point blank, your connections with the 'Kennedy Dynasty,' and exactly how you stand with Jack and Bobby Kennedy."[66] Roy Strasburger, gauging Hollings's support in Columbia, encountered a similar difficulty: "I seem to run into a particular problem which stems from your enthusiastic support of Mr. Kennedy during the presidential election. These people seem to fear that you will support any or all of Mr. Kennedy's programs simply because he is Mr. Kennedy."[67] Hollings's Kennedy problem replayed across the state. Notes detailing a meeting to discuss his Senate campaign in Sumter recount that "Mr. Lee stated that the biggest thing Mr. Hollings had to over-come in Sumter County was the fact that he went all out for Kennedy after the convention was over."[68]

The recollection of the Charlestonian Charles "Bud" Ferillo, a longtime South Carolina civil rights and education advocate, of the local reaction to the president's assassination in 1963 gives some indication of the depth of antipathy many white South Carolinians felt toward him. Ferillo remarked, "I can't begin to tell you what it was like. . . . I remember hearing reports that afternoon that the Citadel corps of cadets had let out cheers throughout the campus. To me, that symbolized the . . . majority of white South Carolinians' attitude about the Kennedys."[69] Journalist Nick Kotz recounted similar macabre celebrations taking place at Mississippi State University.[70] The charge that Hollings did the Kennedys' bidding politically followed him in each of his future political campaigns. In 1992, thirty-two years after John Kennedy's election, GOP fliers were stressing Hollings's connections with another Kennedy, this time Edward.[71]

Ironically, given the burden of Hollings's support for the Kennedys, the Kennedy administration did not support him over Johnston. He was convinced that the White House was working against him. In his memoir he claims that the White House supported Johnston, since his power over postmaster appointments could help Edward Kennedy in his Massachusetts Senate campaign that year. One particular event stuck with Hollings. During the primary campaign, he and Johnston were giving speeches at the Parker High School football field in Greenville. Democratic congressman Mendel Rivers, chairman of the House Armed Services Committee, had told Hollings that the nearby Donaldson Air Base was due to be closed, a point Hollings raised in his address.[72] However when Johnston came to speak, "Dick Donohue and O'Brien at the White House sent a telegram to Olin, and he announced that he had just got a telegram from President Kennedy and that Donaldson Air Base would stay open. Of course, right after the general election they closed Donaldson."[73]

The increased respectability of the state-level Republican Party in South Carolina also played against Hollings going into the 1962 primary. Such respectability was an apparent extension of the foothold the GOP had gained at the presidential level in the 1950s. For the first time in the twentieth century, the party fielded a serious candidate for senator in the form of conservative newspaper reporter William Workman. For decades South Carolina's Republican Party had been inconsequential in statewide elections. Certainly many South Carolinians continued to view Republicanism as something shameful. When Floyd Spence became a Republican in 1962, he was socially ostracized. Many of his former courthouse friends would not speak to him, while his children were made social outcasts at their school.[74] Yet the open support of the Republican ticket by former governor Byrnes in 1960 and the GOP's strong showing in the presidential election that year did reduce the stigma of being a Republican. Moreover the GOP elected its first member of the state legislature in the twentieth century in an August 1961 special election in Richland County. The Republican candidate in 1962, Workman, was widely recognized across the state (he signed his columns simply "W.D.W.") and held very conservative racial and economic views.[75] In addition to his close association with the Citizens' Council movement, he published a segregationist polemic in 1960 titled *The Case for the South*, which justified lynching black men to prevent them from "consorting with a white woman."[76]

Writing to Hollings, Charles Gibbs bemoaned the increased presence of voters in the city and Saint Andrews wards of Charleston who "seem to think that by voting Republican one attains a certain fashionable status. I have heard a good many otherwise sensible people indicate that they may stay out of the Primary in order to vote for Bill Workman with no strings attached. . . . Unless we can figure out some way to fight this attitude we may lose perhaps as much as 2500 votes in Charleston County in the Primary."[77] Had there been no viable Republican alternative, many of those who later voted for Workman in the 1962 general election might have voted for Hollings over Johnson in the Democratic primary, given that Hollings's economic policies hued closely to those Workman espoused. As the state Democratic Party still had a loyalty oath, voters in the primary were honor bound to vote for the successful Democratic candidate in the general election.[78] Hollings saw something more conspiratorial in the nonparticipation of business-oriented voters in the Democratic primary: "I knew of Hollings voters on account of the Chamber of Commerce, the Main Street merchant, the industrial developer, the contractor, the builder, all of that crowd. I was making their livelihood for them, and I was the toast of the town, but not politically. They were saying, by gosh, we're going to put Workman in, and the best way to do it was to beat Hollings now because Workman will never beat Hollings in a general election."[79] While it is difficult to quantify the number of voters who sat out of the 1962 Democratic primary so they could vote for Workman in the general election, the nonparticipation of these voters in the primary undoubtedly increased the margin of Hollings's defeat. As around nineteen thousand more South Carolinians voted in the 1962 general election than in the June Democratic primary, historically the only relevant election in the state, Hollings may well have received those nineteen thousand votes had there been no Republican candidate.[80]

On election eve the *State* newspaper predicted that the race between Hollings and Johnston was too close to call.[81] The next day Johnston won by a two-to-one margin.[82] Against an opponent with considerable patronage powers and harmed by both his own association with the Kennedys and the defection of business-oriented voters to the Republican Party, Hollings suffered a blowout loss. Out of South Carolina's forty-six counties, Hollings carried only rural Calhoun County, and that only narrowly. Given Johnston's influence over appointments, it was ironic that the only county Hollings carried was through the support of the local senator, Marion Gressette, who thought that Johnston had double-crossed him in overlooking his U.S. marshal candidate.[83]

Despite their bitter primary campaign, Hollings immediately sought to mend political fences with Johnston: he showed up at the senator's victory party and subjected himself to mild ridicule dealt out by Johnston and his brother Bill, who served as the mayor of Anderson.[84] Hollings endorsed Johnston in the general election, which he won by a margin of twelve points, 56–44.[85] His rapprochement with the Johnston people bore fruit after Johnston died in office in 1965. In 1962, however, Hollings's loss meant that he would leave public office once he completed his gubernatorial term and return to practice law in Charleston.

Shortly after urging peaceful acceptance of the racial desegregation of Clemson College in his closing gubernatorial address in January 1963, Hollings and his family left the governor's mansion. They took some furniture with them, a decision that ignited controversy in the state. There was no clear precedent for the items governors were entitled to take from the mansion upon completion of their terms; several former officeholders were presented with their desks and office chairs as mementos of their time in office.[86] After rumors circulated that Hollings might have removed some furniture unlawfully, Laurens County senator King Dixon called for a state senate investigation into the matter. Hollings charged that the probe was a political maneuver intended to tarnish his record in case he ran for governor again in 1966 against the newly elected lieutenant governor, Robert McNair, an ally of Johnston. He told the *Daily Mail* in Anderson that Dixon "understood I had intentions of running for governor again—and . . . he was going to kill me off so that I wouldn't be in Bob McNair's way."[87] After Hollings himself had testified before Senator Gressette's Judiciary Committee, the motion to investigate him was gutted on the floor of the state senate following a fierce debate. Gressette demanded "more than hearsay and rumors" to indict the former governor on such a charge.[88]

Particularly irksome for Hollings was the contention that he should return a pair of "Dowdy birds," a valuable set of ornamental china birds given to him by state senator Edgar Brown. One of the birds was later found to be broken. Hollings's wife at the time, Patricia Salley, allegedly smashed it.[89] Years later the investigation still irritated Hollings. In an oral history he remarked: "Just to try and befriend the incoming crowd, there were certain ones . . . [who] tried to spitball me about taking furniture. Hell, I wasn't even there when they moved it. I found out they were talking about the birds that Edgar Brown had literally given to me. I said—'Why raise the argument? Give them the damned birds back. I don't have to have china birds.' [The furniture] was my dining room set. I had to take personal furniture up to the Governor's mansion, because they didn't have anything up there when I got up there. You'd be amazed. I had to add a wing on for children and guests."[90] The allegations of moral impropriety, and the story of the Dowdy birds in particular, followed Hollings into subsequent political campaigns. Kent Krell, an Associated Press reporter who shadowed Hollings's U.S. Senate primary race in 1966, heard him exclaim one evening after speaking on the phone that "they're trying to make me out to be Ali Baba!"[91] In 1968 the campaign of Hollings's Republican opponent devised a song based on the Dowdy birds story, to the tune of "Old MacDonald."

> Fritz Hollings had a house
> E–I–E–I–O
> And from this house he took some birds
> China Dowdy–O.[92]

Somewhat bizarrely Hollings's opponent in his 1992 reelection contest, Tom Hartnett, returned to this theme. Hartnett claimed that if it was fair for Hollings to call him a draft dodger, it was reasonable for him to accuse Hollings of "looting" and "ransacking" the governor's mansion when he left it in 1963.[93]

Despite the charges of wrongdoing leveled at Hollings, he did not withdraw totally from politics in 1963. On October 26 he gave a speech at the Vance-Aycock fundraising dinner in Asheville, North Carolina, where he praised both John and Robert Kennedy and predicted that the president would be reelected. He further counseled the audience, which included partisans for the segregationist North Carolinian gubernatorial candidate I. Beverly Lake, that southerners should no longer decide partisan affiliations based on the national parties' civil rights planks.[94] A conservative *News and Courier* editorial suggested that Hollings might find it easier to campaign for office in North Carolina than in his native state. Moreover "while our former governor finds life good under the Kennedys, great numbers of South Carolinians believe the New Frontier is the worst thing that ever happened to America."[95]

Kennedy was assassinated in November 1963, and Texan Lyndon Baines Johnson succeeded him as president. Exploiting to the full the grief over Kennedy's death and the visceral images of racial injustice aired on national television screens, Johnson shepherded a landmark civil rights bill through Congress and signed it into law in July 1964. The presidential election that year marked a watershed in

★ *Clash between Goldwater and Johnson supporters in Charleston, October 1964.*
SOURCE: Bill Barley and Assoc., Inc.

South Carolina politics. The passage of the Civil Rights Act made South Carolina and other southern states fertile ground for Republican gains. Moreover the nomination of the conservative Barry Goldwater on the GOP presidential ticket allowed the party to "go hunting where the ducks are," as the Arizona senator colorfully remarked. One of only six Republican senators to vote against the Civil Rights Act in 1964, Goldwater, who attended the South Carolina party's convention in 1960, had been a favorite of state Republicans for some time.[96]

The general election campaign itself was an ugly affair in South Carolina. President Johnson was advised to avoid the Deep South for his own safety. In his place his wife, Lady Bird Johnson, took an eight-state southern campaign train tour on the "Lady Bird Special" in October 1964. She was booed and heckled in Columbia and greeted with signs reading "Black Bird Go Home," "Lady Bird is a Nigger Lover," and "Johnson is a Communist" in Charleston.[97] Hollings apparently sought to attend these rallies, but he heard from Governor Donald Russell's supporters: "You're not invited and we want you to know you're not invited."[98] In addition to the racial epithets directed toward the first lady, racial tensions were obvious in clashes between white Goldwater supporters and black Johnson partisans at a Republican rally in Charleston in October.

In the general election that year, Johnson won in a landslide, winning all but six states nationally. However Goldwater made significant strides in the Deep South: alongside his home state of Arizona, he carried Alabama, Georgia, Louisiana, Mississippi, and South Carolina. In Mississippi, the state whose white citizens held most tenaciously to Jim Crow race relations, Goldwater won a remarkable 87 percent of the vote. With South Carolinians giving him 59 percent of their votes, his victory was the first for a Republican presidential candidate in the state since Reconstruction. In contrast in presidential elections from 1968 to 2012, Democrats carried South Carolina only once.[99]

In another important development for the respectability of the South Carolina GOP, Strom Thurmond changed his party affiliation from Democratic to Republican in September 1964 and won reelection to his Senate seat in the November election. Thurmond, once described by Hollings as "the best political weather vane I know," was not a politician to move against the prevailing currents of his state's politics.[100] His decision to switch parties stemmed as much as anything from a sense that it would become increasingly difficult for him to win nomination from a Democratic primary electorate that was incorporating a significant number of African Americans and would acquire even more by the time he faced a Democratic primary in 1966.[101] Even before the passage of the Voting Rights Act, the number of blacks registered to vote in South Carolina had increased by more than 50 percent between 1962 and 1964.[102] Although Thurmond rarely highlighted his newly acquired affiliation, his reelection as a Republican highlighted the growing comfort with Republicanism in the state while also ensuring a battle within the state party between the original, racially moderate business wing and its growing ultra-segregationist component.[103] The dominance of the latter faction was apparent in the appointment of Thurmond aide Harry Dent as the chairman of the state Republican Party in September 1965. He replaced Arthur Ravenel, the leader of the party's racial moderates.[104]

Despite the willingness of politicians in the Republican Party to capitalize on racial disaffection, the actions of South Carolina Democrats were not much different. In the same month that Harvey Gantt was peacefully admitted to Clemson—January 1963—Gov. Donald Russell introduced a tuition grant plan to the almost entirely Democratic state legislature to provide tuition grants to public school pupils, thus allowing white children to avoid the impact of school desegregation by attending private, segregated, schools instead.[105] Meanwhile after the passage of the Voting Rights Act in August 1965, which allowed for the large-scale registration of previously disfranchised black citizens, South Carolina was the first state to challenge the law. *South Carolina v. Katzenbach*, decided in March 1966, unsuccessfully contested the preclearance provisions of the law. As

Crespino notes, "in the mid-1960s, backlash politics was still fluid, not the domain of any one party."[106] This fluidity was readily apparent in Hollings's campaigns for the U.S. Senate in the late 1960s.

After a short period of ill health, Olin Johnston died in office on April 18, 1965.[107] Four days later Donald Russell, a fierce rival of Hollings's who had lost to him in the state's 1958 gubernatorial race, resigned from the governorship and had his successor, Robert McNair, appoint him to Johnston's Senate seat. Russell performed this maneuver without speaking with the late senator's wife, Gladys Johnston, who might reasonably have expected Russell to offer her or Johnston's brother Bill the interim appointment. Although Russell held the seat, he faced a special election for the remainder of Johnston's Senate term at the next election cycle in 1966. Russell's "self-appointment" provided Hollings with the chance to run again for the Senate. There was a strong antipathy between him and Russell. Hollings was angered both by Russell's apparent tampering with state programs that he had initiated, especially the Technical Education Program, and by efforts made to freeze him out of Democratic politics once he left the governor's office. Hollings later recalled: "He'd tried to really close down the damn programs, so hell, I was going to run."[108]

Although there is little doubt he intended to reenter politics, Hollings's personal correspondence suggests that he was planning to run for the governorship again in 1966 rather than the Senate, much like Johnston had done in 1942.[109] Hollings recognized that it would be almost impossible to unseat Thurmond, who was up for reelection in 1966. Hollings's internal polling suggested that Thurmond was not vulnerable at all. Phone conversation notes from March 1966 point to this realization, in addition to the growing acceptability of Republicanism in the state: "Survey shows that in South Carolina the word Republican isn't horrible any more. Even if Jesus Christ ran against Thurmond, the Senator would be elected." The Johnson White House knew of Hollings's pragmatic preference for facing Russell. Asked about his intentions in May 1965, Hollings remarked that Russell, not Thurmond, was "[his] cup of tea," as "he'd be easier for me to beat."[110]

Hollings's successful 1966 Senate campaign highlighted the continued importance in South Carolina politics of local kingmakers, especially the Johnston family's extensive political network. Following Olin Johnston's death, Hollings met with Gladys and spoke with her at length, a connection that helped him greatly in his bid to capture Johnston's seat in 1966. The late senator's support base resembled a political machine, and even after his death, Gladys Johnston's approval or disapproval could still sway many votes. Her graciousness was not a certainty: the state's most prominent Republicans, Thurmond and Congressman Albert Watson (who ran for governor in 1970), also visited her Columbia home, but she asked them to leave.[111] At Johnston's funeral, Hollings later recalled, Gladys encouraged him to run in 1966.[112] Cook, who later served as Hollings's campaign manager in 1966 and 1968, counseled him on the wisdom of continued rapprochement with the Johnston family in June 1965. He wrote that "the animosity between the Johnstons and Russells has not abated and shows no signs of doing so any time soon. Continued overtures in the right direction may neutralize what would ordinarily have been many anti-Hollings votes here."[113]

As a result of his smoothing over of relations after the bitter 1962 primary, Hollings received the tacit support of the Johnston family in 1966. This quiet endorsement was achieved by having a former legislative assistant and close family friend of Senator Johnston, Bubba Meng, work on Hollings's 1966 Senate campaign. Meng, who had even dated Johnston's daughter while they were both at college, later spoke of Gladys Johnston as "like a second momma to me." Meng recalled the conversation he had with her before choosing to work for Hollings in 1966: "Miss J. [Gladys Johnston] called on the phone and said, 'Bubba, I want you to do something for me. . . . Brother Bill is going to come out and endorse Governor Hollings [for the Senate]. I can't come out and do that. All of our friends would know if you would go to work for him that I want him to be U.S. Senator. And I want to ask you to do that.'"

When campaigning in 1966, Hollings emphasized Meng's Johnstonite credentials. Meng recollected that "we'd go in stores or if we'd run into a post office, he would often say, 'Bubba, come here and meet this fellow. Bubba used to be with Senator Johnston.'"[114] As Cook noted, Meng also "[kept] us clean with the Johnston people. Whatever we needed to do to make things good or better, you let us know. . . . That was our key to maintaining open and good relations with the Johnston family."[115] Hollings announced his formal entry into the Senate race against Russell on March 22, 1966, in a campaign that offered insight into the contemporary dynamics of racial politics in the state. A November 1965 Kraft poll conducted for Hollings's campaign highlighted the salience of race in the vote choice of whites. A majority of both Hollings's and Russell's white supporters declared that "race" was the most important problem facing the state (54 percent and 67 percent, respectively). Moreover the pollster noted that undecided voters not only were more attached to racial segregation than those who had already declared their candidate preference but were "even feistier about it," a situation that helped explain the subsequent racial campaigning by all concerned parties.[116]

The South Carolina electorate was more racially diverse in 1966 than the last time Hollings had run a statewide race. As a result of registration drives by the Voter Education Project and other civil rights groups, the number of black people registered in South Carolina rose from 90,901 in 1962, to 139,000 in 1964, an increase from 23 to 37 percent of the eligible black population. Black voter registration efforts in South Carolina were moderately successful in a regional context: a far higher percentage of eligible blacks registered to vote in the state than in Mississippi or Alabama, yet South Carolina's registration figures lagged behind

★ *Voter registration line in Richland County, 1964.*
SOURCE: Bill Barley and Assoc., Inc.

the majority of eligible blacks registered in Tennessee, Texas, and Florida.[117] With the passage of the Voting Rights Act in 1965, South Carolina's African Americans accounted for roughly 20 percent of the total electorate by 1966.[118] Despite this increase black registration still lagged behind white in South Carolina and across the South, while politicians remained reluctant to embrace African American voters openly and sought to avoid association with the "bloc vote."[119]

An example of the perceived toxicity of being supported by the black "bloc vote" came in the textile-dominated upstate. John West, who was campaigning for the lieutenant governorship at the time, remembered seeing at the mill shifts in Anderson County photos distributed by Hollings supporters of Russell shaking hands with the state NAACP field secretary I. DeQuincey Newman. When West quizzed Hollings's campaign staff about where they had found the photo, they replied that Newman had given it to them. "He was supporting Hollings and he realized that it was a political asset for Hollings's crowd to distribute it."[120]

Elsewhere in the primary, the ultrasegregationist South Carolina Independent Party, headed by Maurice Bessinger, charged that black voters favored Hollings. A pamphlet produced by the Independents informed readers that "while the NAACP, CORE and the SCLC are secretly supporting Hollings, the infamous

Modjeska Simkins [a former secretary of the state NAACP with Socialist Party connections] has publicly endorsed Russell to embarrass him and make it appear as if he has the Negro support. DON'T BE FOOLED! The Negro Bloc Vote will go to Hollings because of his Shady Deals."[121] Actually Simkins was a longtime opponent of Hollings. At a Charleston meeting of the black Palmetto State Voters' Association in 1962, she had argued against supporting Hollings in the Senate primary that year and reminded those present of "what happened in the Orangeburg strike" in 1960, when local police forces "wet up all those girls out in the yard . . . with the water hoses." Simkins never warmed to Hollings: in a 1976 oral history, she expressed doubt whether "any of them [former segregationists] change their hearts. They're that kind—'till they get ready to die."[122]

Despite any claims of "bloc voting," Hollings rode his own record as governor and Russell's "drop-out" governorship to victory in the June primary, which he won with almost 61 percent of the vote.[123] Hollings's slogans—"Great governor—greater senator" and "Four years of excellence versus two years of mediocrity" (referencing Russell's incomplete gubernatorial term)—highlighted these themes.[124] As in the 1958 gubernatorial contest, Hollings probably outworked Russell too. Cook noted that he "would be at a mill shift at five-thirty or six o'clock in the morning, campaign all day, and would be at the mill shift at midnight. He just worked his ass off."[125] The AP reporter Kent Krell agreed: Hollings "benefited from seeming to enjoy meeting people on the mill shift at 7am in the morning, whereas Russell . . . was stiff and ineffective."[126] Russell's defeat was easy to predict. Alongside alienating the Johnston family, precedent dictated that he would have difficulty. Before him only one governor had himself named to the U.S. Senate and won the following election.[127] Krell identified Russell's "self-appointment" as the key factor in the primary.[128]

In the general election campaign, Hollings's Republican opponent was Marshall Parker, a North Carolina native and a state senator from the upstate county of Oconee. Parker had been a floor leader of legislation Hollings sought to pass as governor and had run unsuccessfully as a Democrat for the lieutenant governorship in 1962. Hollings ran a complacent campaign after winning the Democratic primary, an oversight than nearly proved fatal to his Senate hopes. His campaign manager in 1966, Cook, later recalled that Hollings "did not think it would be a serious race. He did not let us change the image of the campaign. We, in effect, ran the same campaign in November that we ran for June and our people were tired. The campaign was stale and didn't excite them. . . . The campaign was simply never energized for November as it was for June."[129] One of the oddities of the 1966 campaign was that Cook was a close friend of Parker's. Before he agreed to manage the Hollings campaign, he had gone so far as to seek Parker's assurance earlier in 1966 that he would not run for the Senate. However Parker subsequently announced his candidacy as a Republican and was nominated without opposition at the state Republican convention. The convention was an all-white affair, with proceedings taking place underneath a Confederate battle flag, demonstrative of the lily-white front the party presented to voters.[130]

Although some Klansmen boasted of chairing county-level Republican organizations in 1966, it is unclear how active the group was in South Carolina in the 1960s.[131] Hollings was proud of the crackdown on Klan activity during his time as governor, but the Klan experienced a remarkable expansion in membership in the mid-1960s.[132] The photographer Bill Barley, who later worked in the McNair administration, shadowed Klan rallies in South Carolina for nine months in 1965 as research for a style piece for a German periodical on a local Klan leader, Esters Cox.[133] Cox was the Grand Kladd of South Carolina and head of the lodges of the United Klans of America (UKA) in the town of Hemingway.[134] Barley recalled significant Klan activity in South Carolina in the mid-1960s, especially in the state's rural counties, an impression corroborated by Department of Health, Education, and Welfare (HEW) school desegregation reports that noted Klan activity in several rural school districts.[135] However, UKA membership was highest in supposedly progressive North Carolina, at its 1966 peak eclipsing the combined UKA membership in all the other southern states.[136] In explaining this trend, David Cunningham, in the only book-length treatment of the 1960s Klan, argued that Klan activity was likely to be highest where three conditions were present, namely, where civil rights reforms were judged to be most deleterious to the status of whites, where there lacked "mainstream outlets for segregationist resistance," and where policing efforts were limited to preventing organized violence.[137]

While the gubernatorial leadership of South Carolina was more moderate than in other Deep South states, white politicians still exhausted all possible legal defenses of racially segregated facilities before accepting changes to the racial status quo. In his biography of Governor McNair, Philip Grose attributed the "strategy of using up all the courts" as a "middle path through the political thicket of desegregation that would spare the state bloodshed and at the same time protect the political flanks to the right of vulnerable decision-makers."[138] The existence of mainstream outlets for vocal segregationist sentiment in South Carolina's Democratic and Republican Parties likely depressed Klan membership in the state compared to its northern neighbor, whose politicians accepted the 1964 Civil Rights Act, albeit reluctantly.[139]

Political scientist Bruce Kalk has argued that Parker fit not with the ultrasegregationists who fled the Democratic Party in the early 1960s but rather with the antisocialist business conservative wing of the embryonic state GOP. Although the modern-day South Carolina GOP originated from conservative economic forces, such an interpretation overplays the nonracial component of Parker's appeal. Parker was on the committee that recommended the reopening of South Carolina's park system on a racially integrated basis, and he contended that "the best hope of curbing the rush toward the collectivist state is thru [*sic*] the ranks of the Republican party."[140] On race, then, Parker's approach bore similarities to Hollings's own record. Newspaper reports at the time noted how he did not fit comfortably into the ultrasegregationist stereotype of new South Carolina Republicans.[141] Parker, however, adopted an antiblack posture for the 1966 campaign. On several occasions he publicly disavowed the black vote in the state. At one event he claimed that Hollings had "100 per cent of the Negro vote" and that he needed one hundred thousand white votes for himself to ensure "a fair race."[142] At another he commented that he wanted "no part of the Negro vote."[143] At other times Parker connected the Democratic Party's supposed socialistic direction with racialized language. In a September speech, he declared that he desired "no part of the Negro bloc vote" before continuing to state that the sole means of halting "socialistic tendencies" in the United States was to elect more Republicans.[144]

Parker also received the backing of the South Carolina Independent Party in 1966, which supported the Republican slate of candidates in November after it had backed Russell in the Democratic primary. The group connected the Democratic Party's supposed reliance on black voters with black rioting and civil disobedience. A pamphlet produced by the Independents proclaimed:

> Now in South Carolina we see the same fatal symptoms [as in Atlanta and Northern cities]. We see our so-called "leaders" openly courting the bloc vote, and slyly justifying their actions as "wisdom" and "progress." . . . We cannot afford to have our State Government in the hands of politicians elected by the Negro bloc vote. WE MUST HAVE STRONG LEADERS, and we must have men in Congress who will speak out for, and protect, the people. Stand Up For South Carolina! Support . . . Strom Thurmond—Joe Rogers—Marshall Parker/ They Will Fight To Protect Your Rights And Safety![145]

Moreover, the pamphlet noted, Parker "has promised to introduce legislation to repeal the hated 1965 Voting Rights Bill. This bill was designed solely to register illiterate Negroes to vote for LBJ and his cronies. . . . He is your man, not LBJ's or RFK's." Elsewhere in the pamphlet there was an article titled "Bobby-Fritz Alliance Revealed; Hollings Backed by S.C. Negroes," which claimed that Hollings had received the "ACTIVE SUPPORT" of NAACP leaders in the Democratic primary.[146] According to the Independents' rationale, given Hollings's reliance on African American votes, the white voters of South Carolina could not afford to have him represent them in the Senate.

In a similar fashion to the Independents, Parker focused relentlessly on Hollings's alleged ties to the Kennedy family and to the deeply unpopular Johnson administration. In June he contended that he could "prove the relationship" between Hollings and Robert Kennedy and offered to produce evidence, an accusation he repeated on television at the close of his campaign.[147] Parker's campaign literature also exploited this association: a letter to campaign committee members repeatedly substituted Hollings's name with "Bobby Kennedy's man."[148] The state GOP organization also sought to connect Hollings with Johnson and the Kennedy family, as when Harry Dent somewhat comically alleged that "everybody in South Carolina knows Fritz is a Kennedy man. It's bad enough to have LBJ as your leader, but worse to have someone as far left and as ruthless as Bobby Kennedy pulling strings for you, even if it is all the way from South Africa."[149] For his part Hollings sought to distance himself as much as possible from the Kennedys, as he had done in the buildup to the 1962 Senate primary. In June he assured Wayne Freeman, the editor of the *Greenville News* who had also served on the state's school segregation committee with him, that Kennedy had no involvement in his campaign. "I don't intend to be hamstrung," Hollings claimed, . . . "by the influence of anyone from outside South Carolina, particularly someone with an ultra-liberal philosophy. . . . Senator Kennedy has not contributed to any of my political campaigns and he will not influence or contribute to our November campaign."[150] Hollings went to some lengths to separate himself from the backlash against the national Democratic Party, as his criticisms of Johnson in 1966 made apparent. He presented himself as independent from the national party and claimed in October that "whenever the President is right, we will support him. Whenever the President is wrong, we will oppose him."[151] Hollings even declared late in the campaign that he would not vote for Johnson in 1968.[152] Mayor Bill Johnston of Anderson, the brother of the late Senator Johnston, captured Hollings's appeal in his endorsement: "First, I think you are the best qualified man. And, second, you are a Democrat—a South Carolina Democrat."[153]

On race Hollings's tone was recalcitrant, though he did not express opposition to existing civil rights laws. Rather he opposed the passage of further legislation, such as the open-housing bill that was defeated in 1966, and alluded in speeches to the need for greater law and order. His drafted speeches from September 1966 stressed these factors. In one he argued that Democrats should receive "a vote of appreciation" for the defeat of the open-housing measure, since "the actual vote in opposition to this legislation was 42 Democrats and 12 Republicans . . . almost four times as many Democrats voted against it as Republicans."[154] In another he partly acknowledged the legitimacy of urban unrest—he noted that "social conditions for a portion of our population are bad to the point of being unbearable"—though he counseled that "substituting black injustice for white injustice is a poor alternative."[155] While not counseling continued massive resistance to civil rights pressures, Hollings's position was far removed from that of the national Democratic leadership.

Hollings's view of the conduct of the Vietnam War, an issue of widespread concern in South Carolina, further distanced him from the national Democratic Party. He claimed that President Johnson had entered Vietnam with "a lot of hoopla" but no clear plan for victory.[156] Hollings's speeches promoted escalation of the conflict in order to bring about a rapid end to the war. A speech draft for the 1966 general election noted that "our basic philosophy in Vietnam must be to get in or get out," but "once we commit our men and our material to such a cause then our overriding effort should be to win our victory and return our men home as quickly as feasible."[157] His rhetoric mirrored the approach of the Senate Armed Services Committee chairman, Richard Russell, to American involvement in Vietnam and the critique of Johnson's war policies by the Armed Services Committee, of which the South Carolinian Thurmond was also a member, more generally.[158] Hollings's support for escalation in Vietnam was consistent with his contention during his time as lieutenant governor that the Korean War could have ended in U.S. victory and with fewer casualties if the American commanders been given greater leeway to act.[159] Hollings's support for escalation in Vietnam further allowed him to contrast himself with the locally unpopular Johnson. Mike Joy, an aide who later served as Hollings's administrative assistant, counseled that "right now I think it is almost impossible to hit [Johnson] too hard. I think you should criticize him *constructively*, but thoroughly."[160] In the campaign and in office, Hollings's Vietnam War convictions distanced him from the president.

Going into the final weeks of the fall campaign, an internal poll suggested Hollings would win some 57 percent of the white vote, which coupled with the overwhelming support of blacks he was expected to gain (who made up about 20 percent of the electorate in 1966), would ensure a comfortable election victory.[161] Likewise a poll of state legislators (still overwhelmingly Democratic) at the end of October revealed that they believed Hollings and Thurmond would win the Senate elections handily.[162] Yet in the closing weeks, Parker noticeably closed the gap. Part of this competitiveness was a result of the Hollings campaign's complacency, no doubt a result of having never faced serious state-level Republican opposition before.

Parker, too, proved to be an adept campaigner. Cook believed that "if that race had gone on another two weeks, Fritz would probably not have been elected."[163] Moreover by the end of the campaign, the Parker campaign became closely tied to that of the popular Senator Thurmond, despite Thurmond's usual reticence to engage in party building. Some 230 billboards were placed across the state that carried giant pictures of Parker and Thurmond facing each other, urging the voter to send both of them to Washington.[164]

Hollings carried the state by only eleven thousand votes in November, with 51 percent of the vote. Fearful of a challenge to the final vote tally, at Vice President Hubert Humphrey's sugggestion, Hollings was quickly certified by the Democratic secretary of state, O. Frank Thornton, and traveled to Washington, D.C., by charter plane to be sworn into office by Humphrey. After all, Humphrey reportedly quipped, "possession is ninety percent of the law."[165] Hollings's early swearing-in allowed him to gain a head start in seniority over the other freshman senators elected to the ninetieth Congress (1967–68). In the other Senate race, Thurmond led the state with 62 percent of the vote, forty thousand votes more than Hollings. Thurmond's presence on the Republican ticket undoubtedly benefited Parker.

The election provided support for both economic and backlash-motivated explanations of Republican growth in South Carolina. Parker had his best showings in the upstate, relatively higher-income counties of Greenville and Pickens.[166] These were areas of Republican strength in the 1950s. An upstate senator himself, Parker's strength in that area might also have reflected the "friends and neighbors" pattern of voting evident in many southern political contests.[167] Meanwhile Democrats won the vast majority of black votes: Hollings took an estimated 97 percent, which provided his margin of victory in the Senate race. Democrat Robert McNair also received his victory margin from black voters. Throughout the campaign, while Parker was less strident in his segregationist pronouncements than either Thurmond or the GOP gubernatorial nominee, Joseph Rogers, all of the statewide GOP candidates appealed to white resentment at black voting and activism, as did the state organization itself. The party distributed some five hundred thousand copies of the *Had Enough News*, which depicted Governor McNair shaking hands with African American voters and smiling aboard the Lady Bird Special in 1964, an unsubtle reminder of the Democratic Party's relationship with African Americans and McNair's apparent closeness to the Johnson administration.[168]

In the weeks following the election, Hollings and his advisers dissected the returns and their polling information to see how their candidate had come so close to losing. He entered the Senate keen to consolidate his position before he faced his next contest in 1968. Hollings subsequently played his bona fides as a states'-rights "South Carolina Democrat" to their fullest extent. On high-profile issues, such as civil rights bills and judicial confirmations, he sided firmly with the conservative southern bloc in the Senate. That he was able to do so without fear of ultimately losing African American backing highlighted the limited choices available to the black electorate in the late 1960s.

★★★ CHAPTER 4 ★★★

Backlash

Two years after squeaking into office, in 1968, Hollings had consolidated his position in the U.S. Senate and beat his Republican opponent—again Marshall Parker—by some 150,000 votes. How Hollings established himself in the U.S. Senate, and how he avoided repeating the near debacle of 1966, deserves closer examination. While his path involved courting the supporters of former Senator Johnston, coming out for a more sustained bombing of North Vietnamese targets, and passing a bill to limit foreign textile imports into the United States, this period is particularly interesting for the light it sheds on racial politics in South Carolina.

Shortly after his election victory in November 1966, the junior South Carolina senator took steps to ingratiate himself with the most influential southern Democrat in the Senate, Richard Russell of Georgia. Immediately after his swearing in, Hollings traveled to Winder County, Georgia, to meet with Russell at his home and seek his advice on committee assignments.[1] Russell's suggestion was to gain a seat on the powerful Appropriations Committee, a position Hollings eventually achieved in 1971. For the 1967–68 Congress, however, Hollings took seats on the Commerce Committee, where legislation concerning the textile industry, dominant in South Carolina, was passed; the Agriculture and Forestry Committee, where farm subsidies and food stamp regulations were instituted; and the Post Office and Civil Service Committee, which the late South Carolina senator Olin Johnston had chaired. In addition to seeking his advice on committee posts, Hollings also heeded Russell's counsel on the nature of politics in the Senate. He repeatedly used Russell's dictum that in the Senate "you're given a six year term, the first two years to be a statesman, the second two years to be a politician, and the last two years to be a demagogue."[2] The 1966–68 period, then, was Hollings's "demagoguing" interval, even though the circumstances of the 1966 special election had rearranged the Georgia senator's sequence of stages.

Democratic activist Joseph Sapp reminded Hollings in a November 1966 memorandum that, alongside the apparent need to demagogue, appearances mattered as much as accomplishments when running for reelection: "Our friend on the Federal Bench [former senator Donald Russell] is a good example of the fallacy of the notion that you can run a campaign by being an effective Senator. A senatorial reputation certainly helps a candidate, but it is a fringe benifit [*sic*] rather than the basis for a campaign."[3] In keeping with this line of thinking, Hollings used an ingenious method to increase his prestige at home while improving his understanding of policy and the rules of the Senate. By presiding for such long periods over the Senate, regarded by many as an unpleasant duty, Hollings received a "Golden Gavel Award" at the end of the session, which he later touted in his campaign speeches. He claimed that presiding for so long allowed him to know senators' "likes and dislikes, getting to know them personally, and do them favors." Consequently, he asserted, "when I brought my textile problem to their attention I was able to talk on a first name basis and secure 68 co-sponsors."[4] The textile amendment Hollings referred to would have allowed the president to preserve domestic textile jobs by restricting imports, but it never became law.[5] Hollings successfully attached his textile quota amendment to a Senate excise tax bill in 1968, but it faced determined White House opposition.[6] In May 1968 White House aides made a deal with Arkansas Congressman Wilbur Mills, the chairman of the House Ways and Means Committee, to eliminate the Hollings amendment in conference.[7] Crawford Cook later joked about the "Golden Gavel Award" that "we took what was one of the very undesirable jobs in the Senate . . . and we made it seem like a real event. Hollings has done this wonderful thing. We made big press about it. The next campaign we had tie pins made in the shape of a gavel."[8]

During his first Senate term, Hollings also courted the supporters of the late Senator Olin Johnston, whose seat he filled when he ran in 1966. Coming into the Senate, Hollings kept Johnston's former assistant Bubba Meng on his staff; working in Hollings's Columbia office, Meng remained with the senator until 1985. At the beginning of the ninetieth Congress, Hollings joined the Post Office and Civil Service Committee, which Johnston had chaired from 1950 until his death in 1965. Johnston had used the patronage power of this chairmanship to great effect, which had ensured the presence of a loyal body of Johnston supporters around South Carolina and also in Washington, a fact that greatly helped the logistics of Hollings getting set up in the Senate. As Cook remembered, Johnston had political appointees throughout the Senate's administrative buildings: "Olin's appointees were everywhere. . . . All of those people literally worked for him, and a hat full of them were from South Carolina. So they were more than willing to help."[9] Upon his own appointment to Post Office and Civil Service, Hollings paid tribute to Johnston as "the greatest champion" of the nation's government workers.[10]

Hollings campaigned aggressively throughout his 1966–68 term. Cook, his campaign manager in 1966 and his administrative assistant once he entered the Senate, contended that Hollings "recognized the problem after that '66 almost-fiasco and he wasn't about to let that happen again. So he campaigned very aggressively the whole time."[11] Similarly Ike McLeese, who was part of the so-called diaper brigade (a group of students with little previous involvement in politics) who assisted Hollings's 1966 campaign and then worked in Hollings's Spartanburg office, recalled the brutal schedule Hollings kept:

> We never quit campaigning. I got [Hollings] most Thursdays and would have just a schedule that would wear me and him both to death now. . . . I would pick him up at 4:30, 5 o'clock flight out of Washington on Thursday, and we would work Thursday night shifts at textile plants, and the political event, barbecue, fish fry all day Friday, and either put him on the plane for another part of the state down here [the midlands] or the lowcountry. Sometimes he would start off in the lowcountry, and I would get him on Saturday and work his rear end off until Monday afternoon and put him on a flight back to Washington.[12]

Hollings, set on assuring reelection, showed great attentiveness to the perceived political climate in South Carolina at this time.

During the 1966 campaign, Hollings had advocated for an increased U.S. military presence in Vietnam.[13] After being sworn in on Thursday, November 10, he met with Deputy Secretary of Defense Cyrus Vance and relayed the contention of military personnel around South Carolina, especially Gen. Mark W. Clark, the retired major general Joseph P. Sullivan, and Gen. Hugh Pate Harris, that the United States was pursuing a "no-win" policy in Vietnam. Vance countered that Hollings should visit Vietnam to judge for himself. Consequently Hollings flew out from Washington on November 13 and reached the quarters of Gen. William Westmoreland by the following evening.[14]

Westmoreland was a native South Carolinian and had briefly attended Hollings's alma mater, the Citadel, before completing his studies at West Point. Extremely popular in South Carolina, Westmoreland was later recruited by the state Republican Party to run for the governorship in 1974. Hollings was effusive in his praise for Westmoreland: in a speech to the Spartanburg Lions Club in May 1967, he claimed that Westmoreland was leading "one of the greatest endeavors ever undertaken by the United States."[15]

Consistent with his strategy of attrition, Westmoreland emphasized in November 1966 that ten Vietcong soldiers were dying for every one American and informed Hollings that the army needed only 35,000 more troops to win, in addition to the 535,000 troops already there in November 1966. After visiting the Gulf of Tonkin, Hollings was shocked to learn that certain military targets in North Vietnam were off-limits. As a result he took a list of seventy-five prohibited military targets from Lt. Gen. Joe Moore, another South Carolinian, and passed the list on to President Johnson once he returned to the United States. Were these targets to be authorized, Moore contended, the war would be won within a few months.[16] After the trip to Vietnam, Hollings claimed that "our military is doing an outstanding job in the north, but with the artificial environment created by restrictions on the military, the war in the north is a stalemate and therefore we are losing."[17]

Hollings repeatedly attacked Johnson's conduct of the Vietnam War. In January 1967 at the annual Rock Hill Jaycees Distinguished Service Award banquet, he claimed that the president had failed to unite the United States behind the war effort.[18] Hollings later recounted his November 1966 meeting with Johnson in a sharply critical constituent newsletter from October 1967. (Throughout his career Hollings wrote the final version of the newsletters his office sent out.)[19] He wrote: "The President explained that he was bombing as much as public opinion would permit. . . . I agree that we should not pursue a total war of annihilation. But when you couple the high purpose of Johnson [*sic*] strategy with the Johnson penchant for polling and politics, the people are left distraught." Johnson's "deliberate gradualism," Hollings argued, had cost the United States the opportunity to end its involvement in Vietnam before the 1968 elections.[20]

In another newsletter from June 1967, he urged for previously prohibited targets to be permitted. In a nod to the locally popular South Carolina general, he declared that "we must destroy the enemy's ports and sources of supply. We should bomb the dikes, manufacturing facilities and military targets. We must give Westmoreland the divisions the commanders have been asking for."[21] Hollings continued to attack Johnson's supposedly political approach to the Vietnam War as the 1968 elections approached. In August 1968 before a crowd of one thousand in Charleston, Hollings claimed that "the one thing we haven't tried in Vietnam is a military settlement."[22] Vietnam was particularly important to the South Carolina electorate in the late 1960s, as a Kraft poll conducted for Hollings in November 1967 confirmed.[23]

Cook saw Hollings's position on Vietnam, particularly his attack on Johnson's policies, as highly beneficial to his standing among South Carolina's voters: "All of a sudden South Carolinians were looking at Fritz in a different light. He was on *Meet the Press* and *The Today Show*. He was a big man among big men. It added credibility and stature to him here at home. The war was so unpopular that being opposed to the president's position on the war had to help."[24] Likewise Hollings's Republican opponent in 1968, Marshall Parker, who had run against him in 1966, believed that his criticism of the president on his Vietnam policy nullified a potential Republican line of attack for the 1968 campaign. In an oral history, Parker recalled how Vietnam "was one of our big issues." He expected to be able to "give him [Hollings] a fit for some of the things that were happening [in Vietnam], as Republican-Democratic differences," but Hollings simply "out-cussed Johnson. . . . He called him things I would never call the President of the United States."[25]

Alongside whatever concerns Hollings had about the conduct of the war in Vietnam, there were clear political advantages to opposing Johnson's stewardship of the conflict. South Carolina's voters rejected the president overwhelmingly in the 1964 presidential election, the first time Republicans had carried the state in the twentieth century. Johnson was extremely unpopular in South Carolina aside from disaffection over his position on the war in Vietnam, not least for his successful advocacy for both the Civil Rights Act of 1964 and the Voting Rights Act of 1965 and his nomination of the first African American Supreme Court justice in June 1967.

In keeping with Hollings's public statements on the Vietnam War, throughout his first Senate term, Hollings's voting on military funding was in keeping with a hawkish, conservative foreign policy outlook. He approved all funding increases to cover operations in Vietnam and, according to his 1968 campaign literature, voted for the "strongest possible defense posture." As with many other conservative senators, he also opposed foreign aid: he voted against giving aid to Communist countries and voted to prohibit the Export-Import Bank from providing credit to countries that traded with North Vietnam.[26] Hollings's position also mirrored the disparaging view of foreign aid offered by the conservative insurgent presidential candidate George Wallace.[27]

There were also racial implications to Hollings's proescalation position on Vietnam. Vietnam had the effect of splintering the coalition of pro–civil rights groups that had come together to protest effectively for new legislation to protect the legal rights of African Americans in the early 1960s. Once civil rights leaders began to oppose the war as racist and unjust, Hollings was able to portray these activists as unpatriotic, a theme he merged with his distaste for "peaceniks" and civil disobedience more generally.[28] In a newsletter written to constituents in May 1967, Hollings asked them to "put [themselves] in Ho's shoes": "Would you negotiate if you heard that the churches and universities and scholars were petitioning the President and the Congress constantly to withdraw? Would you negotiate if the leader of the civil rights movement, Nobel Prize winner Martin Luther King said that the U.S.A. was 'the greatest purveyor of violence'—when champion Cassius Clay leads the draft evaders—and Stokely Carmichael says to cheering thousands, 'Hell No!' Would you negotiate when thousands paraded in New York cheering the Viet Cong, cheering you as a communist leader—burning their draft cards and burning the American flag?"[29] Given the disaffection of many white South Carolinians with the pace of racial change, it is unsurprising that all the supposedly unpatriotic individuals mentioned by name were black.

Alongside his initial hawkish moves on foreign policy, Hollings took pains to portray himself as a fiscal conservative concerned with states' rights on domestic policy. The first bill he introduced in the Senate, a measure to return a percentage of federal tax revenue to the states, reflected this concern.[30] He claimed that the measure would provide "local incentive" to deal with problems that could not be effectively remedied by a "Washington solution."[31] Hollings extended his critique of the federal government to the operation of the Office of Economic Opportunity (OEO), one of the centerpieces of Johnson's War on Poverty. In response to one constituent who complained of the unequal provision of OEO projects between Spartanburg, Cherokee, and Union Counties, he claimed that the situation served as "the classic example of a government in Washington trying to run the affairs of the people of the counties of South Carolina. . . . This is another clear example of why we need more local control and local supervision of federally funded projects."[32] Hollings touted his fiscally conservative credentials in materials produced for his 1968 reelection campaign. A record of how he voted on the "important issues" of the ninetieth Congress noted that he "voted against eight billion dollars in unwise or untimely spending in an eight week period."[33] Likewise when campaigning he promised to continue the fight against "blank check" government spending.[34]

Occasionally Hollings's disparagement of federal spending caused trouble in South Carolina, as with his claim that the Training for Tomorrow or "T-Square" program was an example of inefficient government spending.[35] The popular Democratic governor, Robert McNair, supported the OEO program, which was aimed at training some twenty-five thousand educationally deficient South Carolinians at centers across the state and was funded by $19 million in federal funds, at no state expense.[36] After receiving criticism for his contention that the state could educate the same number of people through the TEC program for about a fifth of the cost of the federally funded effort, Hollings apologized for his remarks and pledged to secure all possible federal funds for T-Square.[37]

Hollings's views on poverty and welfare at this time followed a similar line of thinking, prioritizing local involvement in solving local problems. Although those views underwent a transformation in 1968 (privately) and 1969 (publicly), his later antihunger message did not contradict the earlier emphasis he placed on local action. In a letter to a constituent that outlined his opposition to a guaranteed income scheme in 1967, Hollings again touted his revenue-sharing proposal. His solution to the problems of poverty "would lie in the realm of revenue sharing between the states and the federal government in an effort to get the money where the money is needed. I think (1) the economies of a system of this type would provide additional revenues, and (2) the state and local governments are better able to identify the particular problem and tailor-make the particular solution for the particular problem rather than the all-encompassing approach currently being used."[38]

Hollings was not entirely antiwelfare in the ninetieth Congress, either. Although he opposed expanding the funding of the OEO, he supported some poverty programs, notably Head Start, within fiscally conservative boundaries.[39] In January 1968 he publicly praised the Head Start and Neighborhood Youth Corps programs, which he claimed "really allude to the needs of the community and give people an opportunity to train for jobs."[40] In contrast Mississippi senator John

Stennis used his clout with the OEO to defund the Child Development Group of Mississippi, the group that initially ran Head Start centers in the state. Many white Mississippians saw Head Start as threatening since it provided jobs at the local level to poor blacks, who could then register to vote without fear of economic reprisal.[41] Hollings's colleague Thurmond denounced the Economic Opportunity Act in a 1965 newsletter as "wasteful and dangerous."[42] Keeping with Hollings's qualified support for antipoverty programs, campaign material for the 1968 election noted that he "voted to repeal Job Corps and instead double the money put into vocational training (also save 100 million dollars). Voting against funding of a new 1.3 billion dollar poverty program. Voted for an additional 25 million dollars for *Head Start.*"[43] Hollings touted his support for Head Start when courting African American backing for his 1968 reelection campaign.

Clearly Hollings was not a lockstep conservative on economic issues, contradicting the characterization the *New York Times* offered of him in his 1967–68 term as "virtually indistinguishable from his arch-conservative southern colleagues."[44] In addition to his occasional support of antipoverty programs, his voting on education funding demonstrated his efforts to use government in an affirmative role to enhance opportunity: his 1968 campaign literature noted that he voted for additional federal aid to education, Head Start, and funds for Vietnam veterans "to obtain an education under the GI bill," as well as cosponsoring "a *tax credit* for those paying for a student's college education."[45]

Nevertheless Hollings sought to avoid any association with "liberalism," as his response to receiving a rating of only forty-six (out of a possible hundred points) from the Americans for Constitutional Action (ACA) group for his first six months in office highlighted. Hollings was the only member of South Carolina's congressional delegation to score below fifty, while the state's Republican senator, Thurmond, received a perfect one hundred.[46] To concerned constituents Hollings adopted a populist argument. He defended his "wrong" vote for the Presidential Financing Act as one to "eliminate special interest government." He further aligned himself with the Alabama firebrand George Wallace by claiming that Republicans opposed the Financing Act because it would allow a third-party candidate "like George Wallace" to receive funding in the 1968 presidential race. On his other wayward vote, for a bill to allow women to collect limited Social Security assistance at the age of sixty rather than sixty-two, he claimed that while easy for "the wealthy, with their fat retirement programs and big bank accounts," to oppose such relief for seniors "who work hard all their lives just to make ends meet," he could not oppose such a measure.[47] The *Orangeburg Times and Democrat*, which reliably supported Democratic candidates at this time, downplayed the difference in the voting records of Hollings and Thurmond. Its editorial remarked: "Both of our senators can be proud of their votes, and certainly Sen. Hollings cannot be tainted with a charge of liberalism."[48]

Throughout his 1966–68 Senate term, Hollings showed great deference to the sensibilities of conservative white South Carolinians. For many of these voters, race remained a central concern, as opinion polls conducted on Hollings's behalf confirmed. In a letter to *Greenville News* editor Wayne Freeman after the 1968 campaign, Hollings discussed this preoccupation with race and its connectedness with allegedly "coded" issues such as "law and order" in the minds of voters. Having taken information from two different polling companies, he revealed that "in both instances, the number one issue is race. This is disconcerting because a candidate would like to come and talk about jobs and opportunities, but politically he knows this falls on deaf ears, and, instead, he must talk about law and order."[49] Concerns about the breakdown of law in the mid-1960s were well founded, as violence swept across urban ghettos nationwide. The peak of unrest came in 1967. By September of that year, there had been 164 instance of mass violence, of which 33 had brought state police intervention and another 8 had led to the involvement of the National Guard.[50]

The phrase "law and order" was well recognized for its potential to relay racial code to voters. A Kraft poll conducted in November 1967 for Hollings's reelection campaign noted that its discussion of race relations in South Carolina "could just as easily have been classified under the general heading of 'Law and Order.'" Moreover, from the viewpoint of conservative white voters, "the demonstrator—and this includes anti-war demonstrators as well as civil rights demonstrators—is flaunting the law of the land, or at least what they think should be the law of the land."[51] Richard Nixon was well aware of the racial message conveyed by law and order pronouncements. During his 1968 presidential campaign, he claimed that one commercial focused on the breakdown of the rule of law "hit it right on the nose. . . . It's all about law and order and the damn Negro-Puerto Rican groups out there."[52]

More than a quarter of the newsletters sent by Hollings to his constituents in the 1967–68 congressional session railed against the perceived breakdown of the rule of law in the United States and publicized the measures he had introduced to remedy the situation. Only dispatches discussing the Vietnam War outnumbered these law-focused newsletters.[53] In some Hollings railed against recent decisions made by the Supreme Court to expand the rights of the accused, as in his June 1967 "War on Crime" newsletter, in which he referred to the 1957 decision in *Mallory v. United States.* In contrast to the claims of "the sociologists" that crime was a function of "poverty and ignorance," Hollings disagreed: "I believe the reason [for criminal activity] is our Courts' attitude in criminal cases. The civil right of the hardened criminal is upheld to the ridiculous. And completely obscured is the civil right of the average citizen not to be robbed, not to be raped, and not to be murdered. By a set of 5-to-4 decisions the Supreme Court has hand-cuffed the policeman and set the prisoner free."

In the case of the African American Andrew Mallory, "it wasn't long" before he committed another rape. Consequently, Hollings explained, he had cosponsored numerous bills to aid law enforcement alongside Senators John McClellan of Arkansas, Sam Ervin of North Carolina, and Alan Bible of Nevada.[54] Hollings emphasized this theme in his campaign events, too. Notes in his handwriting for an October 1968 lunch listed five points in response to the question "Where stand on crime—what done," including "D.C. Crime Bill—law," "Desecration of flag—law," and "20 Bills with Sen. McClellan."[55]

At other times the racially charged nature of the law and order theme was more obvious, as in the oblique reference to Martin Luther King Jr. in one of Hollings's constituent newsletters from December 1967: "Most of the students and rights leaders who reject society feel like an arrest is a badge of an individual's sincerity. . . . In fact, if you are real good at it, arrest and jail can bring a Nobel Prize."[56] In another newsletter Hollings alluded to the Orangeburg Massacre, in which three black students had been shot and killed by state troopers at South Carolina State College in February 1968. The shootings marked the culmination of an altercation that had begun with black protests over the failure of a local bowling alley to admit black patrons. The newsletter, titled "Clear Call for Law," read: "If you don't like the way a bowling alley is operated, then your right under the law and your responsibility under the law is to cross the street to the Court House and obtain a blue paper and close it down. You have no right to put a brick through the window or burn it down."[57] Although not among the most incendiary language offered by segregationist southern politicians at this time, Hollings's comments were nevertheless a clear nod to the concerns of conservative whites in South Carolina.

Perhaps unsurprisingly Hollings emphasized his solidarity with Wallace, who captured the anxieties of many conservative whites in his 1968 and 1972 presidential campaigns, during which he railed against the breakdown of law and order and the prospect of school busing.[58] Wallace ran as an independent presidential candidate in 1968, challenging the Republican Nixon and the Democratic vice president, Hubert Humphrey. As soon as Hollings had been elected in 1966, his supporters began to theorize how best to deal with the Wallace campaign, as well as the national Democratic Party, in 1968.[59]

Ultimately Hollings endorsed Humphrey, though he kept his distance from the national Democratic Party both physically and rhetorically. Later, in a document written shortly after the November 1968 election, he touted the evasion of "the presidential game" as an important factor in his success that year.[60] Despite his Republican opponent's best efforts, the attempt to tie Hollings to Humphrey was ineffective.[61] Humphrey avoided South Carolina, and Hollings did not attend the Democratic National Convention held in Chicago, which was marred by antiwar protests and police brutality. A radio editorial given by a pro-Wallace WDIX station based in Orangeburg and owned by a member of the John Birch Society, offered a sympathetic account of Hollings and Congressman William Jennings Bryan Dorn's nonappearances at the Chicago convention: "These powerful Democrats want no part of any ticket coming out of the Chicago convention. . . . Would you say that a vote a vote for Hollings and Dorn is a vote for Humphrey? Don't make us laugh."[62]

While endorsing Humphrey, Hollings disavowed the Minnesota Democrat's views. In a letter to one concerned constituent, he presented himself as a captive of the party's loyalty oath. As he had contested and won the state's Democratic primary, "I signed an oath that we will vote for the Democratic ticket." Nonetheless "I made it clear before the vote in the Primary that I was not going to be the presidential campaign manager for anyone. . . . I have my hands full."[63] In one campaign speech, Hollings made his case simply: "Mr. Humphrey quite frankly [runs] on a different platform."[64] A letter written by Hollings's secretary, Betty Bargmann, clarified that while he personally endorsed Humphrey, "he does not advise South Carolinians how to vote."[65]

While personally endorsing Humphrey, Hollings offered a sop to Wallace supporters. Writing to the chairman of the Wallace for President Association of Spartanburg County, he confirmed that should none of the presidential candidates receive the necessary 270 electoral votes to win outright, he would vote in the Senate for the vice presidential candidate whose ticket carried South Carolina in the November election. Given Wallace's popularity across the Deep South, he could have feasibly carried South Carolina. Hollings used his position to separate himself from his Republican opponent in 1968, Marshall Parker, who "said he would vote his National Party's choice and not the choice of the people of South Carolina."[66] In another nod to Wallace supporters, Hollings noted that while he was "obligated ethically" to vote for Humphrey, he thought Wallace offered "the clearest position" on ending the U.S. involvement in Vietnam.[67] Hollings also appeared in public with Wallace when he visited South Carolina, most notably at the high-profile Darlington 500 motor race. As WDIX radio reported: "With 70,000 race fans receiving the greetings of race officials and other distinguished guests, it was Sen. 'Fritz' Hollings, Democrat of South Carolina, who graciously and enthusiastically welcomed George Wallace. The hand of friendship that Sen. Hollings held out to George Wallace at the Darlington 500 was the hand that holds Democrat votes."[68] In his review of the 1968 election, Hollings recalled that "we didn't cuss George Wallace. Instead we took advantage of his coming to the Darlington race to greet him when others were avoiding him. We kept contact with the Wallace movement constantly."[69]

Much as Wallace did in his 1968 presidential campaign, Hollings made overtures to his racially conservative supporters over civil rights legislation and the thorny issue of the methods used to achieve school desegregation. He opposed the 1968 Open Housing Act and referred to it as "the so-called Civil Rights Bill of 1968" in constituent correspondence.[70] Moreover he stressed his support for "freedom of choice" school desegregation plans, a position he endorsed far beyond his 1966–68 Senate term. In June 1968 he cosponsored two bills that sought to shore up the use of freedom of choice plans.[71] As HEW began to pressure southern school districts either to abandon freedom of choice or to lose funds under Title VI of the 1964 Civil Rights Act, Hollings railed against the department on the floor of the Senate and in constituent newsletters. In one August 1968 newsletter, he praised amendments Georgia's Richard Russell proposed to prevent HEW from withholding funds from schools "in order to force a child to attend a school against the choice of his or her parents" and to assign HEW agents proportionately across the United States to review civil rights compliance nationwide. "In other words," Hollings wrote, "Senator Russell wanted the impact of the HEW shenanigans to hit home in the areas whose senators and congressmen were playing politics with our schools."[72] In September 1968 he highlighted the case of the school board in South Carolina's Richland County District no. 1, whose desegregation plan was challenged by HEW before Judge Robert Hemphill ruled in the board's favor. Hollings attacked HEW for pressuring local schools into "accepting the Washington version of how to run a school district" and asked, "Whose health, education, and welfare are being served?"[73]

As with his partial embrace of Wallace and "Wallace issues," Hollings represented the interest of conservative white constituents in his opposition to the confirmation of two of President Johnson's Supreme Court nominees, Thurgood Marshall and Abe Fortas. The way he did so, however, highlighted his effort at the same time to avoid totally alienating black voters.

Marshall, the first African American Supreme Court nominee, was nominated by Johnson in June 1967 and was easily confirmed by a 69–11 Senate vote on August 30. Hollings had actually eaten breakfast and spoken with Marshall at Union Station in Washington, D.C., years previously, on December 6, 1952, shortly before the opening arguments of *Briggs v. Elliot*, which contested the constitutionality of Clarendon County's racially segregated school system.[74] Yet there was little doubt that Hollings, soon to face reelection, was going to vote against him. The votes against Marshall's confirmation closely correlated with the states that had voted for Goldwater: eight of the eleven senators came from the five Deep South states that had gone Republican in 1964, the only states alongside Arizona to do so. No senators from the Deep South voted for Marshall's confirmation: the remaining two senators from the region, John Stennis of Mississippi and Richard Russell of Georgia, both abstained from voting.[75] Hollings later noted that voting for Marshall was never a serious consideration: "If you were for that, you might as well not run [in South Carolina] for reelection in '68."[76]

As Marshall had served as the NAACP's special counsel, it was unsurprising that Hollings's constituents who opposed his confirmation used similar strategies to those that had previously been used to discredit the NAACP, with Marshall's detractors often employing a combination of anticommunist and antiblack themes. A pamphlet published by the "Mothers' Crusade for Victory over Communism" exhibited both of these themes well. It noted that Marshall had been an officer of the National Lawyers Guild, cited as a communist front by the special Committee on Un-American Activities in 1944. Marshall had also submitted "a report denouncing lynching and discrimination" that had been adopted by the guild's executive board.[77] Numerous constituent letters opposing Marshall shared the concern that he would act against the perceived interests of the South once he was confirmed to the Supreme Court.[78] A letter from an E. B. Woodward captured the simplicity of Hollings's decision, should he want to be reelected: "You are in Washington to promote the interest of the majority of the people who sent you there and I assure you the majority are the conservatives." Moreover "disregarding this condition will certainly mark your name as 'MUD.'"[79]

Hollings's justification for his vote against Marshall drew on "judicial philosophy," a term often used euphemistically in reference to the Warren Court's perceived disregard of judicial precedent in its opinions, particularly the 1954 *Brown v. Board of Education* decision. Hollings echoed the line of argument used by the southern conservatives Ervin, Eastland, McClellan, and Thurmond on the Senate Judiciary Committee, who argued in a minority report on the Marshall nomination that he would serve as another member in the Supreme Court's "judicial activist" majority.[80] Hollings wrote to Marshall on June 21, 1967, and asked for written opinions on several recent 5–4 Supreme Court decisions that affected law enforcement and were deemed by many conservatives to be indicative of judicial overreach, such as the *Miranda v. State of Arizona* case.[81] Marshall later noted in his Senate confirmation hearings in July that he would be unable to offer his opinion on any matter he would be likely to rule upon, as to do so would require him to recuse himself from future cases heard once he became a sitting justice.[82] Hollings's inquiry at this point was disingenuous, for by June 20 a staff member had already drafted a letter to concerned constituents that noted that Marshall's testimony on these controversial opinions disqualified him as a candidate. Since this letter draft was written the day before Hollings sent the original letter to Marshall asking his judgment on these cases, it was clear that his negative vote was already decided.[83]

Hollings's justification for rejecting Marshall as a nominee was more temperate than the reasoning given by his conservative South Carolina counterpart, Thurmond. In a speech on the Senate floor before the confirmation vote on August 30, Thurmond not only attacked Marshall's judicial philosophy; after pursuing an arguably esoteric line of questioning over the drafting of the Constitution's Thirteenth and Fourteenth Amendments during Marshall's confirmation hearings, he contended that Marshall was too ill-informed to be a Supreme Court justice. Even Marshall's successful record as a litigator before the Supreme Court could not be used as a basis for his confirmation, since the cases were "decided on bases other than a strict application of the law and the precedents."[84]

Hollings's vote against Marshall infuriated his African American constituents. At a leadership meeting of South Carolinian blacks, the director of the Southern Regional Council's Voter Education Project was cheered when he announced that "Fritz Hollings must understand one thing: The Negro vote giveth and it taketh away."[85] Yet the use of the ostensibly nonracial judicial philosophy argument allowed Hollings to defend his vote to disaffected black citizens in South Carolina. African Americans had given him some 97 percent of their votes in the 1966 general election and certainly had provided him with his margin of victory. Responding to a letter from Samuel Hudson, described by Hollings's secretary as "a responsible Negro with some political influence" and "highly thought of in Georgetown," he sought to square his rejection of Marshall with his supposed support of black advancement.[86] Hollings wrote that "the Court is legislating or acting like a Congress rather than determining the law as a Court must do. I would disapprove anyone bent on continuing this trend. . . . Mr. Marshall's cause is to write into Court decisions what he thinks the law should be rather than what it is. This is one of our greatest dangers."[87]

Abe Fortas's nomination in June 1968 to replace Chief Justice Earl Warren, a nomination that Hollings also opposed, brought about a far more controversial and protracted confirmation fight in the Senate. The nomination was eventually withdrawn after a cloture vote on October 1 fell well short of the necessary two-thirds majority to cut off debate. Seeing an opportunity to curb the perceived excesses of the Warren Court, conservative senators, chief among them Thurmond and fellow Republican Robert Griffin of Michigan, vigorously opposed Fortas's nomination. In confirmation hearings held in July, Griffin contended that Fortas was a lame duck appointment (since Johnson had announced that he was not seeking reelection), decried the jurist's closeness to the president, and sought to filibuster the nomination.[88]

Although he eventually opposed Fortas's confirmation, Hollings had initially told presidential aides that he would support it.[89] Upon the announcement of the Fortas nomination, however, Hollings received an enormous volume of correspondence on the matter, the vast majority of it negative. Constituents were aggrieved on a great range of issues: they railed against Fortas's alleged communist ties, the apparent breakdown of law, efforts to impose regulations on gun ownership, Fortas's supposed permissiveness toward pornography, and, often in a more coded manner, the Supreme Court's recent decisions promoting racial equality. The correspondence written in opposition to Fortas mirrored many of the concerns of the right-wing anti–Warren Court coalition that emerged in the Senate in the late 1950s over disaffection with cases attacking racial segregation, guaranteeing the civil liberties of accused criminals and alleged communists, and relaxing censorship of some materials that had previously been deemed pornographic.[90]

Several letters sent to Hollings attached information from the "Liberty Lobby," a far-right organization whose executive secretary testified at the Fortas confirmation hearings against the "philosophy of 'permissiveness' on the right of the people to live in safety."[91] This right, he claimed, was "far more precious to man than any of the 'rights' that have monopolized the attention of the Supreme Court and the Congress recently."[92] The pamphlets published by the Liberty Lobby revealed how anticommunist, anticrime, and anti-integrationist sentiments often converged in the opposition to the Fortas nomination. One such publication, "The Abe Fortas Record," provided a twenty-point assault on the jurist's career. In addition to citing his alleged ties to subversive groups and his work on designing the "Durham Rule," which "has prevented conviction of killers and rapists," the pamphlet noted that Fortas "helped to write the 'Gesell Report' for the Defense Department, aimed at forcing off-base racial integration in housing, social life, etc., of U.S. servicemen."[93] Fortas believed that much of the opposition to his nomination was motivated by racial considerations. In a letter to Justice William O. Douglas after the nomination hearings ended, he wrote: "Primarily, the bitter response mirrors the opposition to what has happened with respect to the racial question and the general revolution of human dignity, reflected by our decisions in the field of criminal law, etc."[94]

Faced with this feverish opposition to Fortas, Hollings first chose to split the difference politically. He would vote against Fortas's confirmation but would not join the Griffin filibuster, thereby differentiating his position from that of Thurmond, who aggressively opposed the nomination from his position on the Senate Judiciary Committee. In form letters sent to constituents in July, Hollings dismissed as a partisan subterfuge the claim that Lyndon Johnson was making a lame duck appointment: Johnson, he asserted, "not only has the right but the duty" to nominate a new chief justice.[95] Nevertheless on the Senate floor on July 18, he cited judicial philosophy as his grounds for opposing Fortas, as he had for his opposition to Marshall's confirmation: "I oppose the confirmation . . . because I cannot approve the Warren philosophy of the Supreme Court."[96]

Even this position provoked vocal opposition in South Carolina. Several constituents claimed Hollings's stance against Fortas was a meaningless one. Since there was little question that Fortas would receive a majority of votes from the Senate, the only way to prevent his confirmation was to filibuster the nomination.[97] Likewise Hollings's Republican opponent in the 1968 election, Marshall Parker, attacked the decision not to join the Griffin filibuster as "another case of Hollings talking out of both sides of his mouth."[98]

Perhaps unsurprisingly, with him facing reelection in November and the Fortas issue remaining explosive, Hollings altered his position in August. He announced that he would filibuster the Fortas nomination but not for the reasons given in the Griffin manifesto, which alleged that President Johnson should not make a lame duck court appointment. Rather Hollings would filibuster because of Fortas's adherence to the Warren Court's alleged philosophy of judicial activism. In constituent correspondence he contended that "it is the Warren philosophy of the Supreme Court I oppose. On this issue I will filibuster until Christmas, if necessary. However, I will not join in any partisan filibuster which has been instituted for the aggrandizement of any political party during a presidential election year."[99] Hollings joined in the filibuster when the Fortas nomination reached the Senate floor on September 25 and subsequently voted against cloture on October 1. The failure to achieve cloture effectively killed the nomination.

During both the Marshall and Fortas nomination processes, Hollings sought to establish some distance between himself and the state's more ardent conservatives and segregationists, even if the differences were only rhetorical. In response to the chairman of the Beaufort County Democratic Executive Committee, who had noted the "extremely luke-warm" attitude of blacks toward Hollings's reelection, he highlighted both the distinction between his position and that of other South Carolina politicians and the difficulties he had in balancing white and black interests: "Our strongest Democratic candidate, Mendel Rivers, curses these things [President Johnson's Supreme Court nominations] outright and supports the candidate of the other Party. I am squeezed in the middle and do my best."[100]

Why, then, did African Americans support Hollings overwhelmingly in 1968? Part of the explanation lies in the lack of a viable alternative candidate who promised to represent their interests. Even as Hollings offered little difference publicly from South Carolina's stridently segregationist politicians on issues that concerned the black community, there was nowhere else to go. After all they were not going to support the Republican Parker, given his disavowals of the black vote in the 1966 election. Hollings acknowledged this point in correspondence with Wayne Freeman after the 1968 election: "The Negro will apparently remain in the Democratic Party, but due to the antagonism of the Republican leadership. . . . Harry Dent described the bloc vote as 'voting like a bunch of monkeys.' In short, unless the Republican attitude changes, the Negro has no place else to go but the Democratic Party."[101]

Hollings's 1968 campaign sought to minimize the public profile of his black support, an unsurprising strategy given that he had been labeled with some success as the bloc vote candidate in 1966. In a document from November 1968 titled "Reflections on the Election," he noted that he "did not go to the Manning dinner for Roy Wilkins" and "kept the right enemies, like Mojeska [*sic*] Simkins and Billy Fleming," who were both perceived as too radical by many in the white community. Simkins and Fleming were both economically independent African Americans who aggressively confronted South Carolina's segregated system of race relations in the 1950s and 1960s.[102] Moreover the Hollings campaign lined up support from local black leaders before the Senate race received more intense public scrutiny: "We had our meetings earlier during the relative cool of August with the brethren, particularly with the Alex Alfords [an influential African American from Georgetown] who would be offended if you didn't come."[103] From the record of Hollings's correspondence with local African American political leaders in 1968 and the fact that few people would describe August weather in South Carolina as "cool," it seems likely that he intended to write *April* and not *August.*[104]

Nevertheless while Hollings sided with the interests of his conservative white constituents on high-profile issues such as Johnson's Supreme Court nominees, he was responsive to the economic interests of many African Americans. These substantive improvements were most apparent in the fields of health and housing. In 1967 Hollings secured OEO funds to enable the operation of a food stamp program in majority-black Williamsburg after the county's all-white delegation had refused to appropriate the necessary money to fund it.[105] At the time it was not compulsory for a county to sign up for food stamps, while the program's administration costs were to be paid by the county. After Hollings persuaded OEO director Sargent Shriver to allow the use of the necessary eighteen thousand dollars to continue the program, the chairman of the African American Williamsburg Voter's League thanked him for his efforts.[106] In a similar way, after Hollings had sided with Johnson on a vote for a postal-rate increase, he was able to get Shriver to provide OEO funds to establish a health center in Charleston.[107] Crawford Cook remembered the incident humorously. After Hollings told the president that he had been unable to gain Shriver's support, Johnson supposedly replied: "Fritz, I just don't believe that Shriver has understood your request. He'll be up there tomorrow morning at nine o'clock." The next morning Shriver asked, "Alright, Fritz. How big does it have to be and how much do you want?"[108] Hollings's office also expedited approval of Housing and Urban Development (HUD) federal grants for housing projects, benefiting some blacks. A gratified constituent wrote to thank Hollings, whose office helped secure "the approval by HUD of the application made by the Trinity Methodist Church for [an] apartment project" in the Camden area; the church "has a membership of approximately 300 Negroes and these people will be the initial beneficiaries of this apartment complex."[109]

Hollings quietly courted the black vote across the state. Beyond those with statewide influence, such as NAACP field secretary I. DeQuincey Newman and attorney Matthew J. Perry, Hollings's office compiled lists of locally important African Americans for the senator to call.[110] Much of the organization of these lists went through Bubba Meng, the staffer who previously worked for the long-serving Senator Johnston. Johnston, despite his posture as a segregationist, won large majorities of the votes of African Americans in his contests for the Senate in 1950 and 1962, against Thurmond and Hollings, respectively, which suggests that Johnston's operation knew the "right" people to speak with.[111] It also brings to mind the complaint of civil rights activist Modjeska Simkins that the black vote could be bought at election time.[112] One memorandum from Meng written before Hollings traveled to Chester County provided him with the name John R. Hall as well as an address and telephone number. Hall "is a Negro painter who controls the vote. President of Chester County Voters League/ Would be helpful to you if you woudl [*sic*] just give him a call."[113] Another message from Meng provided the senator with a list of "Negro leaders in Fairfield County" to contact personally. Importantly, "even though some are relatives, each controls his own area."[114]

Hollings also corresponded with local black leaders, where he emphasized his support for greater economic opportunity, which would benefit African Americans. Writing in November 1967 to James Felder, the head of the South Carolina Voter Education Project, he asserted that "we'll continue to press for jobs and the training of the unskilled, and of course you know my position on feeding the hungry. When everyone else resisted in Williamsburg, we were able to have the OEO reinstitute the food stamp program."[115] Hollings followed this theme in his correspondence with other influential African Americans in the state, though he supplemented it with a defense of his record in appointing black South Carolinians to positions of influence. After a black Charleston attorney, John Wrighten, asked him "When you are going to get around to appoint or nominate Negroes for something in South Carolina?" and wanted to know "whether or not any of the Negro lawyers in Charleston are qualified, according to your standards, of becoming a U.S. Assistant District Attorney," Hollings provided a lengthy rebuttal.[116] He provided a twelve-point list of African Americans he had appointed or recommended for "posts of responsibility" from 1951 to the present day (and beyond the present day in one instance) and cited his endorsement of economic opportunity programs.

> I instituted technical training in South Carolina [as governor] providing an opportunity for Negroes to learn skills.
>
> I have supported such programs as head start, food stamps, housing and health centers. The point is that I have support [*sic*] programs for the underprivileged and believe that Negroes, as citizens of South Carolina, could and should participate in the progress of our State. Wherein they qualify, I am glad to recommend them.[117]

The Wrighten letter became part of Hollings's appeal to local African American leaders. His office sent out a form letter dated April 18, 1968, shortly after meeting with a group of prominent African Americans, that thanked the recipient for the meeting that morning and enclosed the letter Hollings sent to "our friend" Wrighten, alongside an article on "our work for Head Start."[118]

Although black citizens voted overwhelmingly for Democratic candidates in South Carolina, there was substantial African American dissent toward the behavior of white Democrats. William Saunders, the editor of the *Lowcountry Review*, was heavily influenced by Malcolm X and Stokeley Carmichael. He taunted "Uncle Toms" in March 1968 whose "white bosses have told them to be quiet" before making "their political move—like supporting . . . Hollings."[119] Similarly Modjeska Simkins denounced the slow pace of racial change. She had complained to the Johnson White House in 1966 that away from elections the "Democratic hierachy [*sic*] avoids them [black voters] like the plague." Coming up to election time, white Democrats "nudge up to the vote, use it, and then violate and abandon it as a 'gentleman' does a whore."[120] In a radio broadcast in 1971, she likened occasional black appointments to influential positions to "trying to blacken up a whole quart of buttermilk with one or two drops of ink."[121] Although black dissatisfaction in South Carolina was never as extensive as in Mississippi, where blacks completely separated from the regular state Democratic Party, dissatisfied African Americans launched the United Citizens' Party in 1969 to run black candidates for the state legislature from majority black counties.[122]

Hollings's vocal demonstration of sympathy for the sensibilities of conservative whites on high-profile issues while quietly supporting some African American appointments and economic empowerment more generally brings to mind the later actions of the Georgia politicians Jimmy Carter and Sam Nunn. Carter won the Georgia governorship in 1970, and Nunn was elected to the Senate two years later.[123] Nunn used racial themes to attract white voters in his 1972 campaign: notably he traveled to Alabama to receive George Wallace's endorsement and announced that Wallace "represents the real views of Georgians."[124] Nevertheless African Americans from the state legislature regarded Nunn as a "closet moderate." Bobby Hill, a black state representative from Savannah, remarked: "I know when we close the door and get in a smoke-filled room that we can count on him. And I also know that he's got to win for us to [benefit]."[125]

As in Nunn's case, Hollings's balancing act was conspicuously successful. In November 1968 he beat his Republican opponent by more than 150,000 votes and carried nearly 62 percent of the vote. Part of his success can be attributed to the South Carolina Republican Party being in its infancy at this time. Since there was no candidate with widespread independent popularity on the ticket (as had been the case in 1966 when Thurmond had also run), it was unsurprising that Parker lost. As one local observer remarked in a 1966 publication from the Ripon Society, a liberal Republican organization, "there ain't that many Republicans in South Carolina . . . just a lot of mad Democrats."[126] Any Democrat who could avoid alienating the traditionally Democratic majority in the state would be likely to win statewide. Nevertheless the way Hollings won in 1968 is revealing. A study conducted by the Democratic political scientist Donald Fowler noted "in most counties the votes received by Mr. Humphrey and Governor Wallace when added together closely approximate the vote received by Senator Hollings." In thirty-seven of the state's forty-six counties, the combined vote received by Wallace and Humphrey in the presidential race differed from Hollings's vote by ten percentage points or less. All of this suggests that Hollings received strong support from both Humphrey and Wallace supporters, despite the fact that the two candidates were diametrically opposed ideologically.[127]

Overall the 1966–68 period, Hollings's "demagoguing" interval, allowed him to cement his position in the Senate. By focusing on the conduct of the Vietnam War, he both separated himself from the locally unpopular President Johnson and involved himself in international affairs, despite not holding a position on any of the committees concerned with foreign relations. Hollings highlighted the fiscally conservative elements of his economic positions and sought to present his proposals as compatible with a states' rights view of government. Throughout his term he paid deference to the sensibilities of conservative whites. Yet by quietly courting black political leaders, to whom he emphasized his support for programs that encouraged economic mobility, and because a lack of a viable alternative candidate for black voters, Hollings received almost all of the African American vote in 1968. However his limited responsiveness to the interests of his African American supporters at this time helped ensure that there would be a black third-party challenger in South Carolina's 1970 gubernatorial race, in the form of Tom Broadwater's United Citizens' Party candidacy. The 1968 election did, nevertheless, bring a change in emphasis in Hollings's behavior. Once reelected, he enjoyed more political freedom than before, and he used that freedom to pursue a more progressive agenda in his second term. This willingness to promulgate progressive and locally unpopular policies soon became apparent in his aggressive advocacy for measures to alleviate domestic hunger.

★★★ CHAPTER 5 ★★★

Hunger, USA

In January 1968 a Catholic nun, Sister Mary Anthony, showed Hollings around slums in his hometown of Charleston.[1] It was then, Hollings later wrote, that he lost his hunger "myopia." He realized that "the hungry are not able-bodied men, sitting around drunk and lazy on welfare. They are children. They are abandoned women, or the crippled, or the aged."[2] Unlike the majority of fiscally conservative, states' rights–conscious southern senators, Hollings became a forceful proponent for a federally funded attempt to eliminate domestic hunger in the late 1960s. On the Senate floor in April 1970, the liberal New York Republican Jacob Javits attacked the perception that southern states were antiwelfare and claimed that Hollings "is a living symbol that it is not true."[3] Surprising national observers, Hollings testified on the extent of hunger in South Carolina in February 1969 and advocated a great expansion of the food stamp program.[4]

The poverty issue was politically explosive in the South owing to its intersection with negative stereotypes about African Americans and the perceived threat antihunger programs posed to entrenched economic interests in the region. Nevertheless Hollings remained one of a small number of southern senators who urged the implementation of more generous federal antihunger efforts. He allied with liberal senators who supported more generous food stamp spending and published a book in 1970 proposing solutions to domestic hunger, a problem he dubbed a "national disgrace."[5] He also became a persistent critic of the Nixon administration for its allegedly political approach to the hunger problem. Unlike the moral arguments made by George McGovern and other Senate liberals, however, Hollings stressed economic and antirevolutionary bases for greater food stamp expenditures. Although spending on it never reached the levels urged by food stamp supporters, the food stamp program expanded greatly in the late 1960s and early 1970s. Historian James Patterson has labeled the "liberalization" of the program "unheralded but vitally important" to the alleviation of American poverty.[6]

Though Hollings's antihunger advocacy made him unusual among white southern politicians, his behavior heralded the small-scale accommodation of many other southern Democrats to the economic interests of their black constituents. Campaigns for better nutrition and health care were a logical extension of the earlier civil rights movement, while many civil rights activists subsequently became involved in antihunger campaigns.[7] In South Carolina, I. DeQuincey Newman, the state NAACP field secretary, was especially active in highlighting human deprivation in the late 1960s, while James Clyburn, who had been jailed during sit-in protests in Orangeburg in 1960, subsequently coordinated "hunger tours" conducted by Gov. John West and Hollings in 1971.[8] With the mass enfranchisement of African Americans after the mid-1960s and the ongoing disengagement of many southern whites from the Democratic Party, black voters became essential to the success of southern Democrats at the statewide level. The late 1960s also brought the acquiescence of many southern Democrats to black political participation and demands. By stressing support for ostensibly nonracial issues such as health, education, and economic development while continuing to oppose civil rights initiatives, southern Democrats assembled winning coalitions from African Americans and moderate white voters. This trend was exemplified by the approach of the group of moderate "New South" Democrats elected in 1970, such as Jimmy Carter in Georgia, Dale Bumpers of Arkansas, Reubin Askew of Florida, and West in South Carolina.

Federal antihunger programs had their origins in the Great Depression as a means to resolve the simultaneous presence of large agricultural surpluses and human deprivation on an unprecedented scale.[9] Two methods of disposing of these agricultural surpluses were conceived, namely a commodity distribution program, authorized by the Potato Control Act of 1935, and an early food stamp program begun in 1939.[10] The commodity program allowed local relief agencies to distribute surplus foodstuffs to people already on the welfare rolls on a monthly basis. Although continued through the 1960s, the commodity program was, according to political scientist Jeffrey Berry, "an abysmal failure."[11] It was only available in certain counties, failed to reach many families on welfare, and did not increase demand for agricultural products. Moreover the program's foodstuffs were inadequate for recipients to achieve a nutritious diet: by 1960 the program provided a monthly package worth only $2.20, which contained lard, rice, flour, butter, and cheese.[12]

The prototype food stamp program begun in 1939 provided the basis for the Food Stamp Act of 1964. Under the 1939 effort, people already on public relief could buy orange stamps each week equal to their normal food expenditures. For each dollar of orange stamps bought (which could be used to buy any foodstuff), participants received fifty cents of blue stamps, which could only be used to buy surplus food types. This initiative succeeded both in improving the diet of participants and in increasing demand for surplus products.[13] There was, however, a widely held assumption that the program was used fraudulently by an indeterminate number of participants. Once unemployment levels and farm surpluses decreased as a result of American involvement in World War II, the rationale for the food stamp scheme was judged to have disappeared, and the program was abandoned in 1943.[14]

The National School Lunch Act of 1946 also served as a compromise between nutrition advocates and farming interests. As with the other dual-purpose antihunger programs operated through the Department of Agriculture, it promised both to improve children's nutrition and to dispose of farming surpluses. The program pledged to provide schoolchildren with a hot lunch. To southern senators who advocated the passage of the act, such as Georgia's Richard Russell and Louisiana's Allen Ellender, the program was primarily a subsidy to farmers but also a means to help poor children.[15] The administration of the program catered to the racial concerns of southern Democrats. As with the food stamp and commodity distribution programs, the School Lunch Act did not interfere with local control: the day-to-day administration of the program was left to local officials, and there was no enforcement mechanism to ensure lunches were offered equally to all children.[16]

The next food stamp program was a pilot scheme, announced by President Kennedy in February 1961. Participants would pay a monthly amount, roughly equal to their regular expenditures on food (the "purchase price"), and would receive in return coupons that would allow them to come closer to funding the lowest-cost nutritionally adequate diet devised by Agriculture Department officials, the "economy" food plan. Unlike the 1939 program, stamps could be used to purchase any domestically produced food. Another change was the implementation of a sliding scale for food stamp benefits: while the exact scale varied between different pilot projects, in each case participants with a lower income would pay a lower purchase price and receive a higher bonus value of stamps than those with higher incomes. Although some pilot programs initially included free stamps for the poorest families, this regulation was soon eliminated by food stamp administrators and replaced with a minimum purchase price of two dollars per month. Since Agriculture Department officials considered food stamps to be a "self-help" program, it was essential for all participants to pay a nominal fee.[17] By 1964 the pilot scheme had expanded from its eight original projects to forty-three programs in twenty-two states.[18]

Passed as part of a logrolling compromise between backers of wheat and cotton price supports and the supporters of food stamps, the Food Stamp Act made the pilot programs permanent. Southern Democrats and conservative Republicans on the House Agriculture Committee had tabled it in February 1964; they reported the bill out of committee in return for the protection of wheat and cotton price supports in a tobacco research bill before the House Rules Committee.[19] Under the act the states themselves established the maximum income participants could earn to be eligible for food stamp benefits. Participation in the program was optional for states and counties, with administrative costs for the operation of the program to be paid at the local level (the federal government covered the cost of the bonus stamps). With this stipulation conservative legislators could vote for the program, with the knowledge that their constituents could still decide not to offer the program locally.[20] If a county wanted to establish a food stamp program, it was not permitted to continue operating commodity food distribution. The state welfare agencies themselves established their own regulations for eligibility in the food stamp program, though these regulations needed to be consistent with the maximum incomes allowed for participation in other federally aided public assistance programs.[21] Typically applicants for food stamps were required to travel to a county food stamp agency and have their application processed by a caseworker to determine if they were indeed eligible for the program. Once approved, participants would then collect their bonus stamps (in return for the purchase price) at monthly intervals from the county's food stamp vending office.[22]

The 1964 act had several apparent shortcomings. Alongside the low funding authorization for the Food Stamp Act, the most obvious problem with the program was the great decline in the number of participants once a county changed from the commodity program to food stamps: on average, between 1961 and 1968, the number of participants dropped by 40 percent when this change was made.[23] It is likely that the cumbersome process of establishing eligibility in the program and in collecting bonus stamps, alongside the low bonus value of stamps for participants whose incomes were higher up the sliding benefit scale, accounted for much of the drop-off in participation. Over the next decade, both proponents and opponents of food assistance clashed over the correct operation of the food stamp program: should it function primarily as an antihunger program or as a support for agricultural surpluses?

Hunger in the United States emerged as a national political issue in the late 1960s, with focus directed especially at conditions in the Deep South. Although this emergence had origins in the increased levels of activism and social concern fostered in the Kennedy and Johnson years, "the big change," as one Department of Agriculture official commented, "came when Bobby Kennedy got into the act." The official was referring to Kennedy's tour of poverty areas in the Mississippi Delta in April 1967 alongside Sen. Joseph Clark of the Senate Labor and Public Welfare Subcommittee. Encouraged by Leslie Dunbar, the director of the liberal philanthropic Field Foundation, Harvard University psychiatrist Robert Coles and a team of doctors provided a damning medical report of poverty conditions in Mississippi in July 1967. The report, delivered to Clark's subcommittee, concluded that the children studied were "living under such primitive conditions that we found it hard to believe we were examining American children of the twentieth century." Berry identified three further developments that heightened public awareness of a national hunger problem: the April 1968 publication of a report by the Citizens' Board of Inquiry titled *Hunger U.S.A.*, the airing of CBS's documentary *Hunger in America* in May that year, and the publication of Pulitzer Prize–winner Nick Kotz's indictment of federal antihunger policies, *Let Them Eat Promises*, in 1969.[24]

Because of the reports of Donald Gatch, a white, Nebraska-born doctor who worked in Beaufort and Jasper Counties, South Carolinian poverty was spotlighted specifically in national journals in 1968.[25] An *Esquire* piece was published in June, while the *New Republic* also printed an exposé in its November 1968 edition.[26] Gatch worked with the area's impoverished black population and claimed that rickets, scurvy, beriberi and pellagra, diseases that supposedly did not exist in the United States, were common there. The *New Republic* article's authors further pointed to study results from 1962 indicating that four of every five children examined in Beaufort County suffered from parasitic infections.[27]

Despite the efforts of predominantly urban northern liberals and poor local people to highlight the problems of southern poverty, officials within southern communities routinely denied concerns about hunger. In Beaufort local medical officials denied Gatch's claims of malnutrition, while he was personally ostracized by white community members: the chief of staff at Beaufort County Memorial Hospital contended that Gatch's allegations had "little or no foundation."[28] There was a long tradition of overlooking human suffering as part of efforts to attract new industry. The claims of the Memphis Chamber of Commerce in 1941 are pertinent. Despite being a city with one of the nation's worst housing shortages (four of every five blacks and one in three whites lived in substandard housing), the local chamber contended that "there is no housing shortage in Memphis. . . . Memphis is well housed." Historian David Goldfield described the willful ignorance by local boosters to civic ills as "conscious deceptions to ensure the status quo and to present an attractive image to potential investors."[29]

Meanwhile when the Citizens' Board of Inquiry report named 256 "hunger counties" in the United States, the chairman of the House Committee on Agriculture, Texas Democrat W. R. Poage, simply denied that starvation conditions were present in at least 134 of them.[30] In Virginia the *Richmond Times-Dispatch* largely discounted the findings of the report on the fourteen "hunger counties" in the state.[31] The paper denied the presence of widespread hunger and instead blamed nutrition problems present in these counties on individual failings. It reported "hunger to some degree at times, plenty of low-income families, malnutrition to some degree in all economic brackets, irresponsible parents, some parents—one or both—with a drinking problem, seasonal employment, a need for more industry in some counties and laziness."[32] Numerous South Carolina newspaper editorials agreed with the characterization of poverty as a failure of the individual work ethic: the *Rock Hill Herald* asserted that "for one to live in utter poverty in the United States is ridiculous. . . . So, it would seem to me that the 'poor people' are the 'lazy people.'"[33]

★ *Hollings visiting Columbia slum with I. DeQuincey Newman (left), January 1968.*
SOURCE: South Carolina Political Collections, University of South Carolina, Columbia.

Hollings described himself as a latecomer to recognizing hunger as a problem in South Carolina. He later acknowledged that he had participated in the "public policy of covering up the problem of hunger" during his time as governor (between 1959 and 1963) in an effort to attract industrial investment to the state.[34] His tour with Sister Mary Anthony of Charleston slums in January 1968 cured him of that "myopia," however.[35] Urged on and accompanied by the state's NAACP field secretary, I. DeQuincey Newman, Hollings visited slums in Columbia, Dorchester County, and Greenville later that same month.[36] Uninvited newsmen also arrived to report on these "hunger tours." After he made impolitic comments about the literal fencing-in of slum areas in Greenville, however, and was faced with journalistic accusations that he was chasing the "bloc vote" (a euphemism for African American voters) in his upcoming reelection contest, Hollings abruptly dropped the hunger issue.[37]

Hollings's initial hunger tours bore similarities to those made by Senators Kennedy and Clark in the Mississippi Delta. A key difference, however, was that

Hollings was investigating poverty conditions within his own state. Ever since he had campaigned for John Kennedy in 1960, he had fielded criticisms of his relationship with the family in each of his subsequent political campaigns. It was no surprise then, that Hollings confronted Robert Kennedy when Kennedy told him of his intention to hold committee hearings on the extent of hunger in South Carolina. In his book on hunger, Hollings recounted how he threatened to hold "a New York hunger exposé" if Kennedy came to South Carolina. His brinkmanship worked: hearings were held in Kentucky instead.[38] A file labeled "Poverty" compiled for Hollings by one of his staff members in 1968 illustrates the sensitivity of the issue at the time. It contained two newspaper articles covering calls by local Republican officials for investigations into hunger conditions in urban slums and carried the message: "Be sure the Senator glances over these articles. It would be good to have if we hear to [*sic*] much from the G.O.P. later."[39]

Only once he won reelection to a full six-year Senate term did Hollings return to the hunger problem. The full term, Hollings claimed, gave him the freedom to be "a statesman" and pursue controversial measures.[40] Despite his protestations that approaching the problem of South Carolinian hunger was nonpolitical, greater antihunger spending was particularly important to African Americans, who were four times as likely to live in poverty as the state's whites; almost half of the state's blacks lived in poverty in 1969.[41] As was the case with numerous other southern Democrats, blacks, who made up roughly 35 percent of South Carolinian voters by 1970, were increasingly important for Hollings's electoral prospects.[42] His advocacy for economic policies beneficial to African Americans remained less problematic than supporting explicitly race-related legislation and aligned him with the interests of black voters, a quiet accommodation that successful Democrats across the South mirrored.

Hollings's advocacy of greater antihunger spending was also compatible with his ambitions for higher office. Most notably Georgia's Jimmy Carter parlayed his position as a politically moderate southern governor into the White House in 1976. Hollings was one of many Democrats to reject the vice presidential nomination in 1972 and ran unsuccessfully for the Senate majority leadership in 1976. If he held national ambitions as early as 1969, this interest would have encouraged his course of advocating greater antihunger spending.

In January and February 1969, Hollings traveled across South Carolina with a sizeable entourage, including the state's health officer, Dr. Kenneth Aycock, to examine poverty conditions. Aycock, described by Hollings as "conservative and responsible," later provided a medical estimate that three hundred thousand people suffered from malnutrition in South Carolina, out of a total population of 2.6 million.[43] Following Hollings's investigations several other senators, including Herman Talmadge of Georgia, William Spong of Virginia, and Jacob Javits of New York, carried out similar tours of poverty in their own states. After the "New

South" Democrat John West was elected to the South Carolina governorship in 1970, Hollings toured impoverished areas with him as well.[44]

In February 1969 Hollings appeared as the marquee witness at hearings for Sen. George McGovern's Select Committee on Nutrition and Human Needs. There he affirmed the presence of considerable hunger and numerous malnutrition-related diseases in South Carolina. In doing so he broke what *Time* magazine termed the "disingenuous silence" of southern officials over the region's persistent poverty problems.[45] The recommendations Hollings made before the McGovern Committee remained largely consistent with those he offered nineteen months later in his antihunger treatise, *The Case against Hunger*, published in November 1970. During his testimony Hollings recalled that on one of his hunger tours, Aycock diagnosed within the same household cases of pellagra and rickets, while one child was recovering from scurvy.[46] He was appalled that these diseases presumed nonexistent in industrialized nations, as well as kwashiorkor and marasmus, could be present in the United States.[47]

The immediate impact of Hollings's testimony was the introduction of a pilot free food stamp program in Beaufort and Jasper Counties for the poorest families. Hollings was an opponent of the compulsory purchase requirement for all food stamp recipients that early agricultural department officials deemed necessary to keep food stamps as a self-help program. He bemoaned the inaccessibility of the food stamp program to poor families in the areas he visited in South Carolina. He recalled seeing "literally hundreds of hungry families who never heard of food stamps" but who could not have afforded the purchase price required to receive bonus stamps anyway.[48] Shortly after his testimony, Secretary of Agriculture Clifford Hardin announced the introduction of a free food stamp pilot program for families of four earning less than thirty dollars each month, a measure Hollings had supported in private meetings with Hardin and McGovern shortly before his committee appearance.[49] Although limited—the director of Penn Community Services bemoaned that the maximum income to qualify for free food stamps amounted to one-tenth of the poverty level—the program was a first step toward removing the compulsory purchase price for food stamp recipients, which had inhibited the use of the program by poor families.[50] Hollings continued to oppose the compulsory purchase requirement, and supported later efforts to eliminate it in the Senate's food stamp reform efforts in 1976.[51]

The other immediate consequence of Hollings's February 1969 testimony and the increased visibility of the hunger problem more generally was the restoration of funding to McGovern's hunger committee by a voice vote. The Senate Rules Committee had earlier reduced the group's funding from $250,000 to $150,000. Hollings's South Carolina colleague Thurmond had reportedly called for an even more drastic reduction in its budget to $25,000.[52] Unlike Hollings, Thurmond denied the presence of widespread hunger in South Carolina and did not consider hunger to be a governmental concern.[53] The restoration of funds for the McGovern Committee was central to the maintenance of hunger as a prominent political problem. Since Robert Kennedy's death and the defeat of Senator Clark in 1968, the McGovern Committee had become the major body concerned with investigations into conditions of poverty and malnutrition. Moreover the committee later offered substitute bills for the Food Stamp Act that provided more generous authorizations than the more conservative Senate Agriculture Committee had allowed.[54] Had the McGovern Committee's activities been neutered by a major budget cut, it is likely that the expansion of the food stamp program would have proceeded at a slower pace.

Hollings was a consistent supporter of increased authorizations for the food stamp program. At a November 1970 press conference, he claimed that some $3–4 billion annually would be required to reach the country's "15 million hard-core hungry," far above the Nixon administration's $1.25 billion food stamp budget.[55] His support for expanding the food stamp program marked him as unusual among southern senators. On a substitute measure McGovern offered to replace the Agriculture and Forestry Committee's food stamp bill in September 1969, which passed by fifty-four votes to forty, Hollings joined five other southern senators in voting yea.[56] These were the Republicans Howard Baker of Tennessee and Marlow Cook of Kentucky and Democrats William Fulbright of Arkansas, William Spong of Virginia, and Ralph Yarborough of Texas.[57] Hollings was, however, the only senator from a Deep South state to favor a more liberal food stamp program.

Although Hollings supported greater spending on food stamps and other antihunger programs such as free school breakfast and lunch measures, his support took on a southern slant. Consistent with his calls in his first Senate term for tax revenue to be returned from the federal government to the states and his 1968 campaign pledge to provide "more South Carolina government in Washington and less Washington government in South Carolina," Hollings asserted that any successful effort to tackle poverty required local cooperation.[58] In his testimony to the McGovern Committee in February 1969, he had proclaimed colorfully that the "red-tape-worm of Federal Government must be exterminated" if food aid was going to be effectively distributed.[59] Denouncing the unwieldiness of federal antihunger funding, he often recalled the efforts of the residents of Warsaw Island, South Carolina, to secure federal funding for a clean water plan. On the Senate floor, he claimed that "it is easier to build an ABM [antiballistic missile] or put a man on the moon than to get a comprehensive water plan for a 31-island area with nowhere to look except here in Washington."[60]

In March 1969 Hollings argued that his "biggest problem" was in getting "responsible people" to become involved in antihunger efforts at the local level.[61] Accordingly when a social nutrition program was proposed at upstate Limestone College in 1971, he contacted the Appalachian Regional Commission's federal cochairman to urge the favorable consideration of the college's funding application and congratulated the program director "for trying to see that Limestone has a part in awakening young people to this national tragedy."[62] Hollings often spoke proudly on the Senate floor of the local participation in antihunger efforts in Beaufort and Jasper Counties. The program he described served as the model for the Supplemental Food Program for Women, Infants and Children, a measure he cosponsored with Sen. Hubert Humphrey in 1972.[63] In September 1969 he recalled the "private merchant in the Beaufort area who volunteered the rolling stock to take food to the outside areas. He actually took orders and delivered it to the people at his own expense. . . . That is how the people are getting the food now."[64] His comments in April 1970 left little doubt as to the importance he placed on securing the support of local people in ensuring the success of antihunger programs. He claimed that "under our food stamp program . . . we took cognizance of local participation, local administration, and local leadership. . . . I do not see how we are ever going to solve the hunger problem unless we do have local support and local participation."[65] Hollings's emphasis on local involvement formed a major part of his opposition to the proposed guaranteed income measure offered by the Nixon administration in the Family Assistance Plan (FAP). On the Senate floor in September 1969, he argued against replacing food stamps with a cash payment, since "it does not bring into play local participation. If it were not for the private suppliers, we could not be feeding 2,100 young kids and pregnant mothers in Beaufort County."[66]

Hollings's emphasis on local involvement bore some similarity to the approach of older agriculture-minded southerners such as Russell and Ellender but was more racially inclusive in its scope. Hollings claimed his hunger tours and antihunger advocacy were made to "bring the problem to the public's attention," so people "at least know about the food stamp program," while his February 1969 testimony alleged that many local welfare officials "resent anyone getting onto the welfare rolls."[67] Moreover his 1970 book on hunger denounced the arrangement of power in many rural communities that prevented hungry people becoming aware of antihunger programs.

While he voted with numerous northern liberals in his support of larger federal antihunger efforts, Hollings's argument for this expansion differed from the justifications liberal senators generally provided. McGovern framed the antihunger argument in moralistic terms. In an article he authored in 1970, the South Dakota senator highlighted medical research that demonstrated the "serious, often irreparable damage" caused by malnutrition, and he termed the elimination of hunger "a moral imperative."[68] Hollings recognized the connection between malnutrition and stunted mental development.[69] In his February 1969 testimony, he cited the views of Dr. Charles Lowe, another committee witness, on the connection between malnutrition and early brain cell development and recalled occasions when "my friends have pointed a finger and said, 'Look at that dumb Negro.' . . . He is dumb because we have denied him food. Dumb in infancy, he has been blighted for life."[70] However Hollings argued that unsentimental appeals were required to persuade uninterested observers to act. He emphasized two main arguments to persuade people of the need to increase spending on the food stamp program: an economic argument for their usefulness and the claim that failure to act would leave the millions of hungry poor open to radical ideologies.

Hollings's central selling point for the food stamp program was that spending to eliminate hunger reduced costs in other government areas. It was this argument, and not the national security imperative, that he stressed in his initial February 1969 testimony.[71] Food stamps themselves would also provide direct stimulus to South Carolina's economy and expand the state's tax base via its sales tax. Since almost three hundred thousand South Carolinians participated in the food stamp program in 1971, Hollings reasoned, "just the food stamps means over $75 million to our economy. With a 4 per cent sales tax on food, it means over $3 million tax revenue to South Carolina. The state only spends $700,000 to administer the program so South Carolina is making more than $2 million on the program."[72]

In a staff memo discussing his book on hunger, Hollings wrote: "The most hardened John Bircher could see the logic and economics of solutions if he only realized that hunger in America was to such an extent as to constitute a public problem, a political and governmental problem, rather than a question of social welfare."[73] Defending his record to one enraged constituent, he replied that "my position on . . . poverty and welfare legislation is designed to return the non-producing citizens of our society to a productive role so that they will not be a continuing drain upon our tax structure."[74]

Hollings repeatedly sought to make a causal connection between hunger and economic waste. A report his staff submitted to the U.S. Chamber of Commerce in 1969 titled "The Case to End Hunger" argued: "All evidence points to a direct connection between malnutrition and income. Children without food cannot develop brain capacity. Retarded children cannot learn in school. Uneducated drop-outs can offer nothing to society except trouble and frustration."[75] In his book Hollings tried to suggest an annual monetary benefit to be gained from increasing the calorie intake of the country's low-income population.[76] He then made his case in its starkest terms: "It costs $10 a day to keep a prisoner in jail. For $10 a poor family can buy enough food stamps to eat for seventeen days. It's cheaper to feed the child than to jail the man."[77] Greater spending on antihunger programs was therefore a fiscally conservative position.

Hollings also emphasized the potential for further domestic unrest should the problems of the hungry not be addressed. This contention echoed the justification offered by Richard Russell and other southerners in their arguments for the passage of the 1946 National School Lunch Program, namely that a well-fed populace was a defense against internal subversion. Russell had argued that "a school child who has a good bowl of hot soup and a glass of sweet milk for his lunch will be much more able to resist communism or socialism than would one who had for his lunch a hard biscuit which had been baked the day before and which he had brought with him to school in a tin can."[78] In an interview in 1969, Hollings demanded that the southern states feed their own hungry poor to blunt the impact of the "revolutionary" ideas of supposed black radicals: "The South and its attitudes made the Kings and the Abernathys. I say why give them the argument? Why not just admit that hunger exists and work to get rid of it? Am I going to shout 'no, no, it doesn't exist,' and then force them to show me that it does exist? That just makes Uncle Toms out of the responsible Negro leadership and radicals out of the rest."[79] The interview also illuminated the continued distinction many southern politicians made between "radical" civil rights leaders and other "responsible" black leadership.

Similarly, Hollings admonished his readers in a constituent newsletter, "if public officials, business leaders, and members of the chamber of commerce continue to ignore the hungry children, crying jobs, not handouts, while the militants recognize the problem of the hungry and offer help, what shall come from the ghetto? A Stokely Carmichael or an Abraham Lincoln? We can't afford some 50,000 militant and hostile teenagers roaming the streets of South Carolina 10 years from now just because we insisted on trying to make the irresponsible parent responsible."[80] On the Senate floor, he also highlighted the Black Panthers' Chicago and California nutrition programs in an attempt to refute the notion that hunger "really does not threaten America's security or safety whatsoever."[81] He further attacked a perceived disjuncture between "most Rotarians or any other conservative American" supporting feeding the poor abroad to benefit national security while simultaneously opposing feeding them at home.[82] (The free distribution of surplus commodities abroad was authorized in section 416 of the Agricultural Act of 1949 and in the Agricultural Trade Development and Assistance Act of 1954.)[83] Despite feeding the hungry "to preserve world freedom . . . the hungry who threaten world security apparently pose no threat to America's domestic security."[84]

While Hollings used these arguments for the expansion of federal antihunger efforts, he maintained that the main problem facing opponents of hunger was a lack of public awareness. Moreover, as he had left the Senate Agriculture Committee at the end of 1968 and was not part of McGovern's select committee, the major impact he could have on the food stamp program was through fostering public awareness of the widespread existence of hunger and malnutrition. Accordingly in a December 1969 staff memo he tasked his upcoming book on hunger with "making aware those who are disbelievers." For Hollings "the first step in any solution is to make the public know there is a problem." He consciously differentiated his work from previous publications on the hunger problem, which he contended were inadequate to persuade the skeptical reader of the need for aggressive action. "There have been a hundred articles by Kennedy, Clark, Hollings and 50 others, wandering around in shanties, patting little hungry children on the head," he claimed. "This repulses the reader I want to attract."[85]

Hollings also contended that his antihunger treatise had a different target audience from Nick Kotz's *Let Them Eat Promises*, published that year, which was described by social scientist Jeffrey Berry as "an unremitting attacking on Congress and the executive branch for their lack of commitment to ending hunger in America."[86] Kotz reserved his strongest criticisms for the southern congressmen W. R. "Bob" Poage of Texas and Jamie L. Whitten of Mississippi, who chaired the House Agriculture Committee and House Appropriations Subcommittee on Agriculture, respectively. These two committees were responsible for both the drafting and funding of food stamp legislation. Kotz attacked Poage's and Whitten's apparent hypocrisy in opposing spending on antihunger programs while still supporting generous subsidies for large farmers and ridiculed the "culture of poverty" arguments the two men used to impede the distribution of food aid. Poage's "populism," for instance, "extended to fervent support of liberal government benefits for farmers," yet on assistance programs for the poor, the Texan "became an unreconstructed nineteenth-century conservative."[87] Hollings maintained that the public could not be persuaded of the need to eliminate hunger if they believed that the current inaction stemmed from "a few bigoted southerners in key committee posts." While these influential politicians were a problem to "the professional like Kotz," Hollings argued that "to the uneducated, like me, 'We have met the enemy, and it is us.'"[88] Persuasion rather than denunciation, then, was required.

Although he played down its importance in comparison with Kotz, Hollings acknowledged that a major problem facing any effort to provide food relief to the hungry in South Carolina (or elsewhere) *was* the "politics of hunger." This difficulty played out on both local and national levels. Nationally there were tensions between predominantly southern conservative rural legislators and food stamp advocates, particularly on the House Agriculture Committee, who disagreed over the correct function of the food stamp program: whether it should primarily serve as an agricultural support program or as a welfare program to help poor families eat a nutritious diet. The Food Stamp Act of 1964 itself had provided a dual justification for the program, both to "help achieve a fuller and more effective use of food abundance,' and to 'raise the levels of nutrition among low-income households.'"[89] The National School Lunch Program had the same dual agricultural support and nutrition-based justification.

Opposition to social welfare programs from farming interests had a precedent in the New Deal era, where the southern-controlled House Ways and Means Committee repeatedly blocked efforts to include farm operators, tenants, laborers, and sharecroppers in the Social Security Act's contributory old-age insurance program. Coverage was eventually extended to farmworkers in 1954 after two decades of legislative obstruction. Many southern politicians opposed their initial inclusion in the act because large landowners relied on the precarious economic standing of their agricultural workers to maintain a system of low-wage labor.[90]

At the local level, the arrangement of political and economic power within rural communities inhibited the function of meaningful antihunger programs. Many farmers feared that the distribution of food stamps would disrupt the economic system based around sharecropping, while local industries did not want to lose the guarantee of a cheap labor force. As Hollings noted in an interview in April 1969, "farmers are desperately afraid that if the government feeds their black sharecroppers, they will lose the labor that harvests what little they are able to grow."[91]

In a further break from other congressional southerners who viewed federal antihunger programs primarily as agricultural supports, Hollings attacked the apparent paradox that many politicians simultaneously opposed food relief on the grounds that it would damage the character of the recipient while supporting agricultural subsidies: "Within a forty-mile radius of Timmonsville, South Carolina, there are forty farmers who each received last year over $40,000 from the United States government—for not working! This doesn't affect the character of the *farmer*. . . . But give the poor, little hungry child a 40-cent breakfast and you've destroyed *his* character."[92] In his opposition to funding antihunger programs, Mississippi congressman Jamie Whitten used the same line of argument that Hollings had sought to discredit. Speaking to the Secretary of Agriculture Orville Freeman in late 1967, Whitten claimed, in a statement that further revealed his racial conception of the poverty problem, "You make stamps available at 30 percent discount; then they want them at 50, then 75. Now, I have heard reports that some of the organized minority groups are insisting they be provided free of charge. When you start giving people something for nothing . . . I wonder if you don't destroy character more than you might improve nutrition."[93]

A further problem in the effective operation of a food stamp program in rural counties stemmed from the likelihood that the jobs of administrator and distributor for the stamps relied on the goodwill of local power brokers who opposed the implementation of the program, stultifying any effort to attack poverty. Hollings wrote: "Too often the main effort of the administrator is to make sure the food stamp program doesn't reach the attention of the hands on certain large farms of certain influential farmers."[94] He also confronted the way that the local administration of antihunger program benefits nationwide sometimes acted as a means of social control.[95] He quoted from a four-state White House Urban Affairs Council field study conducted in July and August 1969, which "uncovered clear and unmistakable evidence of manipulation of present qualification criteria to exclude certain families" from food assistance.[96] At Hollings's Nutrition Committee testimony in February 1969, another witness, Paul Matthias, director of the South Carolina Council on Human Relations, cited the case of sixty-two black students in Dorchester County who had previously received free school lunches at all-black schools but were denied them at formerly white schools that had recently been racially desegregated. To receive free lunches again, the students were told, they must move back to the all-black school.[97]

There were clear racial dimensions to the hunger problem in South Carolina and nationally. The high incidence of black poverty in the state and the perception among many whites that Africans Americans were lazy further contributed to a racially coded conception of the poverty problem. President Johnson's secretary of agriculture, Orville Freeman, recalled that there were "a lot of people in Congress who were not too sympathetic" to the food stamp program because "the civil rights issue got into it." These legislators "were not comfortable with a program that reached out into these concentrated black areas."[98] Ike McLeese, a former Hollings staff member from upstate Spartanburg, noted the inherent risk of white backlash in approaching the poverty issue, as it would give the appearance that the senator was "becoming a champion of the black man and the black people."[99] When Hollings began investigating the extent of poverty in South Carolina, he was frequently accused of pandering to black interests. An Orangeburg resident, Macon Garrick, claimed that "the minority groups are getting more than their share of the giveaway programs through the Federal Government, with taxpayers footing the bill." In rebutting this line of criticism, Hollings presented the hunger problem as nonracial. In his reply to Garrick, he asserted that "poverty is not a problem of one race. Of those who are hungry today, approximately 2/3 are white. Most of those receiving food aid are white. . . . The problem is a national one, not a racial phenomenon."[100] He did, however, acknowledge that the rate of black poverty was more acute, especially in the South, where some 42 percent of African American families earned less than the federal poverty level of three thousand dollars annually compared with 13 percent of white families.[101]

Hollings also employed demographic data alongside his gubernatorial record of industrial courtship to rebut claims that he should be pursuing job creation measures instead of antihunger programs. An editorial from the conservative *News and Courier* argued that his focus on antihunger programs was misplaced. "State leaders long have realized that the best way to fight poverty is to attract industry and develop tourism," the editorial contended. "A few thousand dollars worth of food stamps won't uplift the hard core poor. They need jobs."[102] Responding to such criticism, Hollings did not challenge implicit distinctions between "deserving" and "undeserving" poor but rather stressed the number of deserving cases.[103] In response to one constituent who was "sick and tired of the hard working people having to furnish food etc., to people that will not work," he replied: "The people I am speaking of are predominantly old women, children, and invalids; and we have got to get them out of destitution if we are going to move forward. No one knows industry and job training and job attraction better that I. The ones we are talking about can't work."[104] To further advance his case, Hollings often invoked the results of an HEW study that showed only 0.5 percent of the 8.2 million welfare recipients in the United States to be able-bodied males, a striking departure from the portrayal of welfare recipients as work-shy men conjured by numerous newspaper editorialists.[105]

Hollings was also careful to tour poverty areas accompanied by local Republican officials to avoid the charge that he was merely politicking for votes, an accusation leveled at him by Vice President Spiro Agnew. After publicly calling "for every sensation seeking, T.V. worshipping politician to stop running around the country plucking the emotional harpstrings of a compassionate people," Agnew wrote to Hollings in May 1969, where he decried the "general use of the poor as a public relations vehicle" and accused him of "[falling] victim to the desire to be re-elected."[106] However it is likely that Hollings was not wholly interested in the hunger issue for its possible political benefits: if this was his motivation, he would probably have dropped the issue in 1970 when the Nixon administration vacillated in its commitment to attack hunger rather than continuing to promote the worth of expanding antihunger programs.

There is ample evidence to show that Hollings's advocacy of food stamp use was not particularly popular among whites in South Carolina. In May 1969 Crawford Cook, his former administrative assistant, asked for the state's Democratic Party county chairmen to "be made a part of this hunger thing so they can begin defending our position rather than running away from it . . . and believe me the strong feelings about it down here make running the easiest course to follow most of the time."[107] Likewise Karen Kollmansperger, who worked on Hollings's staff until 1970, questioned whether South Carolinians "ever liked it[,] other than people in poverty," despite Hollings's antihunger advocacy being "a popular thing nationally."[108] Polling conducted for his 1974 reelection campaign suggests that Kollmansperger's assessment was correct: aide Mike Copps noted that while the poll "[did] not show terrible disaffection with you [Hollings] because of your stance on hunger and food stamps . . . there is plenty of room in which an opponent can make hay." He also predicted that "public hostility to food stamps will be exploited by any serious opponent."[109]

Antiwelfare sentiment was not just a regional phenomenon. In a 1969 national survey, 58 percent of respondents claimed that poverty derived from a "lack of thrift and proper money management by poor people," while 55 percent attributed it to the "lack of effort by the poor." In the same poll, 84 percent concurred with the statement "There are too many people receiving welfare who ought to be working"; only 34 percent of respondents agreed with the statement "Generally speaking, we are spending too *little* money on welfare in this country."[110]

As his disagreement with Agnew suggests, Hollings's antihunger advocacy brought him into conflict with the Nixon administration. Hollings claimed that the administration was merely interested in the politics of the issue. Nixon seems to have been torn over the worth of expanding the food stamp program. After hearing arguments from advisers both for and against the expansion in food stamp expenditures at a meeting of the Urban Affairs Council in mid-March 1969, the president did not make a firm decision and was shocked at the estimated cost of $3.5 to $4 billion each year for providing a food stamp program in every U.S. county. This uncertainty may have reflected a wider ambivalence Nixon held toward welfare spending. One aide later recalled: "One day he'd [Nixon] be impressed by what Pat [Moynihan, architect of the FAP] said. Then the next day, he'd be pissed off by what some little congressman had told him about welfare cheats." Nixon rhetorically launched his war against hunger on May 6, 1969, although his decision was largely forced by the maneuverings of Senator McGovern and his staff.[111]

Coinciding with the release of *The Case against Hunger* in November 1970, Hollings assailed the president for "trying to weasel out of his responsibility." The food stamp program was still only reaching six of the fifteen million who lived in food insecurity in 1970, yet the Nixon administration had requested only $1.25 billion for the program for fiscal 1971, far short of the $3.5 billion or so required to fund the program fully. He also accused the administration of reneging on its pledge to provide every needy schoolchild with either a free or reduced-cost lunch by its revised target date of Thanksgiving 1970. (It had originally committed to achieving this goal by June of that year.) The Nixon administration used a much lower estimate for the number of eligible children, 6.6 million, than the Senate Nutrition Committee's figure of 8.9 million, a result of "the feeble excuse . . . that the President was only talking about feeding children in schools with existing lunchroom facilities." Moreover Hollings claimed that the results from the ten-state National Nutrition Survey, mandated by Congress in December 1967, had been suppressed "because the facts uncovered are just too disturbing for Richard Nixon to face."[112] In a letter to Nixon dated November 25, 1970, Hollings repeated these criticisms and denounced Nixon adviser Pat Moynihan, "who, in the face of thousands of pages of medical testimony, continues to deny the connection between malnutrition and brain damage."[113]

With the National Nutrition Survey still unreleased, in March 1971 Hollings introduced a Senate resolution urging the disclosure of the survey's findings.[114] On the Senate floor, he claimed that the survey's results showed there to be "15 million hard core hungry and malnourished citizens in the United States," with two out of five people below the poverty line having serious medical problems related to malnutrition. The nutrition survey was eventually released later in 1971 amid charges of data manipulation from Senator McGovern, who claimed the report's information "was tailored to blunt the harsh edges" of the survey's discoveries. Among other apparent failings, the report neglected to include earlier findings from Texas, Louisiana, New York, Kentucky, and Michigan, which included more information on nutritional deficiencies than appeared in the final version. Criticism of the survey was not confined to politicians: Dr. Arnold Schaefer, who had originally headed the survey, decried the final report's near-total reliance on statistical data and lack of interpretative material.[115] In short the nutrition survey *had* been manipulated to minimize its impact on the hunger debate.

Hollings based his opposition to Nixon's proposed Family Assistance Plan (FAP) on his contention that local involvement was necessary to ensure the success of antihunger programs. FAP would have largely replaced welfare recipients' in-kind benefits with a cash payment and a small sum of food stamps. In a 1972 newsletter, Hollings claimed that "throwing money" at the problem with either Nixon's FAP or McGovern's more extravagant welfare reform proposal would lead to inflated food and rent costs and would ignore the wider problems of poverty, such as poor education, housing, and health care and a lack of job training.[116] Elsewhere he used a "culture of poverty" argument to attack the administration's "money stamps" as "the best way I know to legalize abuses" of the food stamp program, which had been so often decried by its conservative opponents. Under Nixon's scheme recipients would be free to spend their money on cigarettes, alcohol, and other nonfood items prohibited under the food stamp program. Hollings described the work requirement of FAP as "a major weak point," given his conviction that the "hard core hungry" who stood to be helped were "not physically able to work." Moreover FAP was "too ambitious" in its doubling of the number of people on welfare, which Hollings claimed would lead to a "revolution between the taxpayers and the taxeaters."[117] FAP died in the Senate Finance Committee both in 1970 and 1972, meaning that Hollings did not have to vote on it. Nevertheless the fact that he opposed it from conservative and liberal positions helps underline the oddity of the bill and the diversity of the opposition to its passage. In its effort to provide both a guaranteed annual income and "workfare," the plan inspired opposition from a liberal-conservative coalition on the Finance Committee, which coupled with the Nixon administration's quiet abandonment of the bill in response to electoral considerations, led to FAP's defeat.[118]

In *The Politics of a Guaranteed Income*, published in 1973, Moynihan claimed that in private Hollings actually "would acknowledge that food stamps were a halfway house toward a guaranteed income, and that a full-fledged proposal such as the Family Assistance Plan would accomplish even more of what he hoped for";

however, feeling that "the South was not ready," Hollings denounced Nixon's proposal and attacked the efficacy of federal food programs under his administration.[119] As Hollings had discussed the possibility of the "federal government [supplementing] farmers' pay like it supplements rent" in March 1969, it is plausible that he was also willing to discuss a more ambitious cash assistance system off the record.[120]

Regardless of whether Moynihan's claim was correct, Hollings took steps to inoculate himself against conservative critiques of his support for antihunger programs as he approached his 1974 reelection contest. The major lines of conservative criticism of the program were twofold: participation fostered welfare "dependency," and the program itself was open to use (and hence abuse) by those who were not truly needy, particularly hippies, college students, and striking workers. In May 1968 Hollings had become embroiled in a minor public relations flap over the eligibility of strikers for food stamps after his office provided information to striking union officials at Celanese Fibers Company, an incident that also reflected South Carolina's pervasive anti-unionism.[121] Subsequently he remained careful to publicize his support for the tightening of eligibility standards to ensure that these less-deserving groups could not use the program, and in 1973 he cosponsored a bill to prevent striking workers from receiving benefits under the program.[122] In a January 1974 memorandum, Hollings aide Michael Copps stressed the apparent need to appear tough on food stamp eligibility standards: "Your concern with hunger is primary, but as you go about looking for solutions you are pragmatic, insistent on tight administration, and certainly not a bleeding-heart."[123] This concern to ensure strikers and students were not eligible to participate in the food stamp program remained steady throughout the 1970s. Facing reelection again in 1980, Hollings remarked: "I have voted against food stamps for strikers and college students—again very consistently over the years. I believe in restricting the program to those in real need and not jeopardizing public support for the program by extending it far beyond its original intent."[124]

Hollings remained a persistent critic of the Nixon administration's poverty policies, despite the president's popularity in South Carolina. After the failure of Nixon's welfare reform proposals, he contended that the poor were actually worse off, thanks to the "massive propaganda campaign . . . to discredit existing poverty programs," which reinforced "the misconception that families on welfare are cheaters, welfare bums, and social criminals living off the work of others."[125] However, as Hollings's aides noted, it was hard to make a popular case against the president for not seriously addressing the nation's hunger problem. Even though the administration had "dragged its heels on seeking the levels of funding necessary to match promises," participation in the food stamp program had rapidly expanded. It grew from three million participants in 1969 to more than ten million in 1972, while the number of schoolchildren receiving free and reduced-cost lunches had nearly doubled.[126] As Nick Kotz, the author of *Let Them Eat Promises*, later noted, "someone painting Nixon as totally opposed to doing anything [to tackle poverty] is not accurate."[127] Even as the Nixon administration's commitment to attacking the continued hunger problems in the United States oscillated, important legislative improvements were made to the food stamp program in the early 1970s. Significantly the program changed from having discretionary budget authority to an open-ended authorization, which in theory allowed the program to expand according to the need of eligible recipients rather than the availability of funds.[128] Also the 1970 reauthorization of the Food Stamp Act nationalized the income and resource eligibility standards for participation in the food stamp program. Previously when states were permitted to set their own eligibility criteria, the maximum allowable income to qualify for food stamps in South Carolina was set at 38 percent of the federal poverty line, the lowest level of all the states.[129]

From the late 1960s, Hollings aggressively pursued the problem of malnutrition in the United States, despite the antiwelfare sentiments of many of his conservative constituents. He recognized the relationship between malnutrition and stunted mental and physical growth. Consequently efforts to eliminate poverty needed to provide poor people with adequate nutrition, so they would then be capable of receiving a good education and job training. This would only be possible through the expansion of the food stamp program and other antihunger programs to ensure that those eligible for assistance actually received it. Unlike earlier southern advocates of agricultural antihunger programs, Hollings's prescriptions presumed racial inclusivity and criticized the power of entrenched local elites. Although poverty remained a persistent problem in South Carolina, the state was far more effective in providing food stamps to its needy citizens than its neighbors by the mid-1970s. A study of food stamp use for 1974 showed South Carolina to have reached 43.2 percent of its prestamp poor population with the program, the highest participation rate in the South and the thirteenth highest in the nation.[130] Despite the potential electoral liability of supporting federal antihunger measures, Hollings remained safe politically in South Carolina. While his aggressive support for expanding the food stamp program marked him out from many of his southern colleagues, in his second Senate term, he played a careful balancing act between the interests of his conservative and more liberal constituents. Although he readily toured areas of human deprivation with the state's NAACP field secretary and championed remedies for a problem that affected many of his poorer black constituents, he remained opposed to legislation guaranteeing voting rights and supported Supreme Court nominees who incited the strenuous opposition of national civil rights groups.

★★★ CHAPTER 6 ★★★

A "common-sense, realistic, South Carolina Democrat"

In his second Senate term, Fritz Hollings gained notoriety as a moderate southern politician: he was, according to historians Jack Bass and W. Scott Poole, "consistent as a progressive voice."[1] Given the antihunger and ocean preservation legislation he promoted, as well as his opposition to U.S. involvement in Cambodia and his support for withdrawal from Southeast Asia more generally, Hollings fits within the moderate group of New South Democratic governors and senators elected around 1970. This group of politicians won election with an overwhelming majority of black voters and a sizeable minority of the white vote and generally finessed issues of race, focusing instead on problems of health, education, and economic development.[2] Yet maintaining such a coalition was challenging, owing to the diverse interests represented.[3] In Georgia one disillusioned Republican dubbed it a "night and day" coalition, given the stark range of ideological viewpoints represented by these politicians.[4] To maintain their biracial support base, southern moderates needed to master what political scientist Alexander Lamis has termed "the art of the political straddle."[5] In his second Senate term, Hollings had to balance competing interests to pursue several progressive policy goals while remaining electable in politically conservative South Carolina.

As with Hollings's growing concern for the prevalence of hunger and malnutrition in the United States in 1968 and 1969, ocean preservation soon became another of his nationally oriented pet projects. His interest in environmental preservation measures was unusual for a politician from a southeastern state whose politicians' voting records were notably unsympathetic to environmental concerns in the 1970s.[6] The 1970s have become known as the "environmental decade" for the large volume of protective legislation authored and the growth of grassroots awareness of environmental issues.[7] An example of such mindfulness was the designation of April 22, 1970, as the first Earth Day, a measure sponsored by Wisconsin senator Gaylord Nelson. As a junior member of the Commerce Committee and the chairman of the Oceans and Atmosphere Subcommittee, Hollings oversaw and pushed through a number of important legislative measures in the

★ *Hollings alongside Commerce Committee colleagues Ted Stevens of Alaska (standing, far left) and Warren Magnuson of Washington (seated, left) and Senate staffers.*
SOURCE: U.S. Senate Historical Office.

1970s that formed a major part of his legislative legacy. Alongside maneuvering to persuade President Nixon to create the National Oceanic and Atmospheric Administration (NOAA), he shepherded several other key pieces of environmental legislation through Congress, including the 1971 Ocean Dumping Act, the 1972 Marine Mammal Protection Act, and the Coastal Zone Management Act, passed in 1972.[8] For his work in ocean preservation, Hollings was recognized by numerous environmental organizations. The National Oceanography Association named him as their oceanography man of the year in 1971 and the Environmental Law Society honored him in 1974, while he was the National Wildlife Federation's legislator of the year in 1975.[9] Upon his retirement from the Senate in 2005, an Ernest F. Hollings Scholarship Program was established to fund undergraduates to undertake internships at NOAA facilities and pursue careers in oceanic and atmospheric science.[10]

In his youth Hollings had worked in the summers of 1939 and 1940 to measure the depth of Charleston Harbor and the Intracoastal Waterway with the

Army Corps of Engineers. He later recalled that his experience of seeing the extent of refuse discarded into the harbor "made a lasting impression. I was an environmentalist even before I got out of my teens."[11] With the assistance of staff member John Hussey, Hollings became active in researching and promoting oceanic legislation. In August 1969 he chaired a Senate special ocean study, while Commerce Committee chairman Warren Magnuson made him the chairman of the newly created Oceans and Atmosphere Subcommittee in November 1969.[12] He used his chairmanship to gain an understanding of complex environmental issues and to author legislation for both the preservation and use of the seas.

Hollings was intimately involved in the establishment of NOAA, established by President Nixon's Reorganization Plan Number Four of July 9, 1970. The stated goal of NOAA was to "make possible a balanced Federal program to improve our understanding of the resources of the sea, and permit their development and use while guarding against the sort of thoughtless exploitation that in the past laid waste to so many of our precious natural assets."[13] NOAA was based on the recommendations of the report by the Stratton Commission, created in 1966 to devise a government organization plan to manage the U.S. relationship with the seas.[14] The central proposal of the commission was the creation of an independent NOAA to head the various marine science agencies, which had previously been uncoordinated. Hollings introduced legislation to the Senate in 1970 to create an independent NOAA, while similar legislation was forwarded in the House. However the White House was less sympathetic: it was, Hollings later claimed, "playing games" over the oceanic program.[15]

Seeing John Ehrlichman, with his background in land development, as a roadblock to the reorganization, Hollings bypassed him and made his proposal to John Mitchell, the attorney general, who then accessed the president directly. Nixon accepted much of the proposal, with the condition that the new agency would not operate independently but instead would be under the jurisdiction of the Commerce Department.[16] Under Reorganization Plan Number Four, NOAA absorbed nine different organizations concerned with the oceans and atmosphere that had previously operated separately.[17] Hollings echoed the president in hailing the reorganization plan as "a sound and significant beginning."[18] The principle of government reorganization embodied in Nixon's plan was consistent with Hollings's earlier support of various independent reviews of state agencies during his time as governor of South Carolina.

However the placement of NOAA under the Department of Commerce rather than as an independent body led some environmentalists to oppose the plan. The major concern was that the thrust of the agency would be to encourage business activity rather than preservation. The Izaak Walton Society summed up this worry in its August 1970 newsletter: "There is nothing in the organic acts of any of the agencies to be transferred to NOAA under Plan No. 4 which require that biological and environmental considerations will be given any attention in deference to the primary mission of the Department—to promote commerce."[19] Reflecting the unease of environmentalists at NOAA's placement within Commerce, Gaylord Nelson introduced "a resolution of disapproval" to the reorganization plan, which was rejected 47–5 on October 1, 1970.[20]

Given the apparently conflicting notions of environmental preservation and commercial development, Hollings's support of preservation measures did not always sit easily with constituents who favored policies to promote economic growth over environmental concerns. This tension was apparent in a public squabble between Hollings and Gov. Robert McNair over the proposed location in the state of chemical plants run by the German corporation BASF. The development was to be at Port Victoria, South Carolina, an area of virgin coastline. Hollings had a minor role in the courting of BASF executives to locate in the economically depressed, rural Beaufort County, a decision the company announced in October 1969.[21] The proposed plants drew opposition from a coalition of residents from the nearby Hilton Head area, a group that included the local chamber of commerce, the Rotary Club, and a black fishing cooperative.[22] These groups claimed that the plants would pollute the waters on the South Carolina coast, harming the area's tourism and seafood industries.[23] After Secretary of the Interior Walter Hickel threatened federal intervention in March 1970 should studies show the proposed industry to harm the ecology of nearby Port Royal Sound, BASF executives initially suspended construction of the sites and later abandoned the Beaufort location altogether.[24]

The fight over the location of BASF in Beaufort County was a sensitive topic given the energetic role Hollings had played in bringing new industrial prospects to the state as governor and the way that the dispute pitted state and federal pollution enforcement against each other.[25] Secretary Hickel noted in his letter to the president of BASF's American branch, Dr. Hans Lautenschlager, that South Carolina's water quality standards were actually "joint State-Federal standards" and so required his approval for any changes.[26] The episode also demonstrated the tension between Washington representatives' concern for enforcing pollution standards and the concerns of local representatives and black leaders from a poor, rural locality that had been passed over for earlier industrial developments in South Carolina.[27]

Hollings's "hunger tours" had brought unfavorable national attention to the extent of poverty in Beaufort County early in 1969. James Waddell, the local state senator, claimed to Hollings in December that year that the location of BASF would prevent further out-migration from Beaufort, Jasper, and Hampton Counties owing to the lack of skilled work in the area.[28] In constituent correspondence Hollings initially supported the plant's construction, provided BASF could comply with state pollution standards.[29] In January 1970 Hollings advised Waddell not to be "the fixer" for BASF but rather "the policeman." That way BASF executives would "get the message and straighten up and spend a little more money than they intended—and still make a hell of a profit."[30] Hollings also asked Lautenschlager to "categorically state that BASF will not pollute in Beaufort," an assurance that was not forthcoming.[31]

In response to calls that a moratorium be placed on the construction of the site pending an investigation into its environmental impact, at first Hollings claimed he could not support any such delay "because it assumes someone is going to violate the law."[32] However he praised Secretary Hickel when he warned the BASF president of the need to comply with federal and state water pollution standards in late March 1970.[33] In April, Hollings clarified his position in a letter to the editor of the *Beaufort Gazette* that was sharply critical of the conduct of state officials. Claiming that the state had been "on the 'sell,'" he complained that "no emphasis was placed on anti-pollution requirements" when courting BASF. So welcoming were the governor, state senator, and mayor that "you would have thought they [BASF executives] were returning astronauts."[34] Simultaneously, however, Hollings queried opponents of the plant who claimed its operations would pollute the Port Victoria area. As BASF itself claimed not to know whether its dyeing process would pollute, "how [could] its critics know?"[35] McNair then hit back at Hollings. He told the *News and Courier* that BASF was "made aware of the implications" of its proposed relocation "from an environmental standpoint." Meanwhile in a speech to the state's General Assembly, McNair remarked that "unlike some in the past, we have not had a public policy of covering up our problems, and overselling ourselves," a thinly veiled reference to Hollings's admission the previous year that he had disguised the problem of hunger while he was governor in order to attract industrial prospects.[36]

By May, Hollings supported the proposed moratorium on construction of the BASF plant. He told constituents that "industry is needed for our state, but not at the expense of our environment."[37] He also defended Hickel from charges that he was enforcing federal pollution laws unevenly across the country.[38] By then Hollings was convinced that BASF executives did not plan to comply with pollution standards. As he wrote to the wife of a local state representative, BASF executives "continue to give lawyers' statements, but then tell me in the office that they are having difficulty complying and have yet to design an operation that will comply," an approach he contrasted with that of Verona, another German chemical company that had recently located in Charleston. Hollings was "for all the industry I can get so long as it doesn't pollute," a point he emphasized in letters to constituents.[39] Seeing a contradiction between Hollings's calls to attack poverty and his environmentalism, conservative columnist John Chamberlain denounced the country's "ecology kick" in May 1970: "The word 'poverty' was forgotten as the public, listening to the conservationists, suddenly began discussing what dredging a couple of humps in the channel leading to Port Victoria . . . would do to disturb the shrimp and fish spawn of the Carolina tidelands."[40]

Away from the BASF controversy, Hollings continued to strive for balance between industrial and environmental impulses, as was apparent in remarks he made on the Senate floor discussing the marine mammal protection bill authored in his subcommittee. The bill was signed into law in October 1972. While noting that the bill established a fifteen-year moratorium on the importation of marine mammals, which would demonstrate that these animals "should be protected and managed on a worldwide basis . . . not simply for commercial purposes," Hollings qualified his comments. "Nevertheless," he contended, "we cannot eliminate thousands of American jobs and millions of dollars worth of industrial investment by acting irrationally on the basis of emotional misinformation from persons who seek to paint over a complex issue with one broad sweep of the brush."[41] The Coastal Zone Management Act, guided to passage by Hollings in 1972, also displayed this balance between environmental and developmental concerns. Its goal was to promote "the wise use of land and water resources for the coastal zone, giving full consideration to ecological, cultural, historic and aesthetic values as well as to needs for economic development."[42] Likewise he voiced his opposition to the stipulations of the Occupational Safety and Health Act (OSHA) in 1973 with the passage of an amendment "to stop OSHA from wrecking South Carolina farmers."[43] Although OSHA was established to regulate the exposure of workers to harmful substances in the workplace, Hollings termed the agency "government bureaucracy at its worst."[44]

Unsurprisingly given that he graduated from the Citadel, a military college, served in the Second World War, and hailed from a state whose economy relied heavily on military spending, Hollings took a keen interest in foreign affairs. When consulting with Georgia's Richard Russell shortly after being elected to the Senate in 1966, Hollings had initially favored seeking a seat on the Armed Services Committee before Russell suggested he try for Appropriations instead. In his initial request for committee assignments in December 1966, he placed the Armed Services Committee as his second priority, behind only Appropriations, a committee he eventually joined in 1971.[45] He routinely kept his constituents informed of his view of world affairs in his newsletters. In 1973 he predicted that he would base his Senate reelection campaign the next year on "what I think is the primary function of the government—and that's national defense."[46] Moreover as a member of the Senate in the late 1960s and early 1970s, Hollings cast a number of votes that impacted the funding of the war in Vietnam and more broadly reasserted the role of Congress in the conduct of foreign policy.

On the most pressing foreign policy issue of the era, the Vietnam War, Hollings balanced between opposing Nixon's management of the war, especially in relation to the Cambodian intervention, and supporting the military personnel still stationed in Southeast Asia. While he had earlier favored a swift escalation and rapid conclusion to the war, he contended publicly in 1970 that the conflict was unwinnable, given the gradual withdrawal policy of the Nixon administration, which Hollings dubbed "surrender on the instalment plan."[47] On May 26 of that year, he asked constituents: "If you're not seeking a military victory, if the policy is retreat, if, from elections, you will accept a Communist government, then what in the devils are we fighting for?"[48] Form letters sent to constituents in 1970 noted Hollings's commitment to a quick withdrawal from Vietnam while reaffirming his hawkish convictions. One form letter read: "It is my information and belief that we could win the war militarily if the military were permitted to fight the war on a military basis rather than a political one. It is clear that this will not be permitted; therefore, I favor a withdrawal of our troops and, even recently, the President has stated that we would accept the self-determination of the government by the Vietnamese—even if it were Communist. Therefore, I see no purpose for further loss of lives."[49] In June 1970 Hollings called for withdrawal on the Senate floor. "We cannot prevail with a war of attrition in Southeast Asia," he argued. "We should get out and in getting out let's not take on any more losing obligations or losing involvements."[50]

After aligning with the Senate's conservative right on foreign policy early in his Senate career, in his second term Hollings showed greater independence. He sided with the doves on April 30, 1970, after Nixon ordered combat troops to attack Communist sanctuaries in neutral Cambodia without congressional approval. Hollings supported the Cooper-Church Amendment to the Foreign Military Sales Act to cut off funding for operations in Cambodia if military activities continued there beyond June 30. Nixon's failure to consult Congress on the invasion, Hollings claimed, "put into question not only the credibility of the President but the credibility of the Congress."[51] Hollings's support of Cooper-Church was controversial in South Carolina. The Nixon administration singled out Hollings as one of the "doubtful senators" in need of special attention from veterans' organizations to ensure that he voted against limiting Nixon's freedom of action in southeast Asia.[52] One of many disaffected constituent groups called on him to "reconsider [his] decision to collaborate with Senators Fulbright, McGovern, Teddy Kennedy, blah, blah Bayh and other radicals in their anti-Cambodian resolution."[53] Hollings then clarified his position. He had independently chosen to support the Cooper-Church Amendment and to oppose the McGovern-Hatfield resolution, a measure that provided him with a degree of political cover for his opposition to the Cambodian invasion. McGovern-Hatfield would have cut off appropriations for all Vietnamese military operations, except for those related to the withdrawal of U.S. troops, and would require all troops to have pulled out by June 30, 1971.[54] Hollings argued that "the war can no longer be prosecuted in the way we Hawks suggest. . . . The good that we are doing in Vietnam is outweighed by the bad it is causing at home." He further framed his argument in constitutional terms: "It is the constitutional duty of the Congress, not the Executive, 'to raise and support Armies.'"[55] In constituent correspondence Hollings highlighted that President Nixon had signed into law in December 1969 an earlier Cooper-Church Amendment requiring congressional approval for the deployment of ground troops in Laos and Thailand, that the pending Cooper-Church Amendment was in harmony with the president's announced plan for withdrawal from Cambodia by July 1, 1970, and that Hollings still believed that escalation of the Vietnam War would have brought a military victory.[56] He was, he contended, "a hawk with [his] wings clipped."[57]

Ultimately Hollings voted both for the Cooper-Church Amendment and the Byrd Amendment to the same bill, a seemingly odd combination of votes, since the Byrd Amendment would have effectively nullified the effect of Cooper-Church. The amendment offered by West Virginia's Robert Byrd would have prevented Cooper-Church from stopping Nixon from taking all necessary action to protect American troops in South Vietnam, the president's public justification for the incursion into Cambodia in the first place. The Byrd measure failed 47–52 on June 11. Hollings was one of only six senators to vote for both amendments. Cooper-Church passed the Senate comfortably but was subsequently killed in the House. As Kentucky senator John Sherman Cooper's staffers recognized, the amendment had only "symbolic value." Hollings subsequently sided with the more dovish elements in Congress when he voted for amendments to hasten the U.S. departure from South Vietnam, conditional on the return of American prisoners of war.[58]

Away from Vietnam, Hollings burnished his hawkish credentials. He supported Nixon on the Safeguard antiballistic missile vote in 1969, on the grounds that it would allow him "to kill missiles rather than people."[59] He also opposed the Strategic Arms Limitation Treaty (SALT I) in September 1972 since it would provide "perhaps irreversible military superiority" to the Soviet Union.[60] Hollings had traveled with Senate Majority Leader Mike Mansfield to Helsinki the previous year to confer with Gerald Smith, the head of the U.S. delegation at the arms limitation talks. Hollings, however, was convinced that the official negotiations were merely "elaborate frauds" for the real negotiations between Henry Kissinger and Anatoly Dobrynin. Only Alabama senator James Allen joined Hollings in opposing the vote to accept Nixon's interim agreement in September 1972.[61]

Meanwhile in response to a Panamanian-led resolution on the status of the Panama Canal at the United Nations in March 1973, and with the special U.S. representative in the Panama Treaty negotiations resigning in July, Hollings joined with a group of conservative senators to reaffirm America's right to sovereignty over the canal.[62] After Kissinger signed a joint statement of principles to guide future treaty negotiations that agreed that the canal territory would be returned to Panamanian jurisdiction, Hollings announced his opposition to this "outrageous" and "foolish" measure in a February 1974 newsletter. He further asserted that "the United Stated has a permanent interest in the Panama Canal. It is ours. We need it for national defense. We need it for commerce. Let's be forthright. Let's tell them it's non-negotiable."[63] Hollings had previously opposed ceding sovereignty over the canal, an issue that became a conservative rallying point later in the 1970s.[64] It seems, however, that in 1973 and 1974, his "demagoguing" interval, he was likely overemphasizing his position on the canal "giveaway."[65] In a letter to a California resident who had previously lived in the Canal Zone, Hollings acknowledged that his newsletter was "beamed to the local folk."[66] A memorandum from Mike Copps in March 1974 lent further credibility to this claim. Attached to a letter from Thurmond and Senator McClellan soliciting support for an amendment that opposed any compromise on American sovereignty over the canal, Copps noted that "while it [the amendment] goes pretty far in supporting continued 'undiluted' American sovereignty over the Canal, we thought it would be difficult for you not to be on it, so we added your name."[67] Later Hollings was one of the first southerners to support the Panama Canal treaties negotiated in 1977. Throughout his second term, and especially in the final two years, he stressed his promilitary record, an area he later used to criticize his opponents when he ran unsuccessfully for the Democratic presidential nomination in 1984.[68]

Hollings generally looked askance at foreign aid payments, a common concern of hawkish southerners. The distaste shown by southern politicians toward foreign aid had been apparent in their voting records since the Eisenhower administration. Historian Joseph Fry concluded that by the 1970s "the southern rejection of foreign aid had become bipartisan and overwhelming."[69] In a December 1972 newsletter, Hollings claimed that "for over a generation we have been the world's Santa Claus. . . . This has to stop." He connected his distaste for foreign aid to balancing the federal budget, one of his persistent concerns.[70] Although a strong supporter of military spending, he also believed that the United States had too extended a presence in the world and so he supported reducing troop levels in nonmilitary roles. He contended that failing to balance the federal budget would lead to a loss of economic and, as a result, military prowess. Decrying the country's gift-giving tendencies on foreign aid, Hollings told his constituents in 1971: "Our country cannot afford to be the world policeman, world banker and world Santa Claus. Thus, I voted to cut America's troop levels in Europe. . . . We must reduce the huge cost of maintaining military personnel and their dependents abroad. You cannot bleed yourself white and maintain an effective, long term military posture."[71] Elsewhere he explicitly likened his views on the level of the U.S. military deployment in Europe to those held by the late Georgia Senator Russell and former President Eisenhower, both of whom commanded the respect of many conservative South Carolinians. "I agree with President Eisenhower and

Senator Richard Brevard Russell of Georgia," Hollings told constituents, "that European interests could be defended with fewer U.S. troops."[72] In 1973 Hollings announced his opposition to sending foreign aid to North Vietnam and passed an amendment he coauthored with Virginia's Harry Byrd to require direct congressional approval for any direct or indirect aid to that nation.[73] He did, however, qualify his skepticism for foreign aid, which he regarded as sometimes necessary for maintaining American strategic interests. He declared in August 1972 that "if a continued American role in Southern Europe and the Middle East helps the long-term goal of denying the area to communism and thereby protecting vital routes of trade for strategic goods—then the best policy is to continue giving aid."[74] In some cases it was not that foreign aid spending was morally wrong but that it was ineffective. Hollings claimed that in Latin America, Asia, and Africa, "the necessary conditions for absorbing and using aid effectively have not been present," a problem that would require "a lot of preliminary work" before the United States should be "tossing billions in aid at them."[75]

Hollings's committee postings gave him greater sway over military construction spending than on other matters impacting foreign policy more directly. From 1971 he was a member of the Appropriations Committee and held a seat on the Military Construction Subcommittee. In keeping with his sincerely held but carefully cultivated image of fiscal conservatism, he supported funds for new weapons systems but also sought to highlight the presence of waste in the Pentagon budget. He told constituents that "if we in the Congress don't keep a watchful eye, the Pentagon would spend us right into the poor house."[76] A favorite example Hollings used to demonstrate such largesse was the navy's request for $876 million to build a new site to house the Trident submarine. Hollings first wrote to his constituents on this matter in August 1972: he suggested instead that Charleston Harbor, once dredged, would be a suitable site and that the necessary dredging would cost only $40 million.[77] The navy was subsequently directed in the subcommittee report to consider existing sites for the Trident program. A site in Bangor, Washington, was eventually chosen, which saved some $400 million from the original estimate. In October 1973 Hollings reported the news as "historic," as it was "the first time since I have been here that the Pentagon has cut its costs rather than have an overrun."[78]

The busing of children to achieve racial balance in public schools became an explosive issue in the late 1960s and early 1970s across the United States. Busing was originally an issue with peculiar resonance in the South, where the rejection of freedom of choice desegregation plans in the Supreme Court's *Green v. New Kent County School Board* (1968) and *Alexander v. Holmes* (1969) decisions promised widespread busing to eliminate the region's previously de jure segregated dual school systems. Busing, however, gained nationwide importance as HEW and the Justice Department began addressing instances of de facto segregation, especially after the *Swann v. Charlotte-Mecklenburg Board of Education* decision of 1971 confirmed the constitutionality of a district-wide busing plan to remedy racial imbalance in the public schools of Charlotte.[79] Busing truly ceased to be a sectional concern by 1973, when *Keys v. School District No. 1 of Denver* acknowledged a judicial remedy for minorities who lived in de facto segregated areas.[80] Amid mounting public pressure against busing, the Supreme Court moved away from the issue in its 1974 *Milliken v. Bradley* ruling, which rejected a comprehensive plan for integrating Detroit's school system across district boundaries.[81] Congress eventually passed legislation prohibiting HEW from demanding the use of busing to promote racial balance in 1977, although the department had already "bowed to political pressure" and ceased to demand busing plans by then.[82]

The salience of the busing issue in the early 1970s was apparent from President Nixon's behavior as he approached the 1970 and 1972 election cycles. Before the 1970 elections, he linked Democrats with his own HEW bureaucrats who "bus children clear across town to achieve an arbitrary racial balance."[83] Meanwhile shortly after George Wallace had played heavily on the busing issue and won the 1972 Democratic presidential primary in Florida, Nixon held a nationally televised address in which he implored Congress to impose a moratorium on future court-ordered busing. After Wallace won the Maryland and Michigan primaries on May 15, Nixon told his adviser H. R. Haldeman that perhaps now his staff would "believe [the] busing issue."[84]

Busing was contentious for a number of reasons. For many who accepted the legitimacy of freedom of choice school plans as an expression of equal opportunity, the rejection of such plans in *Green* and *Alexander* indicated a move toward unnecessary social meddling. The civil rights and education advocate Bud Ferillo later remarked that some "sincere" opponents of busing viewed themselves "as being drafted into an unwanted social experiment."[85] The political editor of the *Florida Times Union* claimed in January 1970 that the protests against busing came from "parents who are sympathetic or have resigned themselves to neighborhood integration of schools but not to integration by gerrymandering or a federal mathematical formula." Many busing opponents contended that it violated the neighborhood school concept and marked a loss of parental agency over their children's education.[86] Naturally those who still opposed the legitimacy of racially integrated public schools also opposed busing as the method to achieve this goal.

Freedom of choice plans were an inefficient means of eliminating dual school systems. They placed the burden of integration on black parents and often resulted in minimal actual school desegregation.[87] As the historian J. Harvie Wilkinson III noted darkly: "Opportunity for pressure, covert and overt, was built into every pore of the 'free' choice system. In the very communities where blacks were most disadvantaged and illiterate, freedom of choice would be least likely to work."[88] The prevailing economic balance of power in many rural locales meant that blacks who wanted to send their children to previously white schools faced economic destitution and physical harm, a circumstance not dissimilar to the economic coercion campaigns orchestrated against black school integration petitioners in the 1950s and early 1960s. Such incidents often occurred in South Carolina. In 1967 the assistant education commissioner, David Seeley, informed Hollings that HEW knew of at least three cases in Florence County of black sharecroppers being evicted from the land of white owners after their families sent their children to white schools. "In the Lynchburg area of Lee County, we have received complaints of shooting into homes, cross-burnings, and credit cut-offs from Negro parents whose children began attending formerly white schools. Similar reports have come to us from Orangeburg and Dorchester Counties. . . . As a result, we have learned through interviews with hundreds of Negro parents throughout South Carolina that most of them fear to try to send their children to a formerly white school."[89]

Many busing supporters claimed that the real complaint opponents of the practice had was not the act of busing itself but that the schools their children were being bused to were racially integrated. In 1970 the chairman of Florida's Dade County school board noted that "we cross-bused in Dade until three years ago, and I never heard a white family complain, because we were busing to maintain segregated schools."[90] Hayes Mizell, a school integration advocate in South Carolina, needled the apparent duplicity of busing opponents by using a *New York Times* advertisement that showcased the spark plugs used in school buses for transporting children to Charleston's First Baptist Church, in Mizell's view a "private segregation academy." Mizell maintained, "It is clearly not busing which is upsetting the patrons of the First Baptist Church. It is race."[91] Ferillo, too, was skeptical of the motives of many busing opponents. For him the antibusing movement "was another last gasp to try and circumvent the integration of schools."[92]

The memoir of former South Carolina governor James Byrnes, first published in 1958, offers a compelling addition to the claims of those who accused busing opponents of hypocrisy. Byrnes boasted that by the time he left office in 1955, some 241,000 South Carolinian schoolchildren traveled to segregated public schools by bus, compared with only 142,000 children four years earlier.[93] Moreover the *Briggs v. Elliot* school desegregation case (later subsumed into *Brown*) grew out of a suit filed by Clarendon County blacks to demand that the local school board provide a school bus for black children to travel to school, a privilege already enjoyed by the school district's white children.[94]

It is likely that Hollings recognized the incongruity of some of the anger directed at busing in the late 1960s. Doug Dent, a University of South Carolina graduate who had worked for him since 1966, wrote a memo on the issue to the senator in January 1970. "A common complaint among white parents," he wrote,

★ *Hollings at a dinner with Strom Thurmond, 1969. Though Hollings and Thurmond developed a working relationship in the Senate, they were never close.*

SOURCE: South Carolina Political Collections, University of South Carolina, Columbia.

"is 'My son now lives five blocks from a school, but in order to achieve racial balance he is being bussed to a school three miles away.' This is a true situation; however, in actuality what is happening is that they are discontinuing the bussing that carries black students from one side of town to another in order to attend a black school and using those same vehicle[s] with new bussing patterns to bus white students to achieve a racial balance in existing facilities."[95] Hollings was a consistent opponent of busing measures throughout his first full Senate term. This decision was probably influenced by his concern to avoid alienating the sizeable bloc of George Wallace supporters in the state. As the Republican operative Harry Dent, by then on the White House payroll, reminded GOP gubernatorial candidate Albert Watson in 1970, "the Wallace-type voters just resent this [school desegregation] to no end."[96] Hollings mirrored his archconservative colleague Thurmond on busing policies. An aide compiled a tally of Hollings's and Thurmond's voting records on the issue between 1967 and 1973: on thirty-eight votes the two senators opposed each other only twice.[97] Hollings also prepared an amicus curiae brief with North Carolina senator Sam Ervin defending the Mecklenburg County

School Board in the *Swann v. Charlotte-Mecklenburg* busing case and coauthored a proposed constitutional amendment to ban the use of busing to achieve racial balance in schools in 1971.[98]

Hollings did not dispute school integration itself but contended that the method to achieve this goal was the freedom of choice plan. On the Senate floor in February 1970, he asserted that "the reason for 'deliberate speed'" provided by freedom of choice "was the human element. . . . We must work together if an effective educational program is to be maintained."[99] This marked a continuation of his pre-1969 rhetoric, in which he maintained that "the Freedom of Choice program is the best way to integrate our schools and maintain the highest level of education possible."[100] Hollings's justification for supporting freedom of choice was that the 1964 Civil Rights Act had itself prohibited the busing of pupils from one district to another, although the use of such plans had been rendered unconstitutional by the Supreme Court's *Green* and *Alexander* decisions.[101] In this assertion he mirrored the remarks of numerous other southern senators, notably Ervin, who by the late 1960s claimed that he agreed with the color-blind principle enunciated in the 1954 *Brown* decision but opposed remedies to eliminate discrimination that took race into account. Ervin's shift away from endorsing de jure segregation to supporting color-blind policies that promised to continue de facto segregation came at the same time that the Kennedy and Johnson administrations gradually moved toward "color-conscious" approaches to eliminate existing discrimination. Much of Hollings's reasoning on busing and civil rights legislation at this time closely mirrored the "soft southern strategy" offered by Ervin.[102] As few questioned the North Carolina senator's hostility to the goals of civil rights activists, Hollings's alignment with him most likely provided him with cover from potential conservative opponents. Ervin, who left office in 1974, remained an avowed foe of civil rights laws. In 1984, two years after Thurmond had voted for the extension of the Voting Rights Act, Ervin dubbed civil rights laws "special privileges enacted by Congress, created by executive regulations, or manufactured by activist Supreme Court Justices for the supposed benefit of members of minority races on the basis of their race."[103]

Despite echoing Ervin's justification for opposing busing, Hollings sought to avoid appearing racist in this opposition. A written opinion prepared for him in which he opposed an amendment offered by Alabama Democrat James Allen to "deny the Supreme Court jurisdiction in the process of public education" offers a useful example of his effort to avoid the appearance of racial prejudice. While asserting that the Supreme Court's unitary schools decision in *Alexander* was "in flagrant disregard of the law of the land," the opinion claimed that supporting the Allen Amendment would "give credence to the charge that our stand for public education in the South is motivated by bigotry."[104]

Although Hollings consistently opposed busing, in the context of contemporary South Carolina politics, he held a middle-of-the-road position. As governor earlier in the decade, he had set the example of reluctant compliance with federal desegregation pressures, contingent on the exhaustion of all legal remedies.[105] As senator he echoed Governor McNair's grudging acceptance of school desegregation and the methods used to achieve it. The clearest enunciation of McNair's position came in a statewide telecast shortly after the Greenville County school system had been issued with a midyear desegregation order in 1970. He remarked, "We've run out of courts, and we've run out of time, and we must adjust to new circumstances."[106] Corresponding with constituents disaffected with the pace of school desegregation, Hollings occasionally echoed McNair explicitly. "Unfortunately . . . I have to agree with the spirit of former Governor McNair's comment that 'we have run out of courts,'" he wrote to Eleanor Pope in July 1971.[107]

There was an ongoing struggle within the state Democratic Party between its racial conservatives and moderates, as was illuminated by the fight over the language for the party's political platform at the 1970 state convention, a gubernatorial election year. That year Ferillo, then the president of the Charleston Young Democrats, led the floor fight to remove segregationist language from the party's declaration on education principles.[108] He was joined by a number of black delegates who attended the convention that year. Ultimately the freedom of choice plank was modified rather than deleted, but Ferillo successfully lobbied for the elimination of a section declaring opposition to interference in public schooling "whether through disruptive judicial decisions or by lawless acts of citizens seeking to destroy public education through the intimidation of innocent children." Added to the statement was the caveat that the party favored freedom of choice "as interpreted within the framework of the laws of the land," a major qualification as recent court decisions had rendered freedom of choice unconstitutional.[109]

The sitting lieutenant governor, John West, ran unopposed for the Democratic gubernatorial nomination in 1970. West, a moderate in the mold of Hollings and McNair, spent his early career opposing the Ku Klux Klan in Camden County. The fact that in 1961 he cast one of only two votes in the state senate against a measure to require the closure of any college forced by court order to integrate spoke of his early openness on racial issues.[110] Although arguably more progressive on race than Hollings—the daughter of I. DeQuincey Newman claimed that the longtime state NAACP field secretary viewed West as a "friend" and Hollings as an "ally"—even West took a tortured path on the busing question in 1970.[111] As polls for his campaign confirmed that race and specifically school integration remained "the dominant issue" in South Carolina, West attacked the actions of HEW as "social experimentation" and claimed that the state "must fight" to avoid the "massive disruption of our public school system threatened by the actions of the federal government."[112] West regretted his court-baiting and told aides who had urged him to continue that if he "had to yell 'nigger' to get elected governor, he didn't want the job."[113] Yet by the end of his successful 1970 campaign, West claimed that busing was a "phony issue" since "we are all against busing."[114] Regardless of white politicians' relative enlightenment on racial matters, opposition to busing remained good politics in South Carolina.

"There is still a lot of hardcore segregationist sentiment in South Carolina," West remarked after the 1970 election, "but South Carolina people are basically law-abiding and won't tolerate violence." In contrast with West's hedging on busing, the Republican gubernatorial candidate, Congressman Albert Watson, appealed to those hardcore segregationist elements and seemed to advocate violent defiance of federal court orders. The Watson campaign leaned heavily on racially inflammatory appeals: in September he ran a television commercial that featured the candidate asking, "Are we going to be ruled by the bloc? Look what it did in Watts . . . in the nation's capital," followed by images of African American rioters clashing with police.[115] The most notorious racial incident of the 1970 campaign, however, came shortly after Watson spoke in Lamar, in Darlington County, where there had been feverish opposition to a recent federal court order to establish racially unitary schools. At a rally there on February 22, Watson proclaimed: "Every section of the state is in for it unless you stand up and use every means at your disposal to defend [against] what I consider to be an illegal order." In an incident that gained national media attention, a mob of whites attacked and turned over school buses carrying black children to desegregated schools on March 3.[116] The reasoning used by some of the assailants offers a fascinating example of the continued overlap of anticommunist themes with anti-integration sentiment. The chairman of the Darlington County Freedom of Choice Committee, Jeryl Best, who spoke to the mob shortly before the attack, later claimed that the group was "just fighting communism."[117] Watson was widely blamed for his apparent role in inciting the violence. The Republican convention in March, dominated by Watson partisans, was unrepentant. Denouncing the supposed "vacillation" of McNair and West on busing, its statement of principles urged that elected officials "speak out firmly and in protest against unwarranted court orders and that every legal avenue to upset these orders . . . be explored to the fullest."[118]

In the same month, Hollings highlighted the "unfortunate thing at Lamar" in his speech to the Democratic state convention. He told his audience: "When law ceases, tyranny begins. . . . It is unfortunate that a petition for redress which used to mean in the halls of Congress now means on the streets."[119] While avoiding an open endorsement of integration, Hollings again provided justification for obeying federal integration orders based on the preservation of public order. As he had implicitly criticized Orangeburg's black protestors in February 1968 for acting outside of the law, he now directed his ire at Darlington County's white rioters. Rather than segregation or integration, the real issue, Hollings contended, was law and order.

Through the 1970 elections, Hollings's Senate colleague Thurmond stridently opposed desegregation. Owing to his support of Nixon for president, who then failed to ease pressure on southern school districts facing the prospect of integration, Thurmond occupied a difficult position of vocally opposing desegregation but being tied to the administration responsible for the wholesale integration of southern schools. Numerous constituents wrote to him expressing their anger at the failure of the Nixon administration to slow the pace of desegregation.[120] In a letter to the county superintendent of schools of Union County, Thurmond wrote that he was urging Congress to appropriate funds to "help school districts reduce the many problems caused by forced integration," an issue that demonstrated the awkward position he occupied as a Nixon ally. "I have strongly opposed forced integration in public schools," he emphasized; yet, "to assist in meeting many of the demands made by HEW or the federal courts, each district should take full advantage of any additional federal funds."[121]

When Hollings defended his antibusing stance to busing proponents, he affirmed his support of the neighborhood school concept. In a form letter from September 1971, he agreed that "racial barriers must come down" but that "there is much to be said in favor of having children attend schools near by their homes, as the best educators long have known."[122] In 1972 Hollings defended his policy to members of South Carolina's League of Women Voters. A legal counsel for South Carolina at the *Briggs v. Elliott* school segregation case, he recalled that Thurgood Marshall's argument in 1952 that busing "because of race" was unconstitutional. Agreeing with Marshall's color-blind reasoning, Hollings wrote that "it is unconstitutional to eliminate a discrimination with another discrimination. . . . In the urban ghetto I am ready to vote more money to put in the best teachers and the best playground, but I do not intend to ignore my 20 year lessons on busing."[123] Rather the way to bring about racial balance in schools was to improve the quality of schools in poor neighborhoods: "If you give the money . . . if you give them a better school in the neighborhood, better teachers, better playground facilities, and better physical facilities, those in the country club will chip in and buy a bus to get down to the good school."[124]

Although Hollings supported measures throughout his career to improve public education and make it easier for parents to fund college education for their children, South Carolina's sorry record in providing adequate funds for its poorer, historically black schools made his suggestion to ensure desegregation by improving poorer schools seem farfetched.[125] One particularly egregious case of a formerly de jure black school remaining undersupported took place in Darlington

County, the site of the Lamar violence. Despite a federal court ordering the elimination of all racially identifiable schools in 1970, there continued litigation over school desegregation for the next twenty-five years. In 1995 the U.S. District Court for South Carolina's *Theodore Whitmore Stanley et al. v. Darlington County School District et al.* offered a damning judgment of the school district's failure to remove the racial identifiability of the historically African American Mayo High School. Mayo "[retained] its racial identifiability" throughout the 1970–94 period. After 1970 the school district provided Mayo with "inferior maintenance, a poor physical appearance, inadequate instructional materials, inferior grounds, inferior resources and substandard facilities." Mayo remained "substantially inferior" to other high schools in the district. For a long time, it lacked "adequate instructional supplies, including current library materials, apparatuses for science instruction, and a computer lab," unlike the nearby Saint John's High School. Mayo failed to offer as wide a curriculum as Saint John's, with students who wanted to study classes only offered at St. John's needing to be bused there during the school day. The school board also "followed a pattern of assigning less competent or problem teachers to historically black schools." For years Mayo had been treated, to some degree, as "a 'dumping ground' . . . for teachers, particularly white teachers, who were not performing satisfactorily elsewhere."[126]

Nevertheless there was some legitimacy to the concern that establishing unitary schools across the state would decrease white support for public education. There had been an appreciable move toward private schooling in the state since the desegregation of the state's public education system had begun. By 1970 more than thirty-five thousand children attended one of South Carolina's 139 private schools; in 1964 there had only been 78 private schools in the state. The trend continued after 1970, the year when school districts were commanded to establish unitary schools immediately. By 1971 another eighteen thousand students abandoned the public school system for one of another 50 new private schools.[127]

Hollings claimed that the South was subject to greater scrutiny on civil rights issues than the rest of the nation. Accordingly in January 1970 he cosponsored an amendment to the Elementary and Secondary Education Act with Mississippi senator John Stennis and Georgia's Richard Russell to apply a single nationwide school desegregation policy "without regard to the origin or cause of such segregation," a measure aimed at exposing perceived northern hypocrisy on school desegregation.[128] Writing to McNair about the amendment, Hollings contended that "if they ever started in the black area of New York and Chicago and started busing to eliminate the dual school system, this country would be in revolt. But this [amendment] is the only way I know to get their attention."[129] Although the Stennis Amendment passed the Senate by 56 to 36, it was gutted in the House-Senate conference committee that followed.[130] Hollings cast his cosponsorship of the amendment in terms of regional fairness. He argued that "if our federal government is going to allow freedom-of-choice in the North, it should be permitted in the South. If not, then it should be denied nationally."[131]

The claims of unequal treatment had some merit. At Senate hearings in October and November 1969, Leon Panetta, the director of HEW's Office of Civil Rights, agreed with Stennis that civil rights laws were being enforced unequally across the country.[132] Panetta also acknowledged at a House Appropriations Subcommittee hearing the next year that, while possible to prosecute nonsouthern school districts for unconstitutional school segregation, "about 15 times more man-hours are needed to establish discrimination in the North than in the South."[133] As of 1971 HEW's own figures showed a higher percentage of black children attending majority-white schools in the South than elsewhere in the nation (38 percent of black children in the South in 1970 versus 28 percent elsewhere in the country that year).[134] Connecticut senator Abraham Ribicoff lent further credence to the claims of unequal enforcement when in a February 1970 speech he accused northern politicians of "monumental hypocrisy in [their] treatment of the black man." "Racism is rampant throughout the country," Ribicoff declared.[135]

Hollings used the same rationale for opposing the extension of the Voting Rights Act in 1970 as he did in supporting the Stennis Amendment: that the South was the victim of regional discrimination. He spoke against the Scott-Hart substitute on the Senate floor, a bill that would retain the same qualification criteria as the original 1965 act for the assignment of federal registrars to localities. (The Nixon administration had put forward a bill that nationalized the scope of the act.) Hollings contended that "if we are to accept the premise that the right to vote is basic in our democracy—and I believe it is—then we must also accept the premise that this right applies nationwide."[136] As with Hollings's opposition to the confirmation of Thurgood Marshall to the Supreme Court, his vote against the Voting Rights Act extension was symbolic. While he voted for all the Ervin amendments to the Scott-Hart substitute aimed at weakening the "trigger" mechanism for the act's coverage and those offered with the same intent by Alabama Democrat James Allen, none of these amendments passed.[137] The Scott-Hart measure replaced the Nixon administration measure by a 51–22 margin, while the bill passed the Senate 64–12.[138] Apart from West Virginia's Robert Byrd, all the nay votes came from southerners.[139] Three Outer South Democrats voted for the bill, namely, Tennessee's Albert Gore, Virginia's William Spong, and Arkansas's William Fulbright.[140] All of them lost their reelection contests, in 1970, 1972, and 1974, respectively. While none of these losses can be reduced to their votes on civil rights measures, in the case of Gore and Spong, their Republican opponents successfully depicted them as too liberal on a host of issues.[141] Hollings's negative vote was politically expedient and likely reflected a belief that race remained a major concern for conservative white voters in South Carolina. Governor West, who had relied on black votes for his election, mirrored Hollings's opposition to the Voting Rights Act and sought assurance from Senator McGovern during the 1972 presidential election that South Carolina would be exempted from the act's coverage. James Clyburn, an African American who worked in the West administration, noted the irony of the situation: "I said to the governor one time when he was raising hell about the Voting Rights Act . . . 'That's a . . . shame. How the hell do you think you got in?'"[142]

Hollings, like other southern Democrats, repeatedly attacked Nixon for duplicity on busing.[143] Closely tied to his criticism was the belief that school desegregation guidelines were being enforced more stringently in the South than elsewhere. In a constituent newsletter from August 1970, he complained that the president "travels to New Orleans grandly proclaiming that he dislikes Northerners pointing the finger at the South. But when we attempt to distribute the agents equally in the North, with the Stennis Amendment, the President has his lieutenants kill that Amendment. The Supreme Court refuses to even hear a northern school case!"[144] Nixon's school desegregation policy *was* misleading and enforced unequally across the United States. As historian Dean Kotlowski wrote, "while making token gestures of political support to conservative whites, Nixon quietly ended de jure segregation in the South. But he declined to tackle de facto segregation in the North and decried busing." After the *Alexander* decision, the president told aides to "do only what the law requires," that is, to ignore de facto school segregation cases, the kind most common outside the South.[145] Nixon's school desegregation policy sought to shift the blame for desegregation away from the administration and onto the federal courts instead.[146] Accordingly he favored a move away from enforcing integration through HEW funding cuts and toward a greater emphasis on Justice Department litigation directed at noncompliant school districts.[147]

Hollings's criticism of Nixon's busing stance was ironic, however, given the similarity of Nixon's public position on desegregation to Hollings's. Before the 1968 Republican Convention, Nixon hedged on civil rights: he opposed busing and backed freedom of choice plans but then reaffirmed his support for the *Brown* decision, hardly different from Hollings's acknowledgement of the necessity for desegregation while opposing busing, the main tool for achieving it. Moreover Nixon's assertion when writing to Ehrlichman that "I don't give a damn about the Southern Strategy—I care a great deal about decent education" closely resembled Hollings's and West's comments on supporting good education rather than integration for its own sake.[148]

Hollings's voting on judicial nominees also demarcated him from the more liberal Democrats in Congress. He voted for all six of Nixon's nominees to the Supreme Court. As part of Nixon's careful courtship of southern whites in the

1968 campaign, he had attacked the perceived excesses of the Warren Court and pledged to appoint only Supreme Court justices who would adhere to a narrow interpretation of the Constitution. The notion of appointing "strict constructionists" had racial connotations to select audiences: many people who opposed the Warren Court's *Brown* decision claimed that the justices had substituted sociological arguments for judicial precedent in their deliberations.

Since Lyndon Johnson had failed in his nomination of Abe Fortas to replace the retiring Chief Justice Earl Warren, Nixon already had one appointment to make upon entering office. This number soon doubled when in April 1969 an article in *Life* magazine detailed a financial relationship between Fortas, still an associate justice, and Louis Wolfson, a convicted stock manipulator. Once John Mitchell, the attorney general, confirmed the conflict of interest to Warren, Fortas resigned on May 14.[149] The first nominee, the conservative Minnesotan Warren Burger, was easily confirmed in June 1969 by a 74–3 vote. Following Harry Dent's suggestion, Nixon sought to fill the other vacancy, traditionally the "Jewish" seat, with a southerner.[150] The eventual choice, Clement Haynsworth, become the subject of a frenzied nomination fight and was ultimately rejected by the Senate on November 21, 1969. Haynsworth, an amply qualified jurist, became the victim of a backlash from Senate liberals against the perceived unfair treatment of Fortas in nomination hearings the previous year.[151]

Hollings played a major role in the nomination process. He suggested that Nixon nominate Haynsworth, a South Carolinian, to one of the court vacancies in May 1969.[152] When Nixon decided to put Haynsworth forward as his nominee, despite Thurmond's supporting Haynsworth, too, Hollings was chosen to head the nomination to ease the confirmation process.[153] Senate liberals still seethed over Thurmond's repeated harassment of Fortas the previous year in Judiciary Committee hearings, which eventually led to Fortas's becoming the first Supreme Court nominee since 1930 not to be confirmed.[154] Thurmond feared a liberal backlash: in a note to Georgia's Richard Russell soliciting quiet support for Haynsworth, he counseled that "Southern and Conservative leaders should not come out too strongly in support of Haynsworth for this could cause a lot of static from Liberals [*sic*] from left-wing groups."[155] Consequently Hollings, perceived as rather more moderate than Thurmond, would marshal the nomination through the Senate.

As the chief judge of the Fourth Circuit Court of Appeals, Haynsworth was a respected jurist. His career, both before and during his time on the bench, however, suggested that he would be unsympathetic toward labor and civil rights interests on the high court. Early in his career he had represented the interests of conservative business leaders in South Carolina and had been closely involved in the passage of the state's right-to-work law in 1954, fiercely opposed by organized labor supporters, who saw the legislation as undermining the potential bargaining power of unions.[156] Haynsworth had repeatedly supported freedom of choice desegregation plans in his judicial opinions and held to the interpretation of *Brown* provided by his mentor Judge John Parker that "the Constitution . . . does not require integration. It merely forbids discrimination."[157] Joseph Rauh of the Americans for Democratic Action (ADA) viewed Haynsworth's support for freedom of choice as disqualifying. Writing to Hollings on September 2, he claimed: "What the supporters of Judge Haynsworth would call 'moderation' is really a record of sophisticated foot-dragging for segregation. . . . Judge Haynsworth is a practicing, judicial segregationist."[158]

Hollings complained that the opposition to Haynsworth stemmed in part from sectional discrimination against southerners. After all Burger, a Minnesotan, held to a similar narrow interpretation of the Constitution but met with nowhere near the same level of opposition.[159] Defending Haynsworth in the Senate shortly before the confirmation vote, Hollings complained that the AFL-CIO "had already gone to work" to undermine the nominee's record even before Nixon announced his appointment on August 18. On August 24 negative headlines about Haynsworth's stock holdings appeared in the *Washington Post*, and by the time the Senate returned from recess to consider the nomination, on September 4, "that same day each Senator received a 59-page brief from the AFL-CIO in opposition to Haynsworth."[160]

Several senators, such as Massachusetts Republican Edward Brooke and New York Republican Jacob Javits, based their opposition to Haynsworth primarily on his civil rights or labor record.[161] However the real fight over the nomination centered on the question of judicial ethics. The opposition in the Senate, led by Indiana senator Birch Bayh, focused on allegations of conflicts of interest in Haynsworth's opinions owing to the judge's large stock portfolio. The most damaging was an alleged conflict of interest in a 1963 case concerning the National Labor Relations Board (NLRB) and Darlington Mills, owned by the notoriously antilabor industrial magnate Roger Milliken. The NLRB had charged that Milliken closed the mill in order to prevent textile workers from organizing. Haynsworth, who owned a small amount of stock in Carolina Vend-A-Matic, a vending machine business with a contract at Darlington Mills, joined in an opinion that ruled in favor of Milliken. Bayh faced a problem in exploiting this possible conflict of interest: Haynsworth had been cleared of wrongdoing in the Darlington Mills case by the Justice Department in 1964 after the Textile Workers Union of America had called for an investigation. Bayh claimed that Haynsworth's behavior constituted a breach of the canon of judicial ethics and, once that argument became untenable, that the judge had provided the "appearance of judicial impropriety." Here he echoed the case made by Michigan Republican Robert Griffin the previous year that the "appearance of impropriety" should be enough to disqualify judicial nominees.[162] On October 8 Bayh released a "bill of particulars" of Haynsworth's supposed misdeeds.

In the Senate Hollings disputed the conflict of interest claims. The day before Bayh unveiled his bill of particulars, Hollings ridiculed the tiny sums involved in some of the apparent conflict of interest cases and noted that "Carolina Vend-A-Matic has never been in court. In spite of all the headlines . . . it was not a party litigant."[163] Hollings contended that the real problem was the ambiguity of the United States Code, which required a judge to disqualify himself should he hold "a substantial interest . . . or is so related to or connected with any party or his attorney as to render it improper, in his opinion, for him to sit on the trial, appeal, or other proceeding therein." Consequently he proposed a bill to amend the code to bar judges from presiding over cases involving litigants in which they held "any investment whatever." Regardless Hollings cited an expert witness, Prof. John P. Frank, that "in the Darlington case, it was [Haynsworth's] plain responsibility to participate, and he would have shirked his duty if he had not done so."[164]

To allay concerns over the alleged conflicts of interest, Haynsworth had promised to place all the stock from the disputed cases into a blind trust.[165] Shortly afterward a cartoon showed Attorney General Mitchell defending the figure of Haynsworth, who had Vend-A-Matic stock tapes falling out of his bag, with the caption "My client hasn't done anything wrong—and he promises to stop doing it." Hollings later remembered the "Vend-A-Justice" cartoons as particularly damaging to Haynsworth's chances. He claimed "that Herblock cartoon lost me five votes."[166]

As pressure against the nominee grew during October and into November, Hollings became increasingly embittered toward Bayh and the efforts of the opposition generally to defeat the Haynsworth nomination. On November 18, 1969, he spoke for two and a half hours in the Senate in support of Haynsworth, denouncing the opposition of the national press to the nomination and responding to each of Bayh's allegations. Bayh "socked the judge with a nine-page bill of particulars dated October 8, 1969. There was no reference here to Justice Fortas or [disgraced former Lyndon Johnson aide] Bobby Baker but rather coldly calculated charges of crime, statutory violations, breaches of ethics, avariciousness, and lack of candor."[167] Hollings railed against Bayh's refusal to debate his bill of particulars on television and contended that Haynsworth's opposition "did not want anyone to answer anything. They do not want debate. They do not want the deliberative processes in the Senate."[168]

On November 21 Haynsworth's nomination was defeated 55–45. Hollings was left frustrated by the White House's apparent failure to court the votes of Republican senators until several weeks after the nomination had been announced, by which stage several of them had come out in opposition.[169] In October he had complained that the White House "dropped the nominee and let him hang there."[170] In the final vote the three top Republicans in the Senate, Minority

Leader Hugh Scott, Minority Whip Robert Griffin, and Conference Chair Margaret Chase Smith, all voted against Haynsworth.[171]

President Nixon's response to the setback was to nominate someone "farther South and further right."[172] The replacement nominee was the Florida Republican G. Harrold Carswell, who was officially nominated on January 19, 1970. Unlike Haynsworth, Carswell was an undistinguished jurist. Much of the nomination debate questioned whether he was intellectually qualified to hold a seat on the Supreme Court. Bryce Harlow, Nixon's main lobbyist for the nomination on Capitol Hill, summed up the problem: opponents of the nomination "think Carswell's a boob, a dummy. And what counter is there to that? He is."[173] Carswell also brought with him more problematic racial baggage than Haynsworth. Unlike Haynsworth's recalcitrant attitude to the ramifications of *Brown*, Carswell was an "ultrasegregationist."[174] In 1948 he had conducted an unsuccessful white supremacist campaign for the Georgia House of Representatives; in 1956 he was involved in the purchase of a municipal Tallahassee golf club, which subsequently privatized to prevent its racial integration; and in 1958 he drafted a charter for a whites-only supporters club at Florida State University.[175]

Alluding to his disappointment at the apparent lack of deliberation in the Senate over Haynsworth, Hollings announced he would "review the hearings on his nomination carefully" before deciding whether to vote for Carswell.[176] The Nixon White House recognized Hollings as an unreliable Carswell supporter, who might "jump ship."[177] A Hollings aide captured the dilemma southern senators faced over the Carswell vote, namely that opposing the mediocre Floridian would mark "another rejection of the South."[178] Although he eventually voted for the doomed nomination, Hollings complained in constituent correspondence that Nixon had failed to "put our [the South's] best foot forward."[179] At the April 6 vote, he supported the nomination despite Carswell's lack of standing as a legal scholar, since "anonymity cannot be equated with mediocrity."[180] A fortnight before the confirmation vote, Hollings summarized his dilemma in a letter to a Sumter constituent: "Carswell can't even carry Haynsworth's law books. . . . In confidence, I will probably vote for him but I am not proud of the vote. I don't believe he is a racist or any of these charges generally about him. I just believe he is a mediocre lawyer and judge and that if I had a case, I would not associate him in it. Therefore, I see no reason why I should promote him to the highest court."[181] The vote for Carswell was a necessary evil to appease Hollings's conservative white constituents, much as his vote against Thurgood Marshall had been. As with busing Hollings's support for Nixon's Supreme Court nominees, especially Carswell, provided him with credibility among conservative voters that gave him greater leeway elsewhere.

In 1972 Hollings faced a presidential election where the Democratic nominee's views were distasteful to a majority of his constituents. As in 1968 he separated himself rhetorically from both the Democratic and Republican presidential candidates while, as long as Wallace was in the Democratic primary contest, retaining a suitable level of sympathy for the Alabama governor.

Hollings's behavior toward Wallace shifted once it became apparent that he would run for the presidency as a Democrat in 1972. In October 1971, when it seemed more likely that Wallace would run as an independent, Hollings asserted at a National Association of Broadcasters conference that the country "does not want the extremism of a Wallace." He extended his criticism to the national Republican and Democratic Parties: the people were "tired of the divide-and-conquer tactics of Nixon-Agnew," while Democrats "seem to be losing touch with the little man who has always been the big part of the Democratic party."[182] When Wallace chose to enter the presidential race as a Democrat in January 1972, Hollings, by then the chairman of the Senate Democratic Campaign Committee, changed tack. While several national Democrats, including the chairman of the Democratic Party, Lawrence O'Brien, criticized Wallace's entry into the primaries, Hollings asserted that he "has as much right to be in the Democratic party as have New York Mayor Lindsay and former Minnesota Sen. Eugene McCarthy," both liberal Democrats. Moreover, "George Wallace expresses the Democratic view on many things as people in my section of the country see it." Continuing the spirit of inclusiveness, he claimed that he would even welcome Thurmond back into the party.[183] When Wallace, who had emphasized his opposition to busing at campaign events, won the Florida primary with 42 percent of the vote from a twelve-strong Democratic field, Hollings argued that the Democratic candidates needed to "get back in the middle or they're lost."[184] With presidential hopeful Ed Muskie claiming that the primary result revealed the "worst instincts" of the electorate, Hollings instead suggested that the other Democratic candidates needed to follow Wallace's lead. "Being against busing that destroys a community is not racist," he commented.[185] He further joked that after the victory of the "Wallace issues" in Florida, Nixon would announce himself as "74 per cent against busing—the same as Florida."[186] Hollings was not far wrong: Nixon urged the federal courts to impose a "moratorium" on busing to achieve racial balance on March 17, less than two days after Wallace's Florida success.[187]

Alongside sympathizing with Wallace's busing position, Hollings was sensitive to other "Wallace issues," especially religious and cultural ones.[188] As the diverse conservative opposition to the Fortas nomination in 1968 had demonstrated, many conservative Americans were concerned about the country's perceived increasing permissiveness toward supposedly immoral behavior and the intolerance of conservative religious and cultural values. Their political mobilization, begun in earnest in the 1970s, remolded national politics in the 1980s and 1990s. Much as he had done in his 1966–68 term with his support for school prayer and making flag desecration a crime, Hollings supported issues that concerned religiously and culturally conservative voters in his 1969–74 term. He was a consistent endorser of amendments to allow prayer in public schools, while in a 1970 newsletter he also denounced the report of President Nixon's Commission on Obscenity and Pornography, which recommended the repeal of federal pornography laws, as "a magna carta for smut."[189]

Despite chairing the Democratic Senate Campaign Committee that year, Hollings distanced himself from the party's presidential ticket in 1972. Once it became apparent that McGovern would be the nominee, he minced few words on the South Dakotan's prospects, though he did announce he would vote for him. In the melee after Tom Eagleton withdrew as McGovern's vice presidential pick, Hollings had been offered the position but had rejected it.[190] After rejecting McGovern's entreaties himself, Florida governor Reubin Askew had suggested that McGovern ask Hollings to be his running mate.[191] In August, Hollings claimed that "the image of Sen. McGovern is such that he will have a difficult time carrying the South and especially South Carolina."[192] In October newspaperman Hugh Gibson wrote in the *News and Courier* that "what seems to worry Democrats most is not the GOP candidates but that awful, looming shadow of McGovern. Some of them are worried sick that voters will carry their resentment of McGovern to the point of pulling nothing except Republican levers in the voting booths."[193] Explaining his politically difficult decision to support McGovern, in constituent correspondence Hollings likened his position within the Democratic Party to Wallace's and contended that he could "be more effective for South Carolina's beliefs by working within the Democratic Party."[194]

While he attacked the president's apparent failure to protect the U.S. textile industry throughout Nixon's first term, Hollings also used the competing welfare reform suggestions from Nixon, McGovern, and the National Welfare Rights Organization to separate himself from the national candidates' apparent fiscal profligacy.[195] He told his constituents in a June 1972 newsletter titled "The Welfare Mess" that "Congress is kept too busy trying to lock the guaranteed annual income plans of the President, Sen. McGovern and the National Welfare Rights Organization. All these proposals for 'Family Assistance' and 'Welfare Reform' will, in fact, create a bigger mess." In Hollings's view "the poverty cycle goes from hunger to poor housing to inferior environment to ill health to faulty training to jail or joblessness to welfare. . . . This is the welfare mess that must be corrected."[196] He stressed this disagreement with the Nixon and McGovern welfare reform proposals in letters to constituents.[197] On the day of the November election, Hollings told an audience of businessmen in Spartanburg that Nixon would be reelected "easily" and that the Democrats would need to "rebuild entirely at the national level. . . . We've got to get the national Democratic candidates more on the right side of the issues."[198] The loss was easy to predict, as Nixon won forty-nine states nationwide and by a 71–29 margin in South Carolina.

After Albert Watson's loss in the 1970 gubernatorial race, there were few obvious candidates to challenge Hollings in 1974. Although polling for the senator placed him in theoretical matchups with Republican congressman Floyd Spence, Gen. William Westmoreland, and White House aide Harry Dent, among others, no prominent opponent emerged.[199] A cartoon published in the *State* in October 1973 captured the situation. Hollings, a runner wearing the number 74, stood by a "Senate Race" sign, while the "official starter" looked through his binoculars into the distance. The caption asked, "Anybody in Sight Yet?"[200]

Hollings would face only nominal opposition in 1974. Gwen Bush, a South Dakota–born Charleston resident with no experience of elective office, was the eventual Republican senatorial nominee. From a conversation with Thomas Hartnett, then a Republican state senator, one of Hollings's secretaries reported that Bush's candidacy was an "ego trip," while members of the state Republican Party "have just all shrugged their shoulders and decided to let her drift." Hartnett was "sorry you [Hollings] have to dignify her campaign with any effort at all."[201]

Bush tried to tar Hollings as a spendthrift liberal and to tie him to the Kennedy family, a familiar theme in Hollings's Senate campaigns. In speeches she attacked "Kennedy-Hollings socialistic" policies.[202] Hollings was an "election year conservative and five year liberal," a politician who lacked "the courage to say 'no' to wasteful and wildly extravagant programs . . . welfare, food stamps, etc."[203] Bush was never a credible opponent. By October 1974 she had raised a minuscule seven thousand dollars, and she garnered only 30 percent of the vote in the November election.[204]

At the same time as Hollings won handsomely in 1974, a Republican captured the governor's office in South Carolina for the first time since Reconstruction when state senator James Edwards beat Congressman William Jennings Bryan Dorn narrowly. Edwards's victory, however, had much to do with the disqualification of the original Democratic nominee, Charles "Pug" Ravenel, in September after the state Supreme Court ruled that he had failed to complete the necessary residency requirements to run for governor. Ravenel, a former Harvard quarterback who had campaigned against the existing Democratic Party apparatus in the primary, refused to endorse Dorn, an old-time Democrat, who was chosen to replace him. In 1974 the Republican Party in South Carolina was still enough in its infancy that, except when facing the personally popular Thurmond (who rarely identified himself as a Republican, anyway), Democrats who avoided alienating large portions of the electorate remained heavy favorites to win. Asked in 1978 about his reticence to identify as a Republican in his campaigns, Thurmond contended that "the Republican party hasn't been in existence long enough to run as a ticket; it isn't strong enough. I'm an independent at heart."[205]

Despite his support for food stamp spending and ending U.S. involvement in Vietnam, Hollings had not sufficiently alienated his more conservative constituents to be vulnerable. A January 1974 memorandum written by Hollings staffer Mike Copps on "matters of image and substance" reflected this reality. Issues expected to hurt Hollings, namely his support of McGovern in 1972, his advocacy for the Cooper-Church Amendment, and his "hunger stance," had not appeared prominently in a Kraft poll from late 1973. While Copps feared that "public hostility to food stamps will be exploited by any serious opponent," he viewed Hollings's support for defense spending and his emphasis on fiscal responsibility (he was a "*common-sense, realistic, South Carolina* Democrat") to be positives in his reelection campaign.[206] The poll itself was revealing: the pollster noted that among respondents who disliked Hollings, they criticized him "for being too liberal, too conservative, and just for being a Democrat," hardly a focused critique for an opponent to exploit.[207]

Hollings, then, successfully straddled the political fence. He advocated increased spending on antihunger programs, championed environmental preservation programs, made qualified calls for withdrawal from Vietnam, and endorsed George McGovern, a candidate who was never likely to carry South Carolina, in the 1972 presidential contest. Elsewhere, as a consistent supporter of heavy military spending and balanced budgets, his views were far more typical of other conservative southern politicians. Although a constant opponent of busing, his position was centrist by contemporary South Carolina standards. The late 1960s and early 1970s witnessed a regional convergence on civil rights, too: as opposition to busing gained a nationwide following in the 1970s, Hollings's simultaneous affirmation of support for *Brown* while opposing its means of implementation became a middle-of-the-road position in national politics. Race still mattered too much for him to support the Voting Rights Act renewal in 1970, though this would soon change. As Copps told Hollings early in 1974, "the South has done some growing up since you last ran a state-wide race, and some of the old demons need no longer be greatly feared."[208] For Hollings 1974 was the year that the demon in his state's politics, race, ceased to be an overriding concern.

Epilogue

By the end of 1974, Fritz Hollings was electorally entrenched in South Carolina. As with many other white Democrats across the region in the 1970s, by being more responsive to African American interests than his Republican opponents while avoiding alienating his more conservative white supporters and his business backers, Hollings amassed comfortable electoral majorities. He remained successful statewide even as the South Carolina GOP gained a foothold in the state's elections and became the dominant party in the 1990s. From lacking a single member in the state legislature in 1960, Republicans held a majority by 1994. Hollings won reelection contests in 1980, 1986, 1992, and 1998 before choosing to retire in 2004. Having entered politics at a time when the Democratic Party was the only avenue to political success, he was the state's last Democrat elected statewide by the time he retired. He served thirty-six of his thirty-eight years alongside Thurmond, which made them the longest-serving pair in Senate history while demonstrating that South Carolinians could routinely return two individuals with differing political outlooks to office.

Though they became more cordial as their service wore on, relations between Hollings and Thurmond were often strained. In 1971 a Hollings staff member complained that thanks to Thurmond's uncanny ability to receive advance notice of grants made in South Carolina, the Republican's office took too much credit for projects that Hollings's people had contributed to: "We don't even get word on construction of an outhouse," the staffer grumbled.[1] Thurmond "never cooperated with me on anything to begin with," Hollings later remarked. "We weren't close." On obtaining federal money for local projects, he contended that lacking a seat on the influential Appropriations Committee, Thurmond "didn't know what was going on. He acted like he did, and announced everything."[2]

In the Senate Hollings continued to moderate his position on race. This evolution was apparent in his approach to the Voting Rights Act, which was up for renewal in 1975. As in 1970 he supported amendments that would have nationalized the act's coverage by eliminating the trigger mechanism in Section IV. Hollings argued that the nationalization of the act would merely provide "equal justice under law." Opponents of these amendments, in contrast, claimed that they were thinly veiled attempts to neutralize the effectiveness of the act. Edward Brooke of Massachusetts, the only African American senator at the time, contended that a Stennis-Nunn Amendment to eliminate Section IV "will gut the Voting Rights Act." Similarly California's John V. Tunney, the bill's floor manager, asserted that the amendment sought to invalidate the law stealthily by removing the section that defined the conditions for the act's coverage. As the Supreme Court's *South Carolina v. Katzenbach* decision, which affirmed the constitutionality of the Voting Rights Act, required "exceptional conditions" to allow for federal intervention in state election procedures, Tunney reasoned, "we are passing a law which is, on its face, unconstitutional, so we can get rid of the entire Voting Rights Act."[3] Unlike in 1970, though, after the amendments to nationalize the act failed in 1975, Hollings voted for final passage of the act's renewal, which passed by seventy-seven votes to twelve. Ten other southerners joined Hollings in his yea vote.[4] From the Deep South states, both Louisiana senators and Georgia's Sam Nunn voted in favor of the act. Despite softening his civil rights posture after the 1970 elections, Thurmond voted against renewal, which he contended "subjected South Carolina and six other Southern States to discriminatory Federal intervention in the administration of their election laws."[5]

When the Voting Rights Act came up for renewal again in 1982, Hollings was more strident in his support. The 1982 renewal included a "results test" compromise that allowed jurisdictions previously subject to the preclearance stipulations of Section V to escape the section's coverage if they proved an absence of voting rights abuses over the previous decade.[6] Hollings supported the measure and contended that the compromise, offered by Kansas's Bob Dole, rendered the act national in scope. On the Senate floor on June 16, he engaged in a heated argument with John East, a conservative North Carolina Republican, over the continued relevance of the Voting Rights Act in the South. Hollings contested East's claim that the act was no longer necessary, which Hollings contended "completely disregard[ed] the historical practice and experience of his backyard and my backyard over the many years."[7] He employed extensively a 1980 decision given by the Republican judge Robert Chapman, in Hollings's view "a pedigree Republican, not a white flight Republican." The legal opinion affected the at-large election system in Edgefield County, Strom Thurmond's birthplace. It noted that "while many of these restrictions [to voting] have been removed . . . there is still a long history of racial discrimination in all areas of life. There is block voting by the whites on a scale that this Court has never before observed and all advances made by the blacks have been under some type of court order." Hollings further attacked the apparent historical amnesia of the Voting Rights Act's opponents: "If this debate is going to continue on as though a bunch of technical nuts got together in the Judiciary Committee and reported an 'ill-conceived and so badly flawed' law, someone has to give the hard, bitter experience of the past 30 years, and even years before that, where the official policy, practices, conspiracies, societal habits, customs, mores, and what-have-you, said, 'No you're not going to come in the door.'"[8]

Since 1970 Hollings had become an ardent defender of the voting rights law. While Hollings's commitment to racial equality was likely sincere, part of his shift can be attributed to the lessening of overt racial politics in South Carolina and the dependence of Democrats and Republicans on the state's increasingly influential black electorate. Even Thurmond, the longtime opponent of federal civil rights legislation, voted for the 1982 Voting Rights Act extension, despite his reservations about its coverage.[9]

Hollings's floor argument with East, however, infuriated Thurmond, who told one reporter that his Democratic colleague "is running for president. Otherwise, it would be an unheard-of thing for a senator to speak against his own state and his own people."[10] In spite of Hollings's protestations that he was merely seeking "to fill a vacuum," Thurmond's complaint had some merit. Hollings *was* readying himself to run for president. He launched his abortive candidacy for the Democratic presidential nomination in 1983.

While Hollings only entered one presidential nomination contest, he had long been discussed as a possible candidate for higher office. This thinking was apparent from at least the early 1970s. Responding to the suggestion that a southerner would be second on the Democratic ticket in 1972, at a December 1970 banquet for the South Carolina Council on Human Relations, Senator McGovern contended that Hollings should be considered as a presidential candidate in his own right.[11] Within his office there had been discussion of Hollings's seeking the Democratic vice presidential nomination at least as early as January 1971.[12] Although Hollings was offered the Democratic vice presidential nomination in the scramble following Sen. Tom Eagleton's withdrawal from the ticket, he refused it. To join with McGovern in 1972, who was deeply unpopular in South Carolina, would have probably meant electoral suicide for him in 1974.

As the 1976 elections approached, Hollings and his staff considered a presidential run.[13] However this time former Georgia governor Jimmy Carter tied up the Democratic nomination. Hollings supported him and introduced Carter at the state capitol in Columbia during the 1976 campaign.[14] Instead Hollings competed for the Senate majority leadership, vacated by the retiring Montana senator Mike Mansfield. He joined a field of three competing for the position alongside Minnesota senator Hubert Humphrey and West Virginia senator Robert Byrd. Hollings sought to portray himself as a compromise between the liberalism of Humphrey and Byrd's conservatism.[15] Despite these efforts, however, Byrd had already secured commitments from many of the Senate Democrats (the majority leadership would be decided by a secret ballot among these senators). After trying to persuade Humphrey to abandon his candidacy in December 1976 to allow him a better chance of beating Byrd in a two-way contest, Hollings left the race on December 13.[16] Humphrey eventually dropped out at the last minute and moved to nominate Byrd by acclamation on January 4, 1977.[17]

Apart from racial matters, Hollings's legislative record remained consistent. This steadiness was especially apparent on bills concerning labor. Hollings had supported right-to-work legislation as a state representative, touted South Carolina's lack of unionization to industrial prospects as governor, and championed the antiunion Supreme Court nominee Clement Haynsworth and sponsored legislation barring striking workers from using the food stamp program as a senator. Given the low levels of labor unionization in South Carolina, it was unsurprising that Hollings was largely unresponsive to labor demands. This generally adversarial approach to labor organizing continued during the debate over the 1978 labor law revision bill, which sought to amend the 1935 Wagner Act. Hollings joined Utah Republican Orrin Hatch in leading the fight against cloture on the bill, which he dubbed a "power grab" on the part of "big labor." In a legislative fight that lasted some six weeks, supporters of labor reform ultimately failed to cut off debate after six attempts by the Democratic Senate leadership to invoke cloture failed.[18] According to labor dispute arbitrator Thomas Terrill, Secretary of Labor Ray Marshall viewed Hollings's opposition to the labor bill as a "betrayal."[19] Based on his earlier record, however, Marshall should not have been surprised. As far as Hollings was sympathetic to labor interests, it was in protecting the textile industry, historically the dominant industry in South Carolina, from cheaper foreign imports. Since worker pay accounted for much of the production cost in the textile industry, mill owners strenuously opposed efforts by workers to unionize. Hollings demonstrated his support for textile workers by seeking to prevent plant closures, not through supporting worker unionization efforts.

Hollings remained an advocate of protectionist legislation throughout his thirty-eight years in the Senate. The closest he came to success in the 1970s was in September 1978 when he introduced an amendment to a trade bill to exempt the textile industry from tariff reductions. Although the measure passed the Senate comfortably, President Carter vetoed it for fear that it would draw retaliation from the country's trading partners.[20] As well as according with Hollings's belief that America's status in the world could not be maintained without a strong industrial base, his efforts to protect the textile industry brought with it local political benefits. In his attempts to limit foreign imports, Hollings cooperated closely with the textile magnate Roger Milliken. As far back as 1961, while he was governor of South Carolina, he had visited Milliken's Spartanburg research facility and conferred with him about the problems facing the industry. Milliken was influential in marshaling support for Hollings's 1978 textile import measure, and he supported Hollings in his future efforts to limit the influx of foreign textiles.[21] Milliken was deeply involved in funding Republican candidates nationwide, a list that included

Thurmond and Ronald Reagan. Despite his agreement with Hollings on trade issues, however, he was minimally involved in the Democrat's reelection efforts; Crawford Cook recalled that Milliken only "signed an ad for Hollings in our last campaign [in 1998]. Other than that, we never got a penny."[22] Ike McLeese, who worked in the textile-dominated upstate for Hollings in the 1960s, joked that "Roger gave money to other people who would give, but he remained pure [as a Republican]."[23] Nevertheless Milliken did not vigorously oppose Hollings. Cook contended that "it was difficult for Roger to openly oppose Fritz because Fritz was the number one person in the United States Senate who tried to maintain some kind of a sensible policy on textiles."[24] In the 1990s Hollings continued his opposition to free trade measures and used his committee seniority to hold up consideration of both the North American Free Trade Agreement and the General Agreement on Tariffs and Trade during the Clinton administration, although both ultimately passed.[25]

As with his positions on labor and textiles, Hollings remained opposed to deficit spending, which he focused on from his position on the Budget Committee. The former Post Office and Civil Service Committee was replaced with Budget after the committee system was reorganized in February 1977. When Senator Muskie was appointed secretary of state in 1980, Hollings assumed the Budget chairmanship. Once the 1980 elections brought a Republican Senate majority, he became the ranking member on the committee. He used this position to attack the Reagan administration's budget proposals and to lay the groundwork for his upcoming presidential bid. Biographical material distributed by his presidential campaign touted Hollings as "the first Democrat to put up a comprehensive and credible alternative" to Reagan's budget proposals in 1982, a plan that "would have saved over $180 billion during the next three years without raising taxes and without cutting spending, only holding up the increase."[26] Several years after his abortive presidential bid, the Gramm-Rudman-Hollings Act of 1986 passed. Gramm-Rudman-Hollings was a sequestration bill that ensured across-the-board spending cuts if Congress did not produce a balanced budget. Hollings later disowned the act, as he claimed that politicians were merely using it to prevent themselves from making difficult budget decisions.[27]

When Hollings declared his presidential candidacy in April 1983, he offered economic, military, and educational arguments for his selection. Reagan, he told his audience at Columbia's Midlands Technical College, "has delivered us disastrous deficits, caused Depression-level joblessness, and he has demolished the consensus we needed for the rebuilding of our depleted defenses." Rather than continued deficit spending, he called for a focus on "America's human infrastructure."[28] Unsurprisingly given his earlier advocacy for more generous food stamp benefits, Hollings opposed the Reagan administration's cuts to social programs. He claimed these cuts did not make budgetary sense. In defending funding for the Women, Infants and Children feeding program (WIC), which he had championed alongside Senator Humphrey in 1972, he returned to his fiscal argument for social spending: "Overwhelming evidence indicates that for every one dollar spent on WIC we save three dollars in medical costs."[29] For Hollings nutrition programs were still fiscally conservative.

Hollings's central proposals—for the reinstitution of the military draft and for a budget freeze—were hardly Democratic staples. He identified as a hawk but contended, as he had done a decade earlier, that the nation "cannot afford all the weaponry that the defense department would ask for." To burnish his credentials, he highlighted his opposition to the B-1 bomber and the MX weapon system in a June 1983 interview.[30] Hollings sought to use his record on defense and spending to distance himself from the other Democratic presidential hopefuls and critique the weaknesses of the party's recent nominees. He asserted that the Democratic ticket lost in 1980 because "every time a problem arose, we had but a single solution: spend more money," while in a press conference shortly before the New Hampshire primary in February 1984 he claimed his opponents were "weak on defense . . . that's why we've lost for the last twenty years [in presidential elections]."[31]

Hollings's presidential campaign fell flat. As one of the more conservative Democrats in the field, he generated little enthusiasm among the primary electorate. Moreover his background as a former segregationist politician proved problematic. In a candidate feature in the *Washingtonian* in December 1983, the writer qualified Hollings's civil rights record: he was liberal "for a southerner." The NAACP gave his voting record an F, the same grade given to President Reagan.[32] Hollings was unlikely to win the nomination, anyway. The chance for an "enlightened" southerner to win the Democratic nomination had likely come and gone in 1976. Hollings was not the only New South politician to seek the nomination, either, as former Florida governor Reubin Askew also entered the primary contest. Hollings chose to focus his efforts on the New Hampshire primary, where despite winning several local newspaper endorsements, he finished far back and dropped out of the race.[33]

In contrast with President Reagan's antigovernment rhetoric, Hollings believed in the usefulness of government involvement throughout his career, apparent from his support for a sales tax to fund school improvements as a state legislator, through his promotion of new educational programs as governor, to his advocacy for food stamps and other antihunger programs as a senator. Though he did not promote large-scale government-led employment programs as older, New Deal–influenced southerners such as Lyndon Johnson and Albert Gore envisaged, Hollings viewed government as capable of a positive societal role.[34]

Two statements given almost fifty years apart demonstrate Hollings's continued faith in active government involvement. In 1956 he told an audience why he advocated a sales tax in South Carolina despite having promised "economy in

State Government" when he was first elected as a state representative in 1948. Hollings had not realized the extent of the state's civic ills. He claimed, "I didn't know at the time that I was elected that we had no school buildings, our transportation system was broken down, and teachers were so poorly paid that they were leaving to go elsewhere. . . . I didn't realize that age old political theory of when in doubt, do nothing, had eaten into our system of Government so that not only was it when in doubt do nothing, we stayed in doubt all the time. And so . . . we faced the issues and began to do something in this State. We imposed the sales' [*sic*] tax, which brings in approximately 45 million dollars, and is really now the anchor to our financial stability."[35] Displaying a similar belief in the positive role of government, in a 2004 interview on *60 Minutes* he remarked that "we believe in feeding the hungry, and housing the homeless, and educating the uninformed and everything else . . . in order to form a more perfect Union."[36] During his 1984 presidential campaign, he recounted a story reminding voters of the major role of government in modern American life. It was about "a guy who came home from the Korean War, went to college on a form of the GI Bill, opened a business with a Small Business Administration loan, made sure his parents' farm was adequately wired through Rural Electrification and irrigated with assistance from the Army Corps of Engineers, saw his kids get subsidized school lunches at a school that received lab equipment from a National Science Foundation grant, got his mortgage from the FHA and hurricane disaster relief from FEMA, and one day, took AMTRAK to Washington to complain to his congressman about getting big government off people's backs."[37]

Hollings's relative moderation during his time as governor of South Carolina and his support for various progressive pet causes as senator distinguished him from many of his southern colleagues. A longtime staff member, Mike Copps, claimed that "you could probably make the case that Fritz Hollings was the first 'New South' Democrat. . . . He was there long before Jimmy Carter, Rubin [*sic*] Askew, Bob McNair, and John West, with this rather bold new leadership for the South."[38] If "New South" is used to describe politicians who moved away from racially and economically conservative appeals and focused instead on issues that promoted greater economic opportunity, Hollings fits into the group. Nevertheless the way these moderate southerners accommodated the interests of newly enfranchised African American constituents is itself informative. John Seigenthaler, Robert Kennedy's administrative assistant in the early 1960s, contended that Hollings "knew what was right" when he was governor but "never would have gone to the Senate if he had committed political suicide" over the race issue.[39] Even if Seigenthaler's sympathetic view of the South Carolinian's motivations for changing his racial policies is not accepted, the timing and extent of Hollings's shift on racial issues was important for understanding the broader adaptation of white southern Democrats to widespread black political participation. As a politician from a Deep South state who remained involved in politics through the 1950s and 1960s and adopted a degree of racial moderation by the early 1970s, Hollings's shift was especially interesting in demonstrating how he remained electorally viable and what his "moderation" entailed.

Although Hollings gave some early indication at the beginning of his career that he wanted to remedy some of the abuses of the Jim Crow system, he made no open challenge to the racial status quo. After the *Brown* decision, he behaved as an ardent segregationist as he campaigned for the lieutenant governorship and governorship. Even then he prioritized maintaining public education over the preservation of the color line in his rhetoric. As governor, after initial defiant gestures, he embraced a degree of moderation on race. Civil rights demonstrations were studiously policed to prevent violent clashes between protestors and hecklers. However protesters were routinely arrested and charged with "breach of the peace," with no consideration given to their demands. Hollings's response to protests was calibrated to deprive protesters of video footage of any altercations that might provide them with leverage when pressuring politicians nationally to pass civil rights laws. At the same time, his drive for economic modernization in the state brought minor improvements in the employment prospects for African Americans. If he did remain committed personally to segregation, the demands of maintaining the Jim Crow system were trumped by economic priorities. His eventual call for the peaceful acceptance of the desegregation of Clemson, even though it was contingent on exhausting all available legal remedies, was a significant and courageous gesture.

Nevertheless Hollings's calls for accepting desegregation did not bring any open endorsement of civil rights in his campaign for the Senate in 1966, even as the rapidly growing African American voting bloc ensured his victory. Similarly in his curtailed first Senate term, Hollings sided with the interests of his conservative white constituents on high-profile issues with racial connotations. At the same time, however, differences between him and the region's most racially conservative figures, such as Thurmond, emerged. During Thurgood Marshall's confirmation process, Hollings sought to square his opposition to the first African American nominated to the Supreme Court with his apparent support for black advancement. Unlike Thurmond's bitter-end approach, in the late 1960s, Hollings professed support for racially integrated schooling, though he opposed the methods used to bring about significant school desegregation. Even before he won reelection in 1968, he promoted programs that improved economic opportunity generally, which also aided poorer blacks. Hollings was not completely unresponsive to the interests of his black constituents at this time, though African Americans were far from equal partners in the biracial coalition that elected him.

After winning reelection with the support of George Wallace voters and African Americans in 1968, Hollings became more vocal in his promotion of issues that stood to benefit economically insecure blacks, most clearly in his demand for a concerted effort to eliminate hunger in the United States. Hollings became a consistent supporter of more generous food stamp benefits and other antihunger programs such as free school lunches and the WIC prescription nutrition scheme. He maintained that greater spending on food assistance reduced the need for more costly expenses in the welfare and penal systems and so was in fact fiscally conservative. Though locally unpopular among many whites, his advocacy also increased his national profile as an "enlightened" southern politician.

Yet alongside his leadership on the racially fraught topic of hunger, in his second Senate term Hollings remained opposed to voting rights legislation and continually opposed busing, much as Thurmond did. Only once he won reelection again in 1974 did he support the renewal of the Voting Rights Act. Despite this relatively late embrace of civil rights legislation, Hollings was one of four Deep South senators, alongside Sam Nunn of Georgia and Russell Long and Bennett Johnston of Louisiana, to vote for the 1975 renewal of the act. Moreover he made tentative but definite movements away from a politics of absolute defiance in the early 1960s, well before Thurmond softened his anti–civil rights stance after the defeat of the ultrasegregationist GOP gubernatorial candidate Albert Watson in 1970. Even then Thurmond's tonal shift was just that: he appointed Thomas Moss, a black staff member, after the 1970 elections, but it was 1982 before he supported the renewal of the Voting Rights Act.

On the major foreign policy issue of the 1960s and early 1970s, Hollings initially promoted a rapid escalation of the Vietnam War, both in terms of troop levels and permitting the bombing of North Vietnamese military targets. This belief in the ability of the United States to bring the war to a rapid and victorious conclusion was consistent with his expressed belief in the 1950s that the Korean War could have been prosecuted more successfully if the generals had been given greater freedom of action. Hollings advanced this view of the Vietnam War throughout his first Senate term, an approach that simultaneously aligned him with the locally favored South Carolina native William Westmoreland and distanced him from the unpopular President Johnson. In the early years of the Nixon presidency, Hollings's prescription for the war changed. He argued that Nixon's policy of de-escalation was actually a slow-paced surrender and claimed that if troops were not fighting to win the war, they should not be in Vietnam at all. Hollings, however, still contended that the war could have been won, if only Johnson or Nixon had pursued a policy of escalation. He subsequently supported measures to limit the geographical scope of the war, though he opposed bills that set a date for U.S. withdrawal from Vietnam. In this way Hollings established his opposition to the conduct of the war while still supporting the troops in the field.

Apart from Vietnam, Hollings's approach to defense spending and foreign policy was hawkish. Although he occasionally chided the Pentagon for fiscal

★ *Hollings scuba diving, c. 1970. As chairman of the Oceans and Atmosphere Subcommittee, he became closely involved in environmental preservation concerns in the early 1970s.*
SOURCE: South Carolina Political Collections, University of South Carolina, Columbia.

profligacy, he supported the funding of expensive new weapons systems such as the antiballistic missile program. Hollings was one of only two senators to oppose the SALT I agreement and also cosponsored a number of resolutions pledging to maintain sovereignty over the Panama Canal as his 1974 reelection contest approached, an issue that soon became a conservative rallying point. As a World War II veteran and a longtime proponent of the military draft, he sincerely believed in the need for a strong national defense. Nevertheless promilitary pronouncements were also good politics in the self-consciously patriotic and defense-industry-dominated state of South Carolina.

From his position on the Commerce Committee, Hollings established an important legacy in ocean preservation legislation in the early 1970s. Appointed the chairman of the newly created Oceans and Atmosphere Subcommittee in 1969, he maneuvered around President Nixon's staff to ensure his support for the creation of the National Oceanic and Atmospheric Administration. He also shepherded numerous significant environmental measures from his subcommittee through the Senate, among them being the Coastal Zone Management Act, the Ocean Dumping Act, and the Marine Mammal Protection Act. At times Hollings's environmentalism did not sit well with constituents who favored the attraction of new industries, and by extension new payrolls, regardless of the environmental cost. This tension was illustrated well during the public dispute over the proposed location of a potentially polluting German chemical plant on an area of virgin coastline in economically depressed Beaufort County, South Carolina.

Hollings's career in the 1960s and 1970s also intersected with the early growth of the South Carolina Republican Party. Although many of the early Republican leaders in the 1950s were economically conservative opponents of the New Deal state, by the early 1960s, white voters disillusioned with the national Democratic Party's support of civil rights legislation joined them. By the time of Thurmond's 1964 party switch, the ultrasegregationist faction had gained dominance in the state GOP. The Republican candidates who contested the 1966 gubernatorial and senatorial elections in South Carolina made numerous appeals to white electoral solidarity. Even though Hollings's Republican opponent, Marshall Parker, had gained a reputation as a moderate on race for his role in reopening the state park system on a racially integrated basis, he denounced the black bloc vote the Democrats would receive on Election Day while claiming that the way to prevent the present socialist direction of government was to elect more Republicans. Interestingly, though, voting returns suggest that two years later, in 1968, Hollings won the votes of Wallace supporters, purportedly the most racially conservative of the whole electorate. Provided that the Democratic candidate was acceptable, these voters seemed willing to remain in the party of their fathers rather than move to the Republicans. Although a Republican captured the governorship of South Carolina in 1974, it was under bizarre circumstances. Aside from the 1974 anomaly, away from the presidential level and the personally popular Thurmond, it was not until the 1980s that Republicans became viable opponents for white South Carolina Democrats who did not alienate their historic base of support.

In the longer view, South Carolina faced similar economic challenges when Hollings left office as when he started his career. As governor he modified the state's industrial development apparatus, raised taxes to balance the budget, and promoted increases in productivity through educational investment. Since then, however, there has been no major alteration in the state's development strategy.[40] Although the state's per capita income rose from 50 percent of the national average in 1950 to 80 percent by 1980, it converged no further between 1980 and 2000. The promise of lower unionization rates and lower wages had successfully brought many industries to South Carolina and the South generally after World

War II, yet increases in global competition led many low-wage industries to relocate subsequently to cheaper locations abroad.[41]

There were ironies to the South Carolina investment approach of courting foreign investment and trade, a process Hollings had begun as governor, while simultaneously criticizing foreign imports that negatively impacted the state's employment prospects. Following a regional and national trend, the number of manufacturing jobs in South Carolina decreased from 380,000 to 330,000 between 1977 and 2001.[42] This decline in manufacturing was most apparent in the virtual elimination of the once-dominant textile industry, which Hollings and other state politicians had tried for so long to protect from foreign imports.[43] The contraction of the industry counteracted some of the employment gains made in the 1960s and 1970s by African Americans, whose numbers had increased from 5.5 to almost 20 percent of the textile workforce between 1964 and 1980.[44] Across the South reliance on low-tax, low-service development strategies left many communities poorly equipped to attract better-paying industries once manufacturing industries moved out.[45]

Though Hollings was a vocal advocate for a concerted federal commitment to eliminating domestic hunger, poverty remained a persistent and racially distinctive problem in South Carolina. Although the black and white poverty rates had decreased from 50 percent and 12 percent, respectively, in 1969 to 33 and 9 percent by 1980, there remained a substantial poverty gap between blacks and whites in the state.[46] While black poverty had declined substantially, South Carolina's African Americans remained more than three times as likely as their white counterparts to live in poverty.

Despite Hollings's push for black and white educational improvements in the 1950s and his subsequent advocacy as a senator alongside his wife, Peatsy, for public schooling, South Carolina's politicians remained reluctant to invest in the state's human capital.[47] South Carolina's educational shortcomings were decried by several business and civic leaders in the twenty-first century. Most notably Darla Moore, a mega-donor to the University of South Carolina, informed state legislators that the state's "permanent state of ignorance" hobbled efforts to succeed in "a knowledge-based economy predicated on technology" and urged a great increase in education funding at all levels.[48]

There were racial connotations, too, to the lack of educational funding, most notably in the state's rural, poor, and largely black public schools. The ramifications of the desegregation of public education and subsequent white flight were still being addressed in 2015. Alongside decisions such as the 1995 Darlington County School Board case, which ruled that the historically black Mayo High School had been systematically discriminated against in the allocation of funding and teaching resources, the state supreme court ruled in favor of the plaintiffs who challenged the state's allocation of funding for poor, rural, and predominantly

★ *Hollings's wedding to Rita Liddy ("Peatsy"), August 21, 1971.* SOURCE: South Carolina Political Collections, University of South Carolina, Columbia.

black public schools in its 2014 *Abbeville County School District, et al., v. The State of South Carolina, et al.* decision.[49] The majority ruled that "the Defendants have failed to provide students in the Plaintiff Districts the requisite constitutional opportunity" through "inadequate transportation," "a corps of unprepared teachers," the grouping of students by "economic class into . . . educational ghettos," and the pushing of students through to graduation despite "large percentages . . . [being] unable to meet minimal benchmarks on standardized tests." Funding was routinely diverted toward popular programs such as sports facilities, "while students suffered in crumbling schools and toxic academic environments."[50] By 2015 the economic and racial legacy of the Jim Crow system was still apparent.

Yet to focus on the continued difficulties facing South Carolinians overlooks the largely positive impact Hollings and his successors McNair and West had on race relations and economics. While the state strategy of using every legal defense before submitting to desegregation was morally ambiguous, it was less troublesome than the ostentatious resistance to desegregation provided by state leaders in Georgia, Alabama, Louisiana, and Mississippi and arguably prevented the perpetration of more violent attacks on civil rights advocates. Moreover despite the reliance of moderate southerners on symbolism to maintain biracial support, their behavior affected the lives of their constituents in concrete ways. Hollings's hunger tours, testimony to McGovern's committee, and advocacy for free food stamps in 1969 *were* important: a pilot free food stamp program was established in Beaufort and Jasper Counties, the McGovern Committee retained its funding, and the food stamp program expanded faster than it would have otherwise. While "enlightened" southerners such as Hollings recognized the positive national publicity that statesmanlike behavior could garner, their actions nevertheless improved the lives of many of their constituents. Hollings continued his reputation for statesmanship after he left office in 2005. In 2015 he urged Republican senator Lindsey Graham to rename Charleston's Hollings Judicial Center as the Waring Judicial Center in honor of the Charlestonian judge Waties Waring. As Graham noted, "not many people in my business would do that." Waring, ostracized by whites in his native city, ruled in favor of black plaintiffs in the 1940s and 1950s on matters of teachers' pay, participation in the Democratic primary, and school segregation.[51]

Although progressive by local standards, Hollings stayed electorally viable in South Carolina. While he promoted some socially progressive policies, his career-long focus on budget balancing protected him from charges of liberalism, as did his promotion of military spending, his antiunionism, and his record of supporting conservative Supreme Court justices. His repeated efforts to pass legislation to insulate the textile industry from job losses helped secure him the financial and electoral backing of textile interests. Though Hollings was skillful in altering his behavior to remain acceptable to both his white and black constituents in the 1960s, his significance extended beyond his quiet accommodation with African American voters and his prolonged electoral success. Hollings's major legacy lies in his many legislative achievements, particularly in education, nutrition, and environmental preservation.

Notes

Introduction

1. John C. West, interview with Herbert J. Hartsook, February 1, 1996, South Carolina Political Collections, University of South Carolina, Columbia (hereafter SCPC).

2. West, "Comments," 28.

3. "Reliable Source; In Vermont, Status May Be More than Governor Can Bare," *Washington Post*, December 19, 2004.

4. "Acid-tongued 'Hollings-isms,'" *Orangeburg (S.C.) Times and Democrat*, December 17, 2004.

5. Joseph Biden, remarks at dedication of the Hollings Library, July 23, 2010.

6. See, for instance, Sproat, "'Firm Flexibility'"; Synnott, "Desegregation"; Synnott, "Federalism Vindicated"; Badger, "From Defiance to Moderation"; Minchin, "Uphill Fight"; Hollings and Victor, *Making Government Work.*

7. See Cohodas, *Thurmond;* Bass and Thompson, *Ol' Strom;* Bass and Thompson, *Life of Strom Thurmond;* Crespino, *Strom Thurmond's America.*

8. *Census of Population: 1940*, vol. 2, pt. 6, 345–47. "Rural farm" areas accounted for almost two-thirds of the total rural population.

9. See Black and Black, *Politics and Society*, 34–43, for a discussion of the decline of the importance of rural voters in the South in the twentieth century.

10. *Census of Population: 1980*, vol. 1, pt. 42, 7.

11. U.S. Census Bureau, 1990 U.S. Census, table 1, https://www.census.gov/population/censusdata/urpop0090.txt (accessed March 27, 2015).

12. Ford and Stone, "Economic Development," 19.

13. In 1950 less than 5 percent of textile employees in South Carolina were black. See ibid., 28.

14. Edgar, *South Carolina*, 510.

15. On the Savannah River Plant in Aiken, see Frederickson, *Cold War Dixie.*

16. Johnson, *Congress*, 159.

17. Schulman, *Cotton Belt*, 141.

18. Foley, *New Senate*, 234–36, 254–56.

19. Shapiro, *Last Great Senate*, x.

20. Gould, *Most Exclusive Club*, 276.

21. Hollings and Victor, *Making Government Work*, 165–69.

22. In his study Foley classed Hollings as "moderate-to-conservative." See Foley, *New Senate*, 298.

23. Political scientist Nicol C. Rae contended that there remained in the 1990s a "persistent (if more muted) regional distinctiveness" among southern senators and observed common voting behavior on "central elements of southern political culture—the military, national security, respect for national symbols, sexual mores, and church/state issues." *Southern Democrats*, 110.

Chapter 1: From Charleston to Columbia

1. Michael M. Hollings, e-mail correspondence with the author, May 1, 2014.

2. "U.S. Senator Fritz Hollings South Carolina Democrat," n.d., Ernest Hollings Papers, 1983–1984, Citadel Archives, Charleston, South Carolina (hereafter HCP), folder 1.

3. Sproat, "Firm Flexibility," 183n23.

4. Kestenbaum, "U.S. District Attorneys in South Carolina."

5. Hollings, interview with the author, September 12, 2011.

6. The Republican Charles Boineau won a special election for a state house seat in August 1961.

7. Ehrenhalt and Healy, *Politics in America*, 1094. See also "Hollings, a Southern Puzzle, Guards the Budget Door," *New York Times*, May 11, 1980.

8. "Service Record of U.S. Sen. Fritz Hollings," n.d., copy in the possession of the author, received from Andy Brack. Brack served as Hollings's press secretary from 1992 to 1996.

9. West, interview with Hartsook, January 31, 1996, SCPC.

10. Hollings and Victor, *Making Government Work*, 8.

11. Brack, "An excerpt from an as-yet unpublished book by Andy Brack," manuscript copy in the possession of the author.

12. Hollings and Victor, *Making Government Work*, 9.

13. Ibid., 14–15. Hollings wrote: "When he [Hollings's father] died, he didn't leave anything but a good name, but that good name elected me."

14. Quint, *Profile*, 4–6.

15. Ibid., vi.

16. Hollings and Victor, *Making Government Work*, 13.

17. Frederickson, *Dixiecrat Revolt*, 237.

18. "The Nitty-Gritty Senator," *Washington Post*, October 14, 2004.

19. Hollings and Victor, *Making Government Work*, 18.

20. Hollings, interview with Jack Bass, September 18, 2008, Citadel Oral History Program, Citadel Archives and Museum, Charleston, South Carolina.

21. Brooks, "Winning the Peace," 588, 584, 580. See also Badger, *New Deal/New South*, 130, for a discussion of the political impact of returning veterans on southern politics.

22. Cohodas, *Thurmond*, 231.

23. Hollings, interview with the author, September 12, 2011.

24. Hollings and Victor, *Making Government Work*, 16–17.

25. Burton, "'Black Squint,'" 176. Between 1896 and 1960, the funding disparity was most extreme around 1915, when $8.70 was spent on each white pupil for every $1.00 spent on a black pupil.

26. Bartley, *Massive Resistance*, 44–45. Byrnes enjoyed one of the most distinguished political careers in South Carolina's history. One of the key southern senators shepherding New Deal legislation, he resigned from the Senate in 1941 to join the U.S. Supreme Court. He

subsequently left the court to become President Roosevelt's director of war mobilization, a position dubbed "assistant president" by many journalistic observers. Denied the vice presidential nomination in 1944, Byrnes served briefly as President Truman's secretary of state before returning to South Carolina, where he won the governorship in 1950.

27. Hollings, interview with Bass, September 8, 2008.

28. Steve Griffith, interview with the author, January 25, 2013.

29. Burton, Burton, and Appleford, "Seeds in Unlikely Soil," 177–80.

30. *Briggs* was later absorbed into the *Brown v. Board of Education* Supreme Court case, which invalidated the constitutionality of racially segregated public schooling.

31. Quint, *Profile*, 14.

32. Bartley, *Massive Resistance*, 45.

33. Sproat, "Firm Flexibility," 167.

34. Marion Gressette, interview with Bass and Walter De Vries, February 25, 1974, Southern Oral History Program Collection (#4007), Southern Historical Collection, Louis Round Wilson Special Collections Library, University of North Carolina at Chapel Hill (hereafter SOHPC).

35. Matthew J. Perry Jr., interview with Robert J. Moore, January 3, 1996, SCPC.

36. "Address of Governor George Bell Timmerman, Jr., Statewide radio-television address November 3, 1955 by Governor George Bell Timmerman, Jr., before a Joint Meeting of the Association of Schools Boards and Association of School Administrators," November 3, 1955, George Bell Timmerman Jr. Papers, box 2, "Speeches, 1955," SCPC.

37. Badger, *New Deal/New South*, 135.

38. "Hollings Is Optimistic on Segregation," *Charleston (S.C.) News and Courier*, December 12, 1952.

39. Hollings, interview with George Terry, Rita Liddy "Peatsy" Hollings, and John Gregory, April 21, 1990, SCPC.

40. In contrast figures such as Donald Russell, Sol Blatt, Edgar Brown, and Strom Thurmond are mentioned on multiple occasions. See Robertson, *Sly and Able;* Byrnes, *One Lifetime.*

41. Cauthern, *Speaker Blatt*, 177.

42. Key, *Southern Politics*, 155.

43. Stone, "Making a Modern State," 454.

44. Renick, "Solomon Blatt," 67.

45. "Session 1952," Ernest F. Hollings Papers, box 687, "Topical, Voting Record in General Assembly, 1949–54," South Carolina Political Collections, University of South Carolina, Columbia, South Carolina (hereafter HP). Hollings did not, however, vote in 1954 on a bill that amended the South Carolina Constitution to abolish the requirement to provide free public schools. See "Session 1954," ibid.

46. Quint, *Profile*, 97–98.

47. Bartley, *Massive Resistance*, 77.

48. Walker, *Ghost*, 7.

49. Bass and Poole, *Palmetto State*, 90.

50. Bass, "Art of Political Biography" panel. The *New York Times* covered the lynching trial extensively. See, for instance, "All 28 Acquitted by Lynch Jurors in South Carolina," *New York Times*, May 22, 1947.

51. A. J. Clement Jr. to Hollings, January 15, 1952, box 604, "General, 1952," HP.

52. Hollings, interview with Bass, September 8, 2008.

53. Brack, conversation with the author, January 24, 2013.

54. Bernard Warshaw, interview with Bass, October 1, 2008, Citadel Oral History Program, Citadel Archives and Museum, Charleston, South Carolina.

55. Maybank Sr. was up for reelection in 1954 and had been running unopposed. He won the Democratic nomination but died in September 1954. His death set off a scramble for the Democratic Party to nominate its own candidate without a primary contest. Barnwell senator Edgar Brown was nominated by the state party, but Thurmond won the November election as a write-in candidate.

56. Hollings, interview with Hartsook, November 10, 1995, SCPC.

57. Brack, conversation with the author, January 24, 2013.

58. In an oral history interview, Hollings remarked: "Clator ran ads that said Hollings is for integration. . . . They ran them in the Greenville, Columbia, and Charleston papers, saying Hollings is for integration." See Hollings, interview with Terry, John Duffy, and Peatsy Hollings, December 12, 1989, SCPC.

59. Anti-Hollings pamphlet, n.d., box 608, "1958, General," HP.

60. "1954 State Campaign Grinds to Halt Here; Election Is Tuesday," *Columbia (S.C.) State*, June 5, 1954.

61. Hollings and Victor, *Making Government Work*, 36.

62. "Hollings Gets Landslide Nod for Post of Lt. Governor; Dozier, Jones Are Renamed in Easy Victories," *Columbia (S.C.) State*, June 9, 1954.

63. Bartley, *Massive Resistance*, 68.

64. Ibid., 70.

65. Lottie D. "Dolly" Hamby, interview with Duffy, October 5, 1999, SCPC.

66. Brooks, "Winning the Peace," 580–88, esp. 586.

67. Quint, *Profile*, 94.

68. Ibid., 117–18, 121.

69. Johnston, "Communism vs. Segregation," 24.

70. Quint, *Profile*, 102.

71. See Timmerman to Edgar Brown, July 20, 1957, "Clemson College's Agreement with AEC for federal funds," George Bell Timmerman Jr. Gubernatorial Records, South Carolina Department of Archives and History (hereafter TR). See also Timmerman to Mr. William L. Watkins, July 29, 1957, "Clemson College's Agreement," ibid.

72. Quint, *Profile*, 104.

73. Bartley, *Massive Resistance*, 214.

74. Ibid., 218.

75. Quint, *Profile*, 86.

76. Badger, *New Deal/New South*, 135.

77. Bartley, *Massive Resistance*, 94.

78. Qtd. by Alfred Maund, writing in the *Nation*, July 23, 1955, cited in McMillen, *Citizens' Council*, 214. Patterson qtd. in McMillen, *Citizens' Council*, 214.

79. McMillen, *Citizen's Council*, 210.

80. Ibid., 212. For more on the black counterboycott in Orangeburg, see Modjeska Simkins, interview with Jacquelyn Hall and Bob Hall, July 28, 1976, SOHPC.

81. See, for instance, "The Clarendon County School Desegregation Case" and "Memorandum to: Mr. Moon, from: Dr Morsell, subject: Racial Reprisals in South Carolina," February 10, 1960, in *Papers of the NAACP*, pt. 20, reel 10, "South Carolina—Briggs, Harry, 1961–1962."

82. Lau, *Democracy Rising*, 210. Across the Southeast region (defined here as Florida, Georgia, Mississippi, Alabama, Tennessee, North Carolina, and South Carolina), membership in the NAACP dropped from 52,375 in 1955 to 26,955 in 1957. See ibid., 211.

83. Quint, *Profile*, 36.

84. Zeigler, *When Conscience*, 152.

85. Edgar, *South Carolina*, 527.

86. Tyson, "Dynamite," 291.

87. Stone, "Making a Modern State," 456.

88. Leslie Dunbar, cited in Bartley, *New South*, 259–60.

89. Stone "Making a Modern State," 5.

90. Crespino, *Strom Thurmond's America*, 50–51. For more on right-to-work laws, see Shermer, "'Take Government out of Business,'" 94–95.

91. Stone, "Making a Modern State," 6.

92. State Development Board Eighteenth Annual Report, 1962–63, 7, South Carolina State Library.

93. Cobb, *South and America*, 56; Maunula, *Guten Tag*, 61–62.

94. Crespino, *Strom Thurmond's America*, 50.

95. Hollings, interview with Terry and Duffy, December 7, 1989, SCPC.

96. Extrapolated from State Development Board Eighteenth Annual Report, 1962–63, 31.

97. Marshall Parker, interview with Hartsook, January 25, 2002, SCPC. See also West, interview with Hartsook, January 31, 1996. Hamby, interview with Duffy, October 5, 1999.

98. Cobb, *Selling of the South*, 77.

99. Stone, "Making a Modern State," 406; handwritten luncheon notes, n.d., box 17, "Industry—States['] Rights," HP.

100. Cobb, *Selling of the South*, 74.

101. Hollings, interview with Hartsook and Trip King, February 3, 1995, SCPC.

102. Hollings, interview with Terry, Duffy, and Peatsy Hollings, December 12, 1989.

103. "Hollings for Governor," in box 608, "1958, General," HP.

104. See, for instance, W. D. Workman Jr., reporting a speech by Hollings at the state capitol in Columbia, January 29, 1958, box 608, "1958, General," HP.

105. Ibid.

106. "Citizen Endorses Hollings," *Greer (S.C.) Citizen*, May 7, 1958. Hollings later recounted that besides the *Citizen*, "all the print media were for Donald Russell." See Hollings, interview with Hartsook, August 7, 1996, SCPC.

107. Black and Black, *Southern Governors*, 82.

108. Anti-Hollings campaign advertisement, n.d., box 608, "1958, General," HP.

109. For Russell attacking the "Barnwell Ring," see Donald Russell to the Voters of Richland County, June 17, 1958, box 608, "1958, General," HP. On the lowcountry-upstate divide over liquor, see Hayes, *South Carolina*, 4.

110. Anti-Hollings ad, attached to letter dated March 24, 1958, box 608, "1958, General," HP.

111. Hollings and Victor, *Making Government Work*, 40.

112. Statement by Senator Wasson of Laurens, n.d., box 608, "1958, General," HP. See also "Hollings Gets Support from Dry Leader," *Florence (S.C.) Morning News*, June 20, 1958.

113. Griffith, interview with the author, January 25, 2013.

114. Black and Black, *Southern Governors*, 81.

115. Hollings, interview with Hartsook, August 7, 1996.

116. Hollings, interview with Terry, Peatsy Hollings, and Gregory, April 21, 1990.

Chapter 2: Segregation with "Dignity"?

1. "Inaugural Address of the Honorable Ernest F. Hollings as Governor of South Carolina," January 20, 1959, as found in "Fritz Hollings: In His Own Words," HP.

2. Hollings and Victor, *Making Government Work*, 82.

3. John C. West dubbed the speech "the best example I've ever seen of raw political courage." See West, "Comments," 28.

4. George McMillan, "Integration with Dignity: The Inside Story of How South Carolina Kept the Peace," *Saturday Evening Post*, March 16, 1963, http://www.clemson.edu/cedp/Press/pubs/gantt/pdfs/003.pdf (accessed November 10, 2015).

5. For positive assessments see esp. Sproat, "Firm Flexibility"; Bast, "Heaven and Hell"; Suggs, "Harvey Gantt." For cynical appraisals see Newby, *Black Carolinians;* Burton, "Dining with Harvey"; White, "Managed Compliance." For skeptical accounts see Badger, "From Defiance to Moderation"; Synnott, "Desegregation."

6. Hollings to Charles E. Viele, November 22, 1961, box 608, "1962, General (1 of 2)," HP.

7. "Hollings to Friends of Aiken County," n.d., box 608, "1962, General (1 of 2)," HP.

8. For his definition of "modernizer" politicians, see Luebke, *Tar Heel*, 23–24.

9. West, interview with Hartsook, July 15, 1996.

10. Jack Bass, conversation with the author, January 24, 2013.

11. Hollings to William D. Workman, August 7, 1958, William D. Workman Jr. Papers, box 37, "Persons, Hollings, Ernest F., General (1 of 3)," SCPC.

12. For a discussion of the legislative battle over the tax increase in 1959, see Stone, "Making a Modern State," 462–67.

13. For examples of the prominence given to the state's AAA rating, see the outgoing correspondence of S. Ernie Wright, boxes 7–9, HP.

14. Stone, "Making a Modern State," 477.

15. See Hollings, interview with Terry, Duffy, and Peatsy Hollings, December 12, 1989.

16. Walter W. Harper, interview with Hartsook, September 12, 1997, SCPC.

17. Hollings and Victor, *Making Government Work*, 65.

18. Cotesworth Means to Hollings, November 13, 1959, Ernest F. "Fritz" Hollings Gubernatorial Records, box 7, "Ports Authority, Puerto Rico," South Carolina Department of Archives and History.

19. Stone, "Making a Modern State," 498–99.

20. Hollings and Victor, *Making Government Work*, 63.

21. See Key, *Southern Politics*, 150–55. South Carolinians practiced "legislative leadership

and hegemony, with Senator Brown functioning as in the manner of a prime minister and the governor little more than a ceremonial chief of state" (155).

22. Griffith, interview with the author, January 25, 2013.

23. See Hollings, interview with Terry, Duffy, and Peatsy Hollings, December 12, 1989.

24. Cobb, *Selling of the South*, 167.

25. Report of Joint Committee Surveying the Needs of the South Carolina State Development Board, 1959.

26. West, interview with Hartsook, July 15, 1996.

27. Harper, interview with Hartsook, September 12, 1997.

28. Cobb, *Selling of the South*, 123.

29. "Segregation Problem," ca. 1958, Anderson County Rotary Club speech, box 688, "Speeches, 1953–June 1957," HP.

30. Cobb, *Selling of the South*, 129.

31. Leslie W. Dunbar, interview with Jacqueline Hall and Helen Breisler, December 18, 1978, SOHPC.

32. Cobb, *Selling of the South*, 125.

33. Ibid., 146.

34. Cramer, "School Desegregation," 387.

35. Kruse, *White Flight*, 149.

36. Crespino, *In Search*, 44. For a questioning of the supposed relationship between racial strife and economic stagnation, see Cobb, *Industrialization*, 115.

37. Crespino, *In Search*, 44.

38. Bartley, *New South*, 253.

39. "What Price Violence?" November 1, 1962, Report L-38, in South Carolina Council on Human Relations Papers, box 11, "SRC, General, 1962," South Caroliniana Library, University of South Carolina, Columbia.

40. Qtd. in Cox, "Integration," 276. Gressette later denied that this conversation had taken place. See ibid., 278.

41. Burton, "Dining with Harvey," 198.

42. Hollings and Victor, *Making Government Work*, 78.

43. See, for instance, Malcolm Seawell, "North Carolina at Crossroad," received March 20, 1959, box 20, "Segregation, 1959," HP.

44. Hollings, interview with Terry, Duffy, and Peatsy Hollings, December 12, 1989.

45. Cox, "1963," 33.

46. Renick, "Solomon Blatt," 61, 67.

47. Statement before the Subcommittees on Constitutional Rights of the Judiciary Committees of the U.S. Senate and U.S. House of Representatives, April 14, 1959, box 688, "Speeches, 1959, January–June," HP.

48. Hollings, interview with Terry, Duffy, and Peatsy Hollings, December 12, 1989.

49. Boxes 18, 19, HP.

50. Qtd. in Arsenault, *Freedom Riders*, 150.

51. Gressette to Hollings, October 24, 1958, box 14, "Education, General (1 of 2)," HP; White, "Managed Compliance," 295.

52. "Annual Report" [1960], South Carolina Conference of Branches, NAACP, Jan. 1–Dec. 8, 1960, *Papers of the NAACP*, pt. 27, series A, reel 13.

53. "Sit-In Student Stabbed in Back," *New York Amsterdam News*, March 11, 1961.

54. Hollings to Farley Smith, February 24, 1960, box 14, "Citizens' Council, 1959–1963," HP.

55. Hollings, interview with Terry, Duffy, and Peatsy Hollings, December 12, 1989.

56. "Memorandum: Summary of Sitdown Demonstrations, Rock Hill, South Carolina," March 14, 1960, *Papers of the NAACP*, pt. 20, reel 10.

57. Synnott, "Crusaders and Clubwomen," 61.

58. Harry Walker, interview with Hartsook, January 27, 1999, SCPC.

59. "Orangeburg Sit-In Protest," *Papers of the NAACP*, pt. 20, reel 10.

60. Walker, interview with Hartsook, January 27, 1999.

61. Catsam, "Into the Maw," 9; Arsenault, *Freedom Riders*, 136–39.

62. "Cleric, 'Riders' Head for Fla. Unknown," *Newsday*, June 15, 1961, William D. Workman Jr. Papers, box 27, "Integration/Civil Rights, General, 1960–1962," SCPC.

63. Badger, "From Defiance to Moderation," 13.

64. "NAACP's Wilkins in Heated Latin Duel with S.C. Governor," March 10, 1961, *Papers of the NAACP*, pt. 20, reel 10.

65. Moore, "Civil Rights Advocate," 159.

66. Ibid., 167–68.

67. Brown, "Civil Rights Activism," 83–84.

68. Walter B. Brown, interoffice memo to Hollings, July 11, 1961, box 14, "Education, Charleston School District 20," HP.

69. Hollings to Charles A. Brown, August 2, 1961, box 14, "Education, Charleston School District 20," HP.

70. Brown, "Civil Rights Activism," 87.

71. Synnott, "Federalism Vindicated," 297. For examples of Turner discouraging student protest, see Hine, "Civil Rights"; Felder, *Civil Rights*, 92–94.

72. McMillen, *Citizens' Council*, 80; White, "Managed Compliance," 3.

73. "Memorandum to: Mr Moon, From: Dr Morsell, Subject: Racial Reprisals in South Carolina," February 10, 1960, *Papers of the NAACP*, pt. 20, reel 10. For a Jasper County example, see "Letter from Matthew J. Perry to Dr. John Morsell re: Vanuel Mitchell," September 26, 1960, ibid.

74. For Barnett's association with the Citizens' Councils, see McMillen, *Citizens' Council*, 326–28.

75. Ralph Kolb to Hollings, December 2, 1960; Hollings to Kolb, December 3, 1960; Kolb to Hollings, December 5, 1960, box 14, "Citizens' Council, 1959–1963," HP.

76. "That Is Mississippi's Problem," September 29, 1962, William D. Workman Jr. Papers, box 37, "Hollings, (1 of 3)," SCPC.

77. Farley Smith qtd. in McMillan, "Integration with Dignity."

78. Hollings, interview with Marcia G. Synnott, July 8, 1980, SCPC.

79. Cox, "Integration," 279.

80. Hollings to E. P Riley, March 25, 1960, box 608, "1960, Democratic Party, General," HP.

81. "2 Governors Reject Pressure on Rights," *New York Times*, November 20, 1960.

82. "Address by Governor Ernest F. Hollings to the General Assembly of South Carolina," January 9, 1963, as found in "Fritz Hollings: In His Own Words," HP.

83. "The election," n.d., box 608, "1962, General (2 of 2)," HP.

84. *Progress*, A Report of the South Carolina Council on Human Relations, 1963, South Carolina Council on Human Relations Papers, cited in Cox, "1963," 10n19.

85. Hollings to J. R. Chadwick, December 15, 1959, Hollings Gubernatorial Records, box 1, "General, 1960."

86. Cobb, *Selling of the South*, 77.

87. Handwritten luncheon notes, n.d., box 17, "Industry—States['] Rights," HP.

88. "An address delivered by Governor George Bell Timmerman, Jr., of South Carolina, in New York City before a group of business and industrial leaders," March 3, 1955, box 604, "General, 1955," HP.

89. "Address by Governor Ernest F. Hollings before the New York Municipal Forum," May 21, 1959, as found in "Fritz Hollings: In His Own Words," HP.

90. South Carolina State Development Board Annual Report, 1956–57, 51, South Carolina State Library.

91. Ford and Stone, "Economic Development," 28.

92. Hollings, interview with Synnott, July 8, 1980. However the geographical location of the technical training schools limited black participation, since a large majority of the facilities were placed in the whiter upcountry part of the state. See Cobb, *Selling of the South*, 170.

93. "State Industrialist Asks Improved Negro Job Opportunities," *Southern School News*, August 1961.

94. Quint, *Profile*, 102.

95. William L. Watkins to Timmerman, "Clemson College's Agreement with AEC for federal funds," June 25, 1957, "State colleges and universities file, 1955–1958," TR.

96. Charles Daniel to Timmerman, "Clemson College's Agreement with AEC for federal funds," July 18, 1957, TR.

97. Timmerman to Bob Cooper, "Clemson College's Agreement with AEC for federal funds," June 29, 1957, TR.

98. Daniel to Timmerman, July 18, 1957; Canup and Workman, *Charles E. Daniel*, 62–63, 146–47.

99. T. C. Callison to J. M. Smith, "Clemson College's Agreement with AEC for federal funds," July 1, 1957; Daniel to Cooper, July 9, 1957, "State colleges and universities file, 1955–1958," TR.

100. Timmerman to Edgar Brown, "Clemson College's Agreement with AEC for federal funds," July 20, 1957, TR.

101. Cooper to Timmerman, "Clemson College's Agreement with AEC for federal funds," August 15, 1957, TR.

102. "Fourth annual message of Governor George Bell Timmerman, Jr. to the South Carolina General Assembly," January 15, 1958, George Bell Timmerman Jr. Papers, box 2, "Speeches, 1958 & n.d.," SCPC.

103. "Third Annual message of Governor George Bell Timmerman, Jr., to the South Carolina General Assembly," January 9, 1957, George Bell Timmerman Jr. Papers, box 2, "Speeches, 1957," SCPC.

104. Hollings to Rev. John S. Cole, August 14, 1959, box 7, "Ernie Wright Correspondence, Outgoing," HP.

105. Synnott, "Federalism Vindicated," 303.

106. "What has happened and what do we want and need to do now?" [1961], SCCHR Papers, box 19, "Economics and Employment, General, 1951–1961." In another example of the limited scope of new job opportunities for blacks, the Greenville Council on Human Relations advertised a meeting it would be having with "three people who have been employed on a merit basis at the Sangamo Electric Company, Pickens, S.C." "Human Relations Newsletter," February 1962, SCCHR Papers, box 19, "Economics and Employment, General, 1962–1963." On the limited pace of African American employment gains at the Savannah River Plant near Aiken, South Carolina, see Frederickson, *Cold War Dixie*, chapter 4.

107. Minchin, *Hiring the Black Worker*, 48.

108. For instance see Tyson, "Dynamite," 291.

109. Workman, *Case for the South*, 188, 218. See also Kalk, *Origins*, 57–58. For a discussion of black illegitimacy rates and teenage pregnancies, see ibid., 171–75; for the alleged black propensity for "thievery," see ibid., 182–83.

110. McMillan, "Integration with Dignity"; Hollings and Victor, *Making Government Work*, 82.

111. "'Fritz' Hollings Speech Was Refreshing Change in Dixie," *Charlotte Observer*, November 2, 1963.

112. "The Nitty-Gritty Senator," *Washington Post*, October 14, 2004.

113. For white interviewees who viewed Hollings's shift as sincere, see, for instance, Charles T. "Bud" Ferillo, interview with the author, April 17, 2012; Ike McLeese, interview with the author, February 21, 2012. For black interviewees who viewed Hollings's change as pragmatic, see Emily M. deQuincey-Newman, interview with the author, April 17, 2012; Modjeska Simkins, interview with Jacquelyn Hall and Bob Hall, July 28, 1976, SOHPC.

114. Sproat, "Firm Flexibility," 170.

115. See, for instance, H. L. Honnicutt to Hollings, February 3, 1959, Hollings Gubernatorial Records, box 1, "General, 1959, February 1–10 (2 of 2)."

116. For other black South Carolinians Hollings stayed in contact with during his governorship, see Hollings, interview with Synnott, July 8, 1980.

117. Hollings, interview with the author, September 12, 2011.

118. "Gov. Hollings Blocks Civil Rights Proposal," *Columbia (S.C.) State*, April 7, 1962.

119. Burton, "Dining with Harvey," 192.

120. Lowe, "Grass Roots," 33.

121. Burton et al., "South Carolina," 203.

122. Kuzenski, "South Carolina," 37.

123. Cox, "1963," 47.

Chapter 3: Hollings, the Kennedys, and Democratic Decline in South Carolina

1. Crespino, *Strom Thurmond's America*, 8.

2. Hollings and Victor, *Making Government Work*, 88–89.

3. Bartley, *Massive Resistance*, 157–61.

4. "Nixon Forecasts Reuther Control If Kennedy Wins," *New York Times*, November 3, 1960.

5. Hollings and Victor, *Making Government Work*, 84, 87–88.

6. Hollings to Olin Johnston, telefax, July 5, 1960, box 608, "1960, Democratic Party, General," HP.

7. Hollings's comments echoed the request of Florida senator Spessard Holland the previous day. See "20 Named on Panel to Map Platform; Democratic Group Weighted with Civil-Rights Backers as Open Hearings End," *New York Times*, July 9, 1960.

8. "10 Southern States Wage Bitter Fight: 10 Southern States Defeated in Fight on Civil Rights Plank," *New York Times*, July 13, 1960.

9. "Spartanburg Acts to Halt Outbreaks," *New York Times*, July 29, 1960.

10. Hollings and Victor, *Making Government Work*, 93.

11. "S.C. Delegation to Cast 21 Votes for Johnson: 3 Candidates Address Group," *Columbia (S.C.) State*, July 12, 1960.

12. "Johnston Backs Ticket: South Carolina Senator Joins Governor in Support," *New York Times*, August 9, 1960.

13. "South Carolina in Kennedy Shift: Leaders Indicate Party Ban on Attempt to Withhold Support from Nominee," *New York Times*, August 15, 1960; "South Carolina Assists Kennedy: Free-Elector Plan Beaten by Democrats, but Ticket Is Facing Opposition," *New York Times*, August 16, 1960.

14. "Excerpts from Speech of Hollings at Democratic Reconvention," August 15, 1960, box 608, "1960, General, February–September," HP.

15. Hollings and Victor, *Making Government Work*, 95.

16. Thomas W. Chadwick, interview with Hartsook, June 26, 1995, SCPC.

17. "South Carolina Leaning to G.O.P: Kennedy's Religion Arouses Fear in Many Voters—Democrats Are Glum," *New York Times*, October 23, 1960.

18. "Democrats Face a Setback in South, Survey Indicates: Democrats Face Trouble in South," *New York Times*, September 7, 1960.

19. Crespino, *Strom Thurmond's America*, 126.

20. The congressman was Bob Hemphill. See West, interview with Hartsook, July 15, 1996.

21. Hollings, interview with the author, September 12, 2011.

22. Hollings and Victor, *Making Government Work*, 95. See also West, interview with Hartsook, July 15, 1996. For an opposing view, see Chadwick, interview with Hartsook, June 26, 1995.

23. See, for instance, Richard K. Donahue, memorandum for Mr. John Bailey, June 2, 1961, John F. Kennedy Papers, White House Central Name File, box 1245, Kennedy Library.

24. Chadwick recalled having a meeting with Hollings where they resolved to cooperate, despite "talk that you're going to run against Olin, my boss." See Chadwick, interview with Hartsook, June 26, 1995.

25. Canup and Workman, *Charles E. Daniel*, 178–79.

26. Ted Riley, interview with Duffy and Terry, July 13, 1989, SCPC.

27. West, interview with Hartsook, February 1, 1996.

28. Bedingfield, "Partisan Journalism," 2.

29. "Draft of Speech by Gov. Ernest F. Hollings before Civic Clubs of Charleston," September 6, 1960, as found in "Fritz Hollings: In His Own Words," HP.

30. See, for instance, "South Carolina Leaning to G.O.P," *New York Times*, October 23, 1960.

31. Minchin, "Uphill Fight," 188, 192–93.

32. Maunula, *Guten Tag*, 46.

33. Minchin, "Uphill Fight," 188–89.

34. Hollings and Victor, *Making Government Work*, 98.

35. In his memoir Hollings recounted speaking with Mike Feldman, a Kennedy aide, about the textile industry's problems as early as May 1960. See ibid. Ted Riley later recalled that "Fritz Hollings and I went to Washington with Gordon McCabe to get Kennedy to write a letter about limiting the import of textiles. . . . Fritz and I talked to Kennedy on the telephone and he said he would go along with us, and so we flew up there." See Riley, interview with Duffy and Terry, July 13, 1989.

36. John F. Kennedy to Hollings, August 30, 1960, box 608, "1960, General, February–September," HP.

37. John K. Cauthen to Mueller Kreps, September 8, 1960, box 608, "1960, General, February–September," HP.

38. Hollings and Victor, *Making Government Work*, 98. For Hollings attacking the GOP's policy on textile imports, see, for instance, "Draft of Speech by Gov. Ernest F. Hollings before Civic Clubs of Charleston."

39. "Draft of Speech by Gov. Ernest F. Hollings before Civic Clubs of Charleston."

40. "South Carolina Leaning to G.O.P," *New York Times*, October 23, 1960.

41. "Draft of Speech by Gov. Ernest F. Hollings before Civic Clubs of Charleston."

42. Ibid.

43. Merritt, "Senatorial Election," 283.

44. See Riley, interview with Duffy and Terry, October 7, 1986.

45. Hollings, interview with Terry, Duffy, and Peatsy Hollings, December 12, 1989, SCPC.

46. Carter, *From George Wallace*, 64.

47. Unnamed memorandum, October 6, 1961, box 608, "1962, General (1 of 2)," HP.

48. Hollings, interview with the author, September 12, 2011.

49. See, for instance, Hollings to R. A. "Bob" Jolley Jr., December 21, 1960, box 608, "1960, Appointments, December 1960–January 1961," HP; Hollings to the Hon. Philip Nichols Jr., April 11, 1961, box 608, "1960, Appointments, Feb/–Sept. 1962 and c. 1961," HP.

50. Chadwick, interview with Hartsook, June 26, 1995.

51. Hollings to Friends of Aiken County [1962], box 608, "1962, General (1 of 2)," HP.

52. During the 1962 campaign against Hollings, Johnston highlighted his support for minimum-wage legislation, rural electrification, and the coverage of medical help for the elderly under the Social Security program. See "Carolinian Maps Campaign Gamble: Hollings Assails Johnston as Pro-Labor in Senate Race," *New York Times*, May 21, 1962.

53. Ibid.

54. *Augusta (Ga.) Herald*, April 20, 1956, box 604, "General, 1956," HP.

55. "State's Top Races End in Landslides," *Columbia (S.C.) State*, June 13, 1962.

56. Simon, "Race Reactions," 239, 252.

57. See Simon, *Fabric of Defeat*, 4; Minchin, "Uphill Fight," 188.

58. "Carolinian Maps Campaign Gamble."

59. Bernard J. "Bubba" Meng, interview with Hartsook, January 21, 1992, SCPC.

60. Johnston beat Thurmond by some twenty-five thousand votes when they contested the Democratic Senate primary in 1950, two years after Thurmond had carried the state as the Dixiecrat presidential candidate.

61. J. Crawford Cook, interview with the author, April 13, 2012.

62. "State NAACP Head Raps Gov. Hollings' Charges," *Charleston (S.C.) News and Courier*, November 12, 1960.

63. "Meddling in Race Issue Hit; Hollings Raps 'Intervention,'" *Columbia (S.C.) State*, May 9, 1961.

64. "S.C. Resents U.S. Vote Probe . . . Hollings," *Spartanburg (S.C.) Herald-Journal*, October 11, 1961; Hollings, interview with Marcia G. Synnott, July 8, 1980, SCPC.

65. William H. Baker to Hollings, May 18, 1962, box 609, "1962, Correspondence, County, Aiken County (1 of 2)," HP.

66. John M. J. Holliday to Hollings, December 6, 1961, box 608, "1962, General (1 of 2)," HP.

67. Roy Strasburger to Hollings, May 18, 1962, box 608, "1962, General (1 of 2)," HP.

68. "Notes from Meeting discussing Fritz Hollings' Senate campaign," February 1, 1962, box 608, "1962, General (1 of 2)," HP.

69. Ferillo, interview with the author, April 17, 2012.

70. Nathan K. "Nick" Kotz, telephone conversation with the author, January 21, 2013. Kotz's brother-in-law was a student at Mississippi State in 1963.

71. "Hartnett Revives Old Charge in Race," *Columbia (S.C.) State*, October 29, 1992.

72. Hollings and Victor, *Making Government Work*, 102–3.

73. Hollings, interview with Terry, Peatsy Hollings, and Gregory, April 21, 1990, SCPC.

74. Floyd D. Spence, interview with Hartsook, July 9, 1992, SCPC.

75. Merritt, "Senatorial Election," 284.

76. Workman, *Case for the South*, 217–18.

77. Charles H. Gibbs to Hollings, January 22, 1962, box 608, "1962, General (1 of 2)," HP.

78. Merritt, "Senatorial Election," 296–97.

79. Hollings, interview with Terry, Peatsy Hollings, and Gregory, April 21, 1990.

80. In the November general election, 298,626 South Carolinians voted, versus 279,448 in the June Democratic primary. Figures extrapolated from "Democrats Face Test in Carolina; Victory by Johnston Assures Battle with Conservatives," *New York Times*, June 14, 1962; "The Vote in Senatorial Races," *New York Times*, November 8, 1962.

81. "Close Vote Seen Certain in Race for Senate Seat; Seniority and 'Working Man' Have Been the Biggest Issues," *Columbia (S.C.) State*, June 11, 1962.

82. "Johnston Winner in Carolina Race; Defeats Hollings, 2 to 1, for Senatorial Renomination," *New York Times*, June 13, 1962.

83. West, interview with Hartsook, February 1, 1996. See also Cook, interview with the author, April 13, 2012.

84. Hollings and Victor, *Making Government Work*, 73–74.

85. "Hollings Will Vote for Olin Johnston," *Sumter (S.C.) Daily Item*, September 27, 1962.

86. "5 Governors Say They Took Nothing," *Greenville (S.C.) News*, May 11, 1963.

87. "Trying to 'Kill Me Off,' Hollings Says of Probe," *Anderson (S.C.) Daily Mail*, May 15, 1963.

88. "Fireworks Roar as Senate Kills Hollings Investigation," *Charlotte Observer*, May 24, 1963.

89. See G. Kent Krell, interview with the author, December 8, 2011; Brack, conversation with the author, January 24, 2013.

90. Hollings, interview with Hartsook, August 7, 1996, SCPC.

91. Krell, interview with the author, December 8, 2011. Hollings's reference is to the story "Ali Baba and the Forty Thieves" from *One Thousand and One Nights*.

92. "To: Crawford, x," "Parker '68 Campaign Songs & Cheers" [1968], box 619, "1968, Persons, Parkers, Marshall," HP.

93. "Hartnett Revives Old Charge in Race."

94. "Hollings' Pro-Kennedy Speech Startles Politicians," *Charlotte Observer*, November 1, 1963. Lake ran unsuccessfully for the North Carolina governorship in 1960 and 1964.

95. "Popular in N.C.," *Charleston (S.C.) News and Courier*, October 29, 1963.

96. Bedingfield, "Partisan Journalism," 7.

97. Hollings and Victor, *Making Government Work*, 113.

98. Hollings, interview with Hartsook, August 7, 1996.

99. Georgia Democrat Jimmy Carter won the state in 1976.

100. Hollings, interview with Herbert J. Hartsook, August 19, 1996, SCPC.

101. Crespino, *Strom Thurmond's America*, 180–81.

102. Kalk, *Origins*, 70.

103. Kalk uses the term *ultrasegregationist* to describe those "who were so preoccupied with civil rights questions that they substantially ignored other issues" (*Origins*, xiii). I use *ultrasegregationist* in the same way.

104. Crespino, *Strom Thurmond's America*, 194.

105. "The Week," *Charleston (S.C.) News and Courier*, February 3, 1963; "Bill for Tuition Grants Introduced," *Southern School News*, February 1963.

106. Crespino, *Strom Thurmond's America*, 195.

107. Grose, *South Carolina*, 106.

108. Hollings, interview with Herbert J. Hartsook and Trip King, February 3, 1995, SCPC.

109. For correspondence suggesting that Hollings was considering another gubernatorial run, see, for instance, D. W. Green Jr. to Hollings, January 28, 1965; "Somebody" [a colleague of Crawford Cook] to Hollings, December 8, 1964, box 612, "1966, General, 1964–1965," HP.

110. "Random thoughts dictated by [Earl] Mazo by phone, 3/19/66," March 19, 1966, box 612, "1966, General, 1966," HP. Ira Kapenstein to Cliff Carter, May 6, 1965, with attached note, Cliff [Carter] to Marvin [Watson], May 7, 1965, Lyndon B. Johnson Papers, White House Central Files Name File, box 361, "Hollings, Ernest F.," Johnson Library.

111. Meng, interview with Hartsook, January 21, 1992.

112. Hollings, interview with Hartsook and King, February 3, 1995.

113. Cook to Hollings, June 3, 1965, box 612, "1966, General, 1964–65," HP.

114. Meng, interview with Hartsook, January 21, 1992.

115. Cook, interview with the author, April 13, 2012.

116. "A Study of South Carolina Voters," prepared by John F. Kraft, Inc., November 1965, box 617, "1966, Poll, November 1965," HP.

117. Lawson, *Black Ballots*, 283–84. The percentages of eligible blacks registered to vote in Mississippi and Alabama by 1964 were 6.7 and 19.3 percent, respectively.

118. White, "Race, Grassroots Activism," 159.

119. By 1969, 54.6 percent of eligible blacks were registered to vote in South Carolina, compared with 71.5 percent of whites. In the eleven former Confederate states, 83.5 percent of eligible whites were registered in 1969 versus 64.8 percent of blacks. See Lawson, *Black Ballots*, 331.

120. West, interview with Hartsook, February 1, 1996. Badger cited West's anecdote in his article on South Carolina governors and racial change. See Badger, "From Defiance to Moderation," 11.

121. "Hollings Sells Out!" n.d., box 617, "1966, Persons, Russell, Donald, General," HP.

122. Modjeska Simkins, interview with Jacquelyn Hall and Bob Hall, July 28, 1976, SOHPC.

123. "Gov. Hollings Unseats Sen. Russell in South Carolina Senate Primary," *Washington Post*, June 15, 1966.

124. "S. Carolina to Vote after Dull Campaign: Bucked Tradition," *Washington Post*, June 13, 1966.

125. Cook, interview with Hartsook, March 26, 1997, SCPC.

126. Krell, interview with the author, December 8, 2011. Although probably inflated, Hollings estimated having made as many as five mill shift visits for every one done by Russell. See Hollings, interview with Terry, Hollings, and Gregory, April 21, 1990.

127. A. B. "Happy" Chandler of Kentucky was the exception. See "S. Carolina to Vote after Dull Campaign."

128. Krell, interview with the author, December 8, 2011. The nearest comparable incident to Russell's self-appointment in South Carolina came in 1954 when the state Democratic Party nominated state senator Edgar Brown for the U.S. Senate without a primary election. (Senator Burnet Maybank had been unopposed in the June primary but had died in September.) Strom Thurmond won a write-in victory over Brown in the general election.

129. Cook, interview with Hartsook, March 26, 1997.

130. "Race, Big Government Are Main Issues in S.C.," *Washington Post*, May 1, 1966.

131. Kalk, *Origins*, 69.

132. Hollings, interview with Terry, Duffy, and Peatsy Hollings, December 12, 1989, SCPC; "A Colorful Maverick: An Achiever with a Solid Senate Record," *Washington Post*, January 10, 1984; Cunningham, *Klansville*, 5.

133. Although unsympathetic to the group's goals, Barley attributed the willingness of local Klansmen to have him shadow them to the fact that his father had been a Klan member. See Bill Barley, interview with the author, January 25, 2013.

134. Barley, "The Klan and Esters Cox: A Remembrance," article in the possession of the author.

135. Barley, interview, January 25, 2013. See attachment to memorandum, Derrick A. Bell, Jr. to Douglass Cater, September 26, 1967, Johnson Papers, White House Central Files, Subject Files, HUbox 54, "Executive, HU2-5/ST 32-ST 50," Johnson Library. The attachment noted that the Ku Klux Klan was "active" in Saluda County School District 1, and "very active" in Barnwell County School District 45.

136. Cunningham, *Klansville*, 5. In 1966 there were 192 klaverns in North Carolina, whose UKA members accounted for 52.2 percent of the total membership of the group, compared with South Carolina's 50 klaverns and 5.6 percent of the overall UKA membership.

137. Ibid., 7.

138. Grose, *South Carolina*, 113.

139. Cunningham, *Klansville*, 87.

140. Kalk, *Origins*, 69. See also "Parker Joins GOP for Senate Race," *Florence (S.C.) Morning News*, March 10, 1966.

141. See, for instance, "Race, Big Government Are Main Issues in S.C.," *Washington Post*, May 1, 1966; "S.C. Issue: 'Resentment'; GOP Choice: Hate Johnson or Kennedy," *Washington Post*, October 23, 1966.

142. "S.C. Issue: 'Resentment.'"

143. Grose, *South Carolina*, 134.

144. "Parker Reveals GOP Thinking since 1952," *Columbia (S.C.) State*, September 9, 1966.

145. Pamphlet "distributed by the South Carolina independents, L. Maurice Bessinger, Chairman" [1966], box 612, "1966, General, 1966," HP.

146. Ibid. In an oral history interview in 2002, Parker acknowledged that some of George Wallace's backers were "a strong part of my support" in 1966. However he attributed his loss in 1966 in part to his refusal to run a more racially tinged campaign, against the advice of these Wallace supporters. See Parker, interview with Hartsook, January 25, 2002.

147. *Columbia (S.C.) State*, June 16, 1966, in compiled typed comments on newspaper articles, box 617, "1966, Persons, Kennedy, Bobby," HP; "Campaign '66: Picking the Winners," *Washington Post*, November 6, 1966.

148. Parker to "Dear Committee Member," n.d., HP, box 617, "1966, Persons, Parker, Marshall," HP.

149. "Dent Predicts GPO [*sic*] to Carry State," *Greenville (S.C.) News*, June 18, 1966, transcription of article in box 617, "1966, Persons, Parker, Marshall," HP.

150. Hollings to Wayne Freeman, June 24, 1966, box 627, "1966, Persons, Kennedy, Bobby," HP.

151. "S.C. Issue: 'Resentment.'"

152. "G.O.P Threatened in South by Loss of Backlash Vote; In Many Races, Democrats Are Even Stronger Foes of Integration Drive," *New York Times*, October 9, 1966.

153. "On the Campaign Trail; Hollings Busy Stumping Anderson, Aiken Counties," *Charleston (S.C.) News and Courier*, November 3, 1966.

154. "Speech, Rough Draft, No. 2," September 1966, box 688, "1966, Campaign Organization Speeches (2 of 2)," HP.

155. Speech [1966], box 688, "1966, Speeches (2 of 2)," HP.

156. "Hollings's Victory in South Carolina Traced to Skill and Issue of 'Dropout Governor,'" *New York Times*, June 16, 1966.

157. [1966 speech draft], box 688, "1966, Speeches (2 of 2)," HP.

158. For Russell see J. Woods, *Richard B. Russell*, 139. For Thurmond see Crespino, *Strom Thurmond's America*, 200. As an example of the Senate Armed Services Committee's Vietnam War critique, in January 1966 the committee inquired into the state of the Vietnam War. Missouri senator Stuart Symington urged the bombing of North Vietnamese industrial targets and Arkansas's John McClellan contended that Johnson's policies prevented the military from "fighting to destroy the enemy that is really responsible for the war in South Vietnam," critiques Mississippi's John Stennis labeled "historic." See R. D. Johnson, *Congress*, 129.

159. See Armistice Day speech, November 11, 1955, box 688, "Speeches, 1953–June 1957," HP. For another example of Hollings's early views on foreign policy, see "Speech before the Washington Light Infantry Annual Banquet," February 23, 1959, box 688, "Speeches, 1959, January–June," HP.

160. "Speech Notes, Joy" [1966], box 688, "1966, Speeches (2 of 2)," HP.

161. John F. Kraft to Henry Techlenburg [*sic*], November 15, 1966, box 612, "1966, General, 1966," HP. Kraft wrote: "The key question, as we're all aware, is how come the 57 percent of the white vote dropped down to 40 percent by election day in just a couple of weeks."

162. "Legislators Say Hollings and Thurmond Will Win," *Charleston (S.C.) News and Courier*, October 31, 1966.

163. Cook, interview with the author, April 13, 2012.

164. "Candidates Enter Homestretch; Parker to Release Paper on National Defense," *Charleston (S.C.) News and Courier*, November 1, 1966.

165. McLeese, interview with the author, February 21, 2012.

166. Kalk, *Origins*, 70.

167. See Key, *Southern Politics*, 131–35, for his discussion of the "friends and neighbors" pattern of voting in South Carolina elections.

168. "S.C. Issue: 'Resentment.'" Grose claimed only two hundred thousand copies were given out. See Grose, *South Carolina*, 140.

Chapter 4: Backlash

1. Cook, interview with Hartsook, March 26, 1997.

2. Hollings, interview with Terry, December 10, 1990, SCPC.

3. Joseph D. Sapp to Hollings, November 28, 1966, box 612, "1966, General, 1966," HP.

4. See Hollings campaign remarks [1968], box 620, "1968, Topical, General," HP.

5. See Minchin, "Uphill Fight," 194.

6. Memorandum for the President, from Joe Califano and DeVier Pierson, April 10, 1968, Johnson Papers, White House Central Files, Subject Files, BE box 14, "Executive, BE 4/Textile," Johnson Library.

7. Memorandum for the President, from Pierson, May 9, 1968, Johnson Papers, White House Central Files, Subject Files, LE box 54, "Executive, LE/FI 11/4, 5/1/68-5/15/68," Johnson Library. On the agreement with Wilbur Mills, see Memorandum for the President, May 8, 1968, Johnson Papers, White House Central Files, Subject Files, LE box 54, "Executive, LE/FI 11/4, 5/1/68–5/15/68," Johnson Library.

8. Cook, interview with Hartsook, March 26, 1997.

9. Ibid.

10. "Hollings Is Assigned to Choice Positions," *Charleston (S.C.) News and Courier*, January 12, 1967.

11. Cook, interview with the author, April 13, 2012.

12. McLeese, interview with the author, February 21, 2012.

13. Cook, interview with Hartsook, March 26, 1997. Cook remarked that "we had oversimplified the Vietnam problem [during the 1966 campaign]."

14. Hollings and Victor, *Making Government Work*, 118–21.

15. "We Must Mean Business, Says Hollings of War," *Spartanburg (S.C.) Herald-Journal*,

May 23, 1967. See also "Hollings Rebukes Vietnam War Critics," *Charleston (S.C.) News and Courier*, April 26, 1967.

16. Hollings and Victor, *Making Government Work*, 121–24.

17. "Mansfield Wants U.S. to Push for Ceasefire in Vietnam," *Washington Observer*, December 15, 1966.

18. "Hollings Accuses Johnson of Leadership Void," *Charleston (S.C.) News and Courier*, January 18, 1967.

19. Cook recalled: "Lee and I would draft some for him, but in the final analysis he would sit down and write it himself." See Cook, interview with Hartsook, March 26, 1997. See also Michael Copps, interview with Hartsook, August 22, 1996, SCPC.

20. "We Lost Our Chance," October 1967, box 82, "Newsletters, 1967–1970," HP.

21. "Confrontation Is the Key," June 6, 1967, box 82, "Newsletters, 1967–1970," HP.

22. "Adm. Dowd Takes Helm at Naval Supply Center," *Charleston (S.C.) News and Courier*, August 31, 1968.

23. John F. Kraft, Inc., "A Report of Voter Attitudes in South Carolina," November 1967, box 619, "1968, Polls, General," HP.

24. Cook, interview with Hartsook, March 26, 1997.

25. Parker, interview with Hartsook, January 25, 2002.

26. "The following is a compilation of how Senator Ernest F. Hollings voted on the important issues of the 90th Congress," n.d., box 108, "Topical, 90th, Voting Records," HP.

27. Carter, *Politics of Rage*, 339.

28. See "The War—At Home and in Vietnam," May 1967, box 82, "Newsletters, 1967–1970," HP.

29. "General Westmoreland's Message," May 1967, box 82, "Newsletters, 1967–1970," HP.

30. See "Senator Fritz Hollings Reports to South Carolina," "Viewpoint on the Issues," August 1972, box 82, "Newsletters, 1971–1972," HP.

31. "The Solution," August 1967, box 82, "Newsletters, 1967–1970," HP.

32. Hollings to Mrs. Alice Gallman, August 16, 1967, box 94, "Topical, 90th, Commerce, Development, Office of Economic Development (OEO), General," HP.

33. "Following is a compilation."

34. "Parker: A Vote for Hollings Is a Vote for HHH and HEW," *Sumter (S.C.) Daily Item*, October 11, 1968.

35. A. Wade Martin to Hollings, February 3, 1967, box 94, "OEO, T-Square," HP.

36. "State of the State Message by Governor Robert E. McNair," January 24, 1967, box 94, "OEO, T-Square," HP.

37. See Hollings to Mr. J. E. Chaffin, February 21, 1967, box 94, "OEO, T-Square," HP; "Hollings Attack on T-Square," *Columbia (S.C.) Record*, February 7, 1967.

38. Hollings to Mr. Jeffrey C. Shaw, November 3, 1967, box 108, "Topical, 90th, Welfare, General," HP.

39. Hollings to Russell Brown, September 27, 1968, box 108, "Welfare, Poverty, General," HP. Brown was a member of the Citizens' Committee of Charleston County, a predominantly black organization. Hollings wrote: "I have worked on the Head Start program, for example, think it is a good program, and do not believe it should be transferred to the Office of Education."

40. "Hollings Cites Problem of Poverty in the State," *Charleston (S.C.) News and Courier,* January 14, 1968.

41. Folwell, "Legacy," 3–6.

42. "Thurmond Calls Anti-Poverty Program a 'Grab Bag,'" *Charleston (S.C.) News and Courier,* July 19, 1965.

43. "Following is a compilation."

44. "Hollings Fight on Hunger Is Stirring the South," *New York Times,* March 8, 1969. See also Peirce, *Deep South States,* 404.

45. "Following is a compilation."

46. Americans for Constitutional Action, September 6, 1967, box 108, "Voting Records," HP.

47. Hollings to Mrs. Charles Edward Bradham, September 18, 1967, box 108, "Voting Records," HP.

48. "Three Kind of Liars," *Orangeburg (S.C.) Times and Democrat,* September 20, 1967.

49. Hollings to Wayne Freeman, January 28, 1969, box 618, "1968, Correspondence, Gen. (3 of 3)," HP.

50. Patterson, *Grand Expectations,* 663.

51. Kraft, "Report of Voter Attitudes."

52. Qtd. in Carter, *Politics of Rage,* 348.

53. Box 82, "Newsletters, 1967–1970," HP.

54. "War on Crime," June 1967, box 82, "Newsletters, 1967–1970," HP.

55. Handwritten notes for luncheon held by South Carolina Association of School Boards, Inc., October 15, 1968, box 618, "1968, General," HP.

56. "Crime Marches On," December 1967, box 82, "Newsletters, 1967–1970," HP.

57. "Clear Call for Law," May 1968, box 82, "Newsletters, 1967–1970," HP.

58. See, for instance, Wallace's 1968 campaign commercial "Busing/Law and Order," http://www.livingroomcandidate.org/commercials/1968/businglaw-and-order (accessed April 25, 2013).

59. Sapp to Hollings, November 28, 1966, box 612, "1966, General, 1966," HP.

60. "Reflections on the Election," November 7, 1968, box 619, "1968, Reflections on Election," HP.

61. For examples of Marshall Parker seeking to associate Hollings with Humphrey, see, for instance, "Parker: A Vote for Hollings Is a Vote for HHH and HEW," *Sumter (S.C.) Daily Item,* October 11, 1968, or "Fritz Hollings—Stands Up for Humphrey!" campaign ad produced by Parker for Senate Committee, *Charleston (S.C.) News and Courier,* November 5, 1968.

62. WDIX radio editorial, "A Vote for Who Is a Vote for Who?" September 5, 1968, box 619, "1968, Democratic Party, General," HP.

63. Hollings to Thomas R. Miller, September 23, 1968, box 619, "1968, Democratic Party, National Convention," HP.

64. Hollings campaign remarks [1968], box 620, "1968, Topical, General," HP.

65. Betty Bargmann to Miss Pauline Kerr Creed, October 24, 1968, box 618, "1968, Correspondence, Gen. (2 of 3)," HP.

66. Hollings to E. E. Watson, October 29, 1968, box 619, "1968, Democratic Party, National Convention," HP.

67. "'Not Telling People How to Vote'; Hollings 'Obligated' to Vote for Humphrey," *Spartanburg (S.C.) Herald-Journal*, October 16, 1968.

68. "Vote for Who?"

69. "Reflections on the Election."

70. See, for instance, Hollings to Norman A. Brinker, March 8, 1968, box 93, "Topical, 90th, Civil Rights, General," HP; Hollings to Leland F. Robertson, March 18, 1968, box 93, "Civil Rights Act of 1964, Compliance," HP.

71. These bills were S. 3569 and S. 3570. See *Congressional Record—Senate*, June 3, 1968, 15758.

72. "Tell it like it is," August 3, 1968, box 82, "Newsletters, 1967–1970," HP.

73. *Congressional Record—Senate*, September 4, 1968, 25618.

74. Hollings and Victor, *Making Government Work*, 31–32. An earlier version of the section examining the Marshall and Fortas nominations first appeared in Ballantyne, "Managing the Backlash: Ernest F. 'Fritz' Hollings and the Marshall and Fortas Supreme Court Nominations," *Proceedings of the South Carolina Historical Association* (2013): 19–28.

75. The following senators voted nay: Robert Byrd (W.Va.); James Eastland (Miss.); Allen Ellender (La.); Sam Ervin (N.C.); Lister Hill (Ala.); Spessard Holland (Fla.); Ernest Hollings (S.C.); Russell Long (La.); John Sparkman (Ala.); Herman Talmadge (Ga.); Strom Thurmond (S.C.).

76. Hollings, interview with Terry, December 10, 1990.

77. "Thurgood Marshall," published by "Mothers' Crusade for Victory over Communism," received June 20, 1967, box 105, "Topical, 90th, Judiciary, Judges, Selection and appointment, Supreme Court, Marshall, Thurgood," HP.

78. See, for instance, G. A. White to Hollings, June 14, 1967; Brian Cisco to Hollings, June 14, 1967, box 105, "Marshall," HP.

79. E. B. Woodward to Hollings, received June 20, 1967, box 105, "Marshall," HP.

80. Ervin provided this apparently race-neutral argument against Marshall's "judicial activism" and dubbed him "a constitutional iconoclast." See Campbell, *Senator Sam Ervin*, 154.

81. Hollings to Thurgood Marshall, June 21, 1967, box 105, "Marshall," HP. Hollings asked for opinions on the following cases: *Miranda vs. State of Arizona*, *Walker vs. City of Birmingham*, *Reitman vs. Mulkey*, and *Berger vs. State of New York*.

82. Davis and Clark, *Thurgood Marshall*, 273. Marshall made this point in his response to Hollings's letter of June 21 as well. See Marshall to Hollings, June 27, 1967, box 105, "Marshall," HP.

83. See "DRAFT," "sj," June 20, 1967, box 105, "Marshall," HP. See also box 688, "Speeches, 1967, June–December & n.d.," HP. "SJ" probably referred to Sheila Joy.

84. *Congressional Record—Senate*, August 30, 1967, 24649–53.

85. "South Carolina Negroes Meet to Push for Voter Registration," *New York Times*, September 25, 1967.

86. Memorandum [Betty Bargmann to Hollings], August 10, 1967, box 105, "Marshall," HP. In his letter Hudson initially cited the fears of a disaffected black youth: "Your vote of 'NO' would make the senatorial delegation of South Carolina 100% against the progress of the Negro. . . . This boy is doubting your integrity, your honesty, and is placing you in the same category with all other racist[s]." See Samuel B. Hudson to Hollings, August 6, 1967, box 105, "Marshall," HP.

87. Hollings to Hudson, August 11, 1967, box 105, "Marshall," HP.

88. On July 12, 1967, Griffin announced: "Never before has there been such obvious political maneuvering to create a vacancy so that an outgoing President can fill it and thereby deny the opportunity to a new President about to be elected by the people." *Nominations of Abe Fortas*, 46.

89. Kalman, *Abe Fortas*, 471n61. According to White House aides, Hollings was one of twelve Democratic senators they contacted who agreed to support Fortas.

90. Campbell, *Senator Sam Ervin*, 164–66.

91. See, for instance, "The Abe Fortas Record," attached to H. C. Johnson to Hollings, July 13, 1968, and to George W. Dargan to Hollings, July 17, 1968, box 104, "90th, Judiciary, Judges, Selection and Appointment, Supreme Court, Fortas, Abe, Opposition, 1968 (1 of 7)," HP. See also Liberty Lobby pamphlet "THERE ARE NO GUNS IN THIS HOUSE," n.d., box 104, "Fortas, Opposition, 1968 (2 of 7)," HP.

92. *Nominations of Abe Fortas*, 283–84. The Liberty Lobby witness was W. B. Hicks Jr.

93. "Abe Fortas Record." The Durham Rule provided an insanity defense for defendants, if a jury decided that there was a causal relationship between a mental disease suffered by the defendant and the criminal act committed. The Gesell Report was produced by the President's Committee on Equal Opportunity in the Armed Forces in November 1964, of which Fortas was a member.

94. Kalman, *Abe Fortas*, 348.

95. Hollings to W. S. "Steve" Weston Jr., July 12, 1968, box 104, "Fortas, Opposition, 1968 (1 of 7)," HP.

96. "Nomination of Justice Abe Fortas to Be Chief Justice of the United States; Speech of Hon. Ernest F. Hollings of South Carolina in the Senate of the United States, Thursday, July 18, 1968," *Congressional Record*, July 18, 1968, box 104, "Fortas, Opposition, 1968 (3 of 7)," HP.

97. See, for example, John C. Bond to Hollings, July 3, 1968, box 104, "Fortas, Opposition, 1968 (2 of 7)," HP.

98. Lee Bandy, "Hollings' Stand Branded 'Farce,'" *Columbia (S.C.) State*, [July 1968], attached to letter received July 24, 1968, box 104, "Fortas, Opposition, 1968 (3 of 7)," HP.

99. Hollings to John D. Attaway Jr., August 7, 1968, box 104, "Fortas, Opposition, 1968 (5 of 7)," HP.

100. Calhoun Thomas to Hollings, July 10, 1968; Hollings to Thomas, July 15, 1968, box 104, "Fortas, Opposition, 1968 (1 of 7)," HP.

101. Hollings to Wayne Freeman, February 4, 1969, box 618, "1968, Correspondence, Gen. (3 of 3)," HP.

102. For more on Fleming, see White, "Managed Compliance," esp. 236, 301–2; for Simkins see B. A. Woods, "Modjeska Simkins."

103. "Reflections on the Election."

104. See box 620, "1968, Topical, Race," HP.

105. The chairman of the county's black voter league informed Hollings that "the Director of the County Welfare and the state Director have agreed to continue to run the program as long as the Williamsburg County Voter's League can solicit enough donations to take care of the part of the administrative cost that is needed." See E. I. Lawrence to Hollings, June 1, 1967, box 90, "Topical, 90th, Agriculture, FNS, Food Stamps," HP.

106. Lawrence to Hollings, August 25, 1967, box 90, "Food Stamps," HP.

107. Hollings and Victor, *Making Government Work*, 133. In his memoir Hollings asserted that the clinic in question was the Beaufort-Jasper Health Center, although in correspondence from the time, he placed the clinic in Charleston. See, for instance, Hollings to the Reverend L. B. Burgess, April 18, 1968, box 620, "Race," HP.

108. Cook, interview with Hartsook, March 26, 1997.

109. Donald A. Campbell Jr. to Hollings, October 29, 1968, box 618, "1968, Correspondence, Gen. (1 of 3)," HP.

110. See, for instance, Waddell Byrd to Meng, April 19, 1968, box 620, "Race," HP; "Political—Negroes," n.d., box 620, "Race," HP.

111. Johnston ran for the Senate unopposed in 1956.

112. In an oral history, she remarked: "They'd pay it [money] over to certain wheelers and dealers who say they can control the black vote. That doesn't happen only in South Carolina, but we know about it here." Discussing Hollings's unsuccessful 1962 campaign, Simkins recalled telling the president of the Palmetto State Voters, a group that worked with the NAACP on voter registration, that "you got money from the Hollings forces; you were paid off." See Modjeska Simkins, interview with Jacquelyn Hall and Bob Hall, July 28, 1976, SOHPC.

113. Typed memo, April 25, [1968], box 620, "Race," HP.

114. Memorandum to Hollings from Meng, May 1, 1968, box 620, "Race," HP.

115. Hollings to James L. Felder, November 14, 1967, box 620, "Race," HP.

116. J. Howard Wrighten III to Hollings, March 8, 1968, box 620, "Race," HP. Wrighten had unsuccessfully sought admission to the all-white University of South Carolina School of Law in 1946, although his application led to the creation of the supposedly "separate but equal" South Carolina State College School of Law the following year.

117. See Hollings to Wrighten, March 8, 1968, box 620, "Race," HP.

118. Hollings to the Burgess, April 18, 1968. Identical letters were sent to George Kline, J. Herbert Nelson, Virgil Dimery, A. J. Whittenberg, Rev. J. E. James, Earl Middleton, Alex Alford, R. N. Beck, Dr. Charles H. Thomas, and Frank E. Cain Jr. See ibid.

119. Fink, "Union Power," 11; March 10, 1968, *Lowcountry Newsletter*, box 620, "Race," HP.

120. Modjeska Simkins to Lyndon B. Johnson, October 8, 1966, White House Central Files Name File, box 340, "Russell, Donald," Johnson Library.

121. "Richland County Citizens' Committee Broadcast, February 10, 1971," as found in "Modjeska Monteith Simkins: In Her Own Words," Modjeska Monteith Simkins Papers. Simkins also refused to attend Benedict College's commencement exercises in 1971 when she learned Hollings would receive an honorary degree. She contended that Hollings's "recent charades of smooth talk on poverty and hunger, and his belated slum strolls and ghetto walks cannot erase from my memory the treatment of protesting State College students during his gubernatorial administration, his praise and support of Citizens['] Councils when he was Lieutenant Governor, and his longstanding callousness toward the sufferings of the masses of disadvantaged and utterly deprived." See Simkins to Benjamin F. Payton, May 4, 1971, as found in "Modjeska Monteith Simkins: In Her Own Words," Simkins Papers.

122. Grose, *Looking for Utopia*, 153, 321 fn15. On Mississippi, see for instance Lamis, *Two-Party South*, 45.

123. For a discussion of Carter's 1970 candidacy, see Lamis, *Two-Party South*, 97–99.

124. "Sam Nunn's Rising Star," *New York Times*, January 4, 1987.

125. Bass and De Vries, *Transformation*, 149.

126. John C. Topping Jr., John R. Lazarek, and William H. Linder, "Southern Republicanism and the New South" [1966], box 620, "1970, Republican Party, General," HP.

127. Donald Fowler, "The 1968 General Election in S.C.," n.d., box 621, "Campaigns, 1974, General," HP.

Chapter 5: Hunger, USA

1. The content of this chapter is largely based on Ballantyne, "'A Public Problem . . . Rather Than a Question of Social Welfare': Ernest F. Hollings and the Politics of Hunger," *The Sixties: A Journal of History, Politics and Culture* 8, no. 1 (2015): 75–98, DOI: 10.1080/17541328.2015.1033834.

2. Hollings, *Case against Hunger*, 20, 22.

3. *Congressional Record—Senate*, April 10, 1970, 11210.

4. See, for instance, "Hollings Fight on Hunger Is Stirring the South," *New York Times*, March 8, 1969.

5. See, for instance, "Hollings Says 'Super Bread' Is Needed," *Sumter (S.C.) Daily Item*, October 6, 1971.

6. Patterson, *America's Struggle*, 163.

7. See, especially, Green, "Saving Babies in Memphis," 135; Kornbluh, "Food as a Civil Right."

8. On Clyburn's involvement in hunger tours, see "South Carolina Governor Visits the Poor and Finds Hunger Big Problem," *New York Times*, February 7, 1971.

9. Berry, *Feeding Hungry People*, 21.

10. MacDonald, *Food*, 2.

11. Berry, *Feeding Hungry People*, 24.

12. Ibid., 21, 24.

13. Ibid., 22.

14. MacDonald, *Food*, 3–4.

15. Levine, *School Lunch Politics*, 72–79.

16. Ibid., 86–87.

17. Berry, *Feeding Hungry People*, 30.

18. United States Department of Agriculture, Food and Nutrition Service [USDA FNS], "A Short History of SNAP [Supplemental Nutrition Assistance Program]," http://www.fns.usda.gov/snap/rules/Legislation/about.htm (accessed October 22, 2012).

19. King, *Budgeting Entitlements*, 48–49.

20. MacDonald, *Food*, 8.

21. USDA FNS, "Food Stamp Act of 1964," http://www.fns.usda.gov/sites/default/files/PL_88-525.pdf (accessed September 12, 2015).

22. See MacDonald, *Food*, 22–27, for an account of the process of establishing eligibility in the program and obtaining food stamps, written in 1977 prior to the passage of another Food Stamp Act that year.

23. King, *Budgeting Entitlements*, 49; MacDonald, *Food*, 8. See also Berry, *Feeding Hungry People*, 29–33, 40–42.

24. Berry, *Feeding Hungry People*, 43–46.

25. For an account of Gatch's attempts to highlight malnutrition in Beaufort County, see Bass, "Hunger?" 274.

26. "Compiled by AB, Excerpts from 'Let Us Now Praise Dr. Gatch,'" *Esquire*, June 1968, 108–111, 152–156, box 108, "Topical, 90th, Welfare, Poverty, General," HP.

27. Coles and Huge, "Strom Thurmond Country."

28. "Let Us Now Praise Dr. Gatch"; "Beaufort Officials Deny Charges of Malnutrition," *Charleston (S.C.) News and Courier*, November 28, 1967.

29. Goldfield, *Cotton Fields*, 160.

30. "134 Counties Deny Starvation Report," *Richmond (Va.) Times-Dispatch*, May 26, 1968.

31. "Statistics Are Old, Criteria Questionable: What the Hunger Report Shows," *Richmond (Va.) Times-Dispatch*, May 26, 1968.

32. "Probe by T-D Fails to Find Hunger as Defined by Board," *Richmond (Va.) Times-Dispatch*, May 26, 1968.

33. "Voice of the People: Who Are the Poor People?" *Rock Hill (S.C.) Evening Herald* [July 1968], attached to letter from Agnes M. Wallace to Hollings, July 29, 1968, box 104, "Fortas, Opposition, 1968 (5 of 7)," HP. See also, for instance, "Hollings' Hunger Battle Offends Working America," *Columbia (S.C.) State*, October 3, 1971. Anthony Harrigan, the executive vice president of the conservative Southern States Industrial Council, wrote the *State* editorial.

34. *Hearings before the Select Committee on Nutrition*, 1165.

35. Sister Mary Anthony to Hollings, February 3, 1968, box 98, "Topical, 90th, Education, General," HP.

36. For reference to the Dorchester County tour, see "Robinson Tapped for U.S. Attorney," *Charleston (S.C.) News and Courier*, January 17, 1968.

37. Hollings, *Case against Hunger*, 29–30, 34–35.

38. Ibid., 33–34. Following his select committee testimony, Hollings's pleading with Kennedy to stay away from South Carolina in 1968 was recorded in the *New York Times*. "Hollings Fight on Hunger," See also Edelman, oral history interview with Hackman.

39. "Bubba to Betty," received March 2, 1968, box 108, "Poverty, 'Poverty' [Hollings' File]," HP.

40. In 1969 Hollings told reporters, "If I'd done this then [before the 1968 election], folks would have said, 'Oh, he's just politicking!'" See "Hollings Fight on Hunger."

41. According to the 1970 Census, in South Carolina 49.7 percent of African Americans lived in poverty in 1969, compared with 12.3 percent of whites. See *Census of Population: 1970*, vol. 1, pt. 42, 127.

42. White, "Race, Grassroots Activism," 159.

43. Hollings to Mr. W. G. Freeman, December 1, 1970, box 129, "Topical, 91st, Persons, Agnew, Spiro (VP)," HP. For South Carolina's population in 1970, see *Census of Population: 1970*, vol. 1, pt. 42, 133.

44. "West to Tour Hunger Areas," *Sumter (S.C.) Daily Item*, January 26, 1971.

45. "Hunger: An Underdeveloped Country," *Time*, February 28, 1969.

46. "There Is Hunger. . . ," *Charlotte Observer*, February 20, 1969.

47. Hollings, *Case against Hunger*, 84. Kwashiorkor and marasmus derive from a severe protein and calorie deficiency, respectively.

48. *Hearings before the Select Committee on Nutrition*, 1163. See also Hollings, *Case against Hunger*, 210. Hollings wrote: "The poor have had to spend a large amount of their meager cash income to be able to take part in the food stamp program. . . . It is very hard for many of them [the very poor] to give up a large amount, at one time, to buy stamps on the limited occasions each month when they are available." Moreover, lacking a cash income, "the poorest of the poor cannot participate at all."

49. United States Department of Agriculture, "Pilot Food Program Offered South Carolina," February 21, 1969, box 109, "Topical, 91st, Agriculture, FNS, Food Stamps, General (1 of 2)," HP; Berry, *Feeding Hungry People*, 62; "Free Food Stamp Plan Is Begun in Carolina, but Few Turn Out," *New York Times*, March 4, 1969.

50. Courtney Siceloff to Robert E. McNair, February 24, 1969, Robert E. McNair Papers, box 54, "Topical, Poverty," SCPC.

51. See, for instance, *Congressional Record—Senate*, April 8, 1976, 10147. The 1976 Senate reform did not eliminate the purchase requirement, but it established a pilot project on its elimination. See ibid., 10156.

52. "Hunger: It Jolts a Senate Coalition," *New York Times*, February 23, 1969.

53. See, for instance, "Playing Politics with Poverty," *Lewiston (Idaho) Morning Tribune*, February 27, 1969.

54. See, for instance, *Congressional Record—Senate*, September 24, 1969, 26850–80.

55. "Text of statements by Senator Hollings at News Conference Regarding Nixon Administration Failure to Attack Hunger Problem in America," November 12, 1970, box 126, "Topical, 91st, Hunger, Statements, Hollings," HP.

56. Here Kentucky is treated as a "southern" state alongside the eleven states of the former Confederacy.

57. Tennessee senator Albert Gore was announced in favor of the McGovern substitute but was not present for the vote.

58. "Biography, U.S. Senator Ernest F. Hollings," n.d., box 618, "1968, General," HP; Crawford Cook to Hollings, July 29, 1966, box 612, "1966. Campaign Organization, Strategy," HP.

59. *Hearings before the Select Committee on Nutrition*, 1166.

60. *Congressional Record—Senate*, September 24, 1969, 26884. See also "Feed the Hungry —Not Just Good Advice," *Chicago Tribune*, March 27, 1969.

61. "Hollings Seeking New Volunteers for Hunger Fight," *Charleston (S.C.) News and Courier*, March 30, 1969.

62. Hollings to Mr. Stuart Lusty Jr., May 25, 1971, box 144, "Topical, 92nd, Education, Higher, General," HP. The Limestone course did not receive approval that year owing to weaknesses in the proposed curriculum, but it did receive a twenty-five-thousand-dollar grant to continue a feasibility study for the program. See James M. Whitmire Jr. to Hollings, July 16, 1971; Memorandum from Mary C. Egan to Susan Horowitz, July 1, 1971, box 144, "Topical, 92nd, Education, Higher, General," HP.

63. Barone and Cohen, *Almanac of American Politics*, 1434. See also *Congressional Record—Senate*, August 16, 1972, 28578, 28581.

64. *Congressional Record—Senate*, September 24, 1969, 26884.

65. *Congressional Record—Senate*, April 10, 1970, 11209.

66. *Congressional Record—Senate*, September 24, 1969, 26885.

67. *Hearings before the Select Committee on Nutrition*, 1170.

68. McGovern, "Politics of Hunger," 55, 64. Similarly New York senator Javits called the existence of hunger an "assault on America's conscience." See "$1-Billion Sought to Attack Hunger; Urban Council Asks Nixon for Funds in Addition to $1.5-Billion Johnson Plan," *New York Times*, March 18, 1969.

69. Dr. Paulus Zee, a doctor at the St. Jude Children's Research Hospital in Memphis, also provided medical, rather than moral, explanations for stunted growth and anemia. See Green, "Saving Babies," 149.

70. *Hearings before the Select Committee on Nutrition*, 1165.

71. He remarked that "the people must learn that it is cheaper to feed the child than jail the man." Ibid., 1165.

72. "A Senator's Reply; Mr. Hollings on Hunger," *Charleston (S.C.) News and Courier*, October 13, 1971.

73. Memorandum, from Hollings to John Hussey and Ruth Singer, December 15, 1969, box 124, "Topical, 91st, Hunger, General, Neutral," HP.

74. Hollings to Alan T. Pidgeon, January 27, 1970, box 131, "Topical, 91st, Welfare, General," HP.

75. "The Case to End Hunger, A report submitted to the U.S. Chamber of Commerce by Mike Joy and John Hussey of the staff of Sen. Ernest F. Hollings, D-S.C.," June 25, 1969, box 126, "Hunger, Statements, Hollings," HP.

76. Hollings, *Case against Hunger*, 123.

77. Ibid., 143.

78. Qtd. in Levine, *School Lunch Politics*, 82.

79. "Interview with Sen. Ernest F. Hollings," April 4, 1969, box 81, "Press, Articles, 1961–1970," HP.

80. "Children," May 2, 1969, box 82, "Newsletters, 1967–1970," HP.

81. *Congressional Record—Senate*, April 10, 1970, 11209.

82. Hollings, *Case against Hunger*, 174.

83. MacDonald, *Food*, 5.

84. Hollings, *Case against Hunger*, 175.

85. Memorandum, Hollings to Hussey and Singer.

86. Berry, *Feeding Hungry People*, 47.

87. Kotz, *Let Them Eat*, 75. For Kotz's criticism of Poage, see ibid., 76, 113–14. On Whitten see ibid., 96.

88. Memorandum, Hollings to Hussey and Singer.

89. King, *Budgeting Entitlements*, 49.

90. Finegold, "Agriculture," 208–10. See also Katznelson, *When Affirmative Action*, 42–48, for a discussion of southern congressional influence over the drafting of the Social Security Act. He contended that "for the first quarter century of its existence, Social Security was characterized by a form of policy apartheid" (43).

91. "Interview with Sen. Ernest F. Hollings," April 4, 1969.

92. Hollings, *Case against Hunger*, 150–51.

93. Kotz, *Let Them Eat*, 96.

94. Hollings, *Case against Hunger*, 153.

95. On the use of federal aid programs to reinforce the control of traditional elites, see especially Kornbluh, "Food as a Civil Right," 143. She contended that in Mississippi "local officials administered the programs in ways that . . . helped sustain planter white supremacy."

96. Hollings, *Case against Hunger*, 246–47.

97. *Hearings before the Select Committee on Nutrition*, 1271.

98. Orville Freeman, Oral History Interview IV.

99. McLeese, interview with the author, February 21, 2012.

100. Macon Garrick to Hollings, June 14, 1971, box 137, "Topical, 92nd, Civil Rights, General," HP; Hollings to Garrick, July 7, 1971, box 137, "Civil Rights, General," HP.

101. See Hollings, *Case against Hunger*, 138.

102. "Undeserved Criticism," *Charleston (S.C.) News and Courier*, March 6, 1969.

103. On the "deserving" and "undeserving" poor categories, see especially Katz, *Undeserving Poor*.

104. James G. Blalock to Hollings, February 21 [*sic*], 1969; Hollings to Blalock, February 12, 1969, box 124, "Topical, 91st, Hunger, General, Con (1 of 2)," HP.

105. See Hollings, *Case against Hunger*, 3. For an example of such editorials, see, for instance, "Hollings' Hunger Battle."

106. Spiro Agnew to Hollings, May 12, 1969, box 109, "Food Stamps, General (1 of 2)," HP.

107. Cook to Hollings, May 19, 1969, box 621, "1974, Correspondence, General (2 of 2)," HP.

108. Karen Kollmansperger, interview with Hartsook, April 27, 1993, SCPC.

109. Memorandum "To: Senator, From: Mike Copps," January 10, 1974, box 622, "1974, Publicity, Radio and Television, General," HP.

110. Patterson, *America's Struggle*, 167.

111. Following reports that Nixon had decided against increasing spending on food stamps, McGovern and his aides leaked a copy of an Urban Affairs Council report that recommended $1.7 billion in additional expenditures on the program, shortly before Secretary of Agriculture Clifford Hardin and HEW Secretary Robert Finch were due to testify before the Nutrition Committee on May 7, 1969. See Berry, *Feeding Hungry People*, 60–62.

112. Berry, *Feeding Hungry People*, 61. "Text of statements by Senator Hollings," November 12, 1970, box 126, "Hunger, Statements, Hollings," HP.

113. Hollings to President Nixon, November 25, 1970, box 124, "Hunger, General, Neutral," HP. Hollings was likely referencing a memorandum Moynihan wrote to Nixon in March 1969 that contended "there is is strong evidence that very severe malnutrition, as seen in the developing countries, may lead to mental retardation, but the entire question of whether less severe malnutrition as seen in the American population can affect intellectual development is just not settled." Memorandum, Moynihan for Nixon, March 17, 1969, White House Central Files, Subject Files, HE box 13, "Executive, HE 3-1 Hunger and Malnutrition," Nixon Library. An article discussing the memorandum appeared in the *New York Post* in May 1969. See "Moynihan and Hunger," *New York Post*, May 1, 1969.

114. "S. Res. 70," March 10, 1971, box 152, "Topical, 92nd, Hunger, National Nutrition Survey, General," HP.

115. Robert E. Anderson Jr., "Whatever Happened to the National Nutrition Survey?" *New South*, Fall 1971, box 152, "National Nutrition Survey, General," HP.

116. "United States Senator Ernest F. Hollings Reports to South Carolina," "The Welfare Mess," June 1972, box 82, "Newsletters, 1971–1972," HP.

117. "The Case against Hunger: An Interview with U.S. Senator Ernest F. Hollings," *Trends*, South Carolina Economic Trends, State Development Board Publication, April 1971, box 81, "Press, Articles, 1971–1976," HP.

118. For a discussion of the failure of FAP to pass the Senate Finance Committee that emphasizes policy difficulties, see Davies, *From Opportunity to Entitlement*, 226–29. For an explanation of FAP's demise that privileges the Nixon administration's quiet withdrawal of support for the measure, see Kornbluh, "Who Shot FAP?"

119. Moynihan, *Politics*, 396.

120. "Hollings Seeking New Volunteers for Hunger Fight," *Charleston (S.C.) News and Courier*, March 30, 1969.

121. See, for instance, "Celanese Strikers Get Food Stamp Help from Hollings," *Charlotte Observer*, May 10, 1968; Mrs. R. V. Yates to Hollings, May 30, 1968, box 90, "Food Stamps," HP. Yates wrote: "These Celanese workers CHOSE to TURN DOWN substantial, higher wages and increased benefits. Does this mean that the government and the legislators approve of laziness, and in turn, reward it with food stamps?"

122. *Congressional Record—Senate*, May 23, 1973, 16707.

123. Memorandum, "To: Senator, From: Mike Copps," January 10, 1974.

124. "Hollings, a Southern Puzzle," *New York Times*, May 11, 1980.

125. Hollings, "The Rural Poor," *Current History*, June 1973, box 81, "Articles, 1971–1976," HP. Other observers perceived a backlash against the "undeserving poor," including Mitchell Ginsberg, the former commissioner for welfare in New York City. On November 9, 1972, he told the *Los Angeles Times* that "the hatred of welfare is unbelievable. . . . We are in the midst of a very sharp swing against doing something for the poor, for minorities." See Davies, *From Opportunity to Entitlement*, 236.

126. "Memo, To: EFH, From: John, Re: 'Hunger and Nutrition,'" n.d., box 152, "Hunger, General," HP.

127. Kotz, telephone conversation with the author, January 21, 2013.

128. King, *Budgeting Entitlements*, 56.

129. Eisinger, *Toward an End*, 39.

130. MacDonald, *Food*, 86–87.

Chapter 6: A "common-sense, realistic, South Carolina Democrat"

1. Bass and Poole, *Palmetto State*, 136.

2. Donald Randy Sanders argued that style was more important than actual issues for these New South Democrats. See Sanders, *Mighty Peculiar Elections*, 6.

3. For the persistent divergence in opinion between black and white southerners on matters related to civil rights and government involvement in ensuring individual economic security, see Black and Black, *Politics and Society*, 206–9, 218–19.

4. Robert Shaw, Georgia's Republican state party chairman, was commenting on the alliance of white rural voters and African Americans that elected Jimmy Carter governor in 1970. See Lamis, *Two-Party South*, 99.

5. Lamis, "Future of Southern Politics," 56.

6. Hays and Hays, *Beauty*, 40–41.

7. Merchant, *American Environmental History*, 198.

8. Hollings authored the ocean dumping bill, which later became law. See "Senator Fritz Hollings Reports to South Carolina," October 1972, box 82, "Newsletters, 1971–1972," HP.

9. "Hollings Cited for Sea Probes," *Milwaukee Journal*, June 3, 1971; "Hollings Receives Award," *Sumter (S.C.) Daily Item*, March 2, 1974; "U.S. Senator Fritz Hollings South Carolina Democrat," n.d., HCP, folder 1.

10. National Oceanic and Atmospheric Administration, Office of Education, "Hollings Scholarship Program," http://www.oesd.noaa.gov/scholarships/ (accessed May 28, 2013); "Program Description," http://www.oesd.noaa.gov/scholarships/hollings.html (accessed May 28, 2013).

11. Hollings and Victor, *Making Government Work*, 153.

12. "Sen. Hollings to Head Ocean Study Committee," *Charleston (S.C.) News and Courier*, August 8, 1969; Hollings and Victor, *Making Government Work*, 152.

13. Office of the White House Press Secretary, July 9, 1970, box 115, "Topical, 91st, Commerce, Oceans, NOAA, Establishment, S. 2841, S. 2802, General (2 of 2)," HP.

14. The Stratton Commission was officially named the Commission on Marine Science, Engineering and Resources, created in 1966 by Congress and headed by Julius A. Stratton. See Hollings and Victor, *Making Government Work*, 152.

15. Ibid., 154.

16. Ibid., 155.

17. Office of the White House Press Secretary, July 9, 1970, box 115, "S. 2841, S. 2802, General (2 of 2)," HP.

18. *Congressional Record—Senate*, July 30, 1970, 26604.

19. Izaak Walton League of America, Washington Newsletter, August 1970, box 115, "S. 2841, S. 2802, General (2 of 2)," HP.

20. Executive Reorganization Plan IV to Establish NOAA, n.d., box 135, "Topical, 92nd, Animals, Marine Mammal Protection Act, 'Ocean Mammals' [Hollings File]," HP.

21. Beaufort County Development Commission to Hollings, October 17, 1969; BASF Corporation, "BASF Group to Invest $100 Million in 1800-Acre South Carolina Industrial Site," October 1, 1969, box 120, "Topical, 91st, Environment, Pollution, BASF, Co. proposing chemical plant in Beaufort (1 of 9)," HP.

22. Gordon F. Craighead Jr. to Robert E. McNair, December 6, 1969; William N. Cork to McNair, December 5, 1969; David Jones and Thomas C. Barnwell Jr. to Hollings, December 8, 1969, box 120, "BASF (2 of 9)," HP.

23. "Conservationists Battle Industrialists in Hilton Head, S.C.; Dye Plant to Be Built Near Resorts," *Washington Post*, December 15, 1969.

24. "BASF Plant Suspension Announced," *Sumter (S.C.) Daily Item*, April 8, 1970; "BASF Finalizes Withdrawal Plans," *Sumter (S.C.) Daily Item*, January 15, 1971.

25. After BASF postponed its construction, Beaufort's Democratic senator James M. Waddell Jr. termed Hickel's ultimatum to the German company over pollution levels "a gross example of federal government interference in states['] rights." See "Anti-BASF Forces Hail Plant Delay," *Charleston (S.C.) News and Courier*, April 8, 1970.

26. "Special Bulletin," *Hilton Head (S.C.) Islander*, April 7, 1970, box 120, "BASF (6 of 9)," HP.

27. Local NAACP representatives supported the creation of the plant in Beaufort County. See Cobb, *Industrialization*, 133.

28. Waddell to Hollings, December 19, 1969, box 120, "BASF (3 of 9)," HP.

29. See, for instance, Hollings to Burke Watson, January 30, 1970, box 120, "BASF (3 of 9)," HP.

30. Hollings to Waddell, January 5, 1970, box 120, "BASF (3 of 9)," HP.

31. Hollings to Hans Lautenschlager, February 25, 1970, box 120, "BASF (5 of 9)," HP. Instead Lautenschlager responded that he had "proposed to Governor McNair on December 24, 1969, that a committee be organized consisting of all agencies involved which should analyze the situation and make the proper recommendations." See Lautenschlager to Hollings, March 26, 1970, ibid.

32. Hollings to Mr. and Mrs. Allan Romanow, March 13, 1970, box 120, "BASF (5 of 9)," HP.

33. "Hollings Lauds Secretary for Anti-Pollution Stand," *Charleston (S.C.) News and Courier*, March 28, 1970.

34. "BASF Controversy: Hollings Gives Views on Plant," *Beaufort (S.C.) Gazette*, April 23, 1970.

35. "Sen. Hollings Questions BASF Construction Critics," *Charleston (S.C.) News and Courier*, April 18, 1970.

36. "Governor Hits Charge by Hollings," *Charleston (S.C.) News and Courier*, April 25, 1970.

37. Hollings to T. J. Roper, May 27, 1970, box 120, "BASF (8 of 9)," HP.

38. Hollings to Mr. and Mrs. James Freeman, May 5, 1970, box 120, "BASF (8 of 9)," HP.

39. Hollings to Mrs. Wilton Graves, May 4, 1970, box 120, "BASF (8 of 9)," HP. For examples of Hollings's stressing his commitment to attracting industry to South Carolina, see, for instance, Hollings to Edwin Creighton Tobias, December 7, 1970, box 120, "BASF (9 of 9)," HP, or Hollings to John R. Smith, April 23, 1970, box 120, "BASF (6 of 9)," HP.

40. See, for instance, "Is It Ecology vs. the Need for Jobs?" *St. Petersburg (Fla.) Independent*, May 15, 1970.

41. News from the office of Sen. Ernest F. Hollings, D-S.C [1972], "Text of Remarks on Marine Mammal Protection Legislation on the Floor of the Senate" [S. 2871], box 135, "Topical, 92nd, Animals, Marine Mammal Protection Act, 'Ocean Mammals,'" HP.

42. Merchant, *American Environmental History*, 224.

43. "Fritz Hollings Reports," August 1973, box 82, "Newsletters, 1973–1974," HP.

44. Merchant, *American Environmental History*, 198; "Fritz Hollings Reports," August 1973.

45. Hollings to Mike Mansfield, December 3, 1966, box 68, "Topical, 90th, Congress, Committee Appointments," HP.

46. Peirce, *Deep South States*, 406.

47. Hollings to President Nixon, November 13, 1969, box 110, "Topical, 91st, Armed Forces, Vietnam, General," HP.

48. "The Cause of the Chaos," May 26, 1970, box 82, "Newsletters, 1971–1972," HP.

49. Vietnam War Machine Letter no. 2, n.d., box 110, "Vietnam, General," HP.

50. "Text of remarks on the floor of the Senate Wednesday, June 24, 1970," "News from the office of Sen. Ernest F. Hollings," box 110, "Vietnam, General," HP. See also "To

Condone or Condemn," April 1, 1971, box 82, "Newsletters, 1971–1972," HP, for a forthright call for withdrawal.

51. "Hollings Opposes Cambodian Invasion," *Charleston (S.C.) News and Courier*, May 13, 1970.

52. Memorandum, George T. Bell for H. R. Haldeman, May 7, 1970, White House Special Files, Staff Member Office Files, H. R. Haldeman Files, box 128, "Cambodia [3 of 4]," Nixon Library; memorandum, William E. Timmons for Harry Dent, Chuck Colson, Jeb Magruder, and Rob Cole, May 20, 1970, Haldeman Files, box 128, "Cambodia [1 of 4]," Nixon Library.

53. "Cambodia," May 20, 1970, box 82, "Press, Newsletter, 1971–1972," HP.

54. Johnson, *Congress*, 168.

55. "Cambodia."

56. See, for instance, Hollings to Henry J. Field, May 29, 1970, box 120, "Topical, 91st, Foreign Affairs, Cambodia, General, 1970 (2 of 14)," HP; Hollings to Leland C. Stoddard, May 26, 1970, ibid. For a description of the December 1969 Cooper-Church amendment, see Fry, *Debating Vietnam*, 156.

57. Hollings to William S. Brockington, May 29, 1970, box 120, "Cambodia, General, 1970 (2 of 14)," HP.

58. Johnson, *Congress*, 166–67, 293–98.

59. "ABM," May 6, 1969, box 82, "Newsletters, 1971–1972," HP.

60. "Senator Fritz Hollings Reports to South Carolina," October 1972, box 82, "Newsletters, 1971–1972," HP.

61. Hollings and Victor, *Making Government Work*, 160–61.

62. "Canal Representative Quits," *New York Times*, July 3, 1973; *Congressional Record—Senate*, July 19, 1973, 24747–48. See also "Fritz Hollings Reports to South Carolina," July 26, 1973, box 82, "Newsletters, 1973–1974," HP.

63. "The Fritz Hollings Report; the Panama Canal," February 1974, box 82, "Newsletters, 1973–1974," HP.

64. See, for instance, "Robo," Hollings to John Smith, September 14, 1971, box 148, "Topical, 92nd, Foreign Affairs, Panama Canal," HP. The letter stated that "any legislation coming before the Senate which would jeopardize American jurisdiction over the Canal would find me in strong opposition."

65. "Surrendering the Canal," February 20, 1974, box 175, "Panama Canal," HP.

66. Hollings to Mr. and Mrs. Homer R. Stutsman, October 1, 1973, box 175, "Panama Canal," HP.

67. John McClellan and Thurmond to Hollings, March 29, 1974; memorandum, Copps to Hollings, April 1, 1974, box 175, "Panama Canal," HP.

68. See "Political Discussion," C-Span, February 23, 1984.

69. Fry, *Dixie Looks Abroad*, 254. For his discussion of southern anti–foreign aid sentiments in the post–World War II era, see ibid., 251–54.

70. "Report to the People," December 1972, box 82, "Newsletters, 1971–1972," HP.

71. "Report to the People from Fritz Hollings" [December 1971], box 82, "Newsletters, 1971–1972," HP.

72. "Fritz Hollings Reports to South Carolina," September 13, 1973, box 82, "Newsletters, 1973–1974," HP.

73. "Report to the People from Fritz Hollings," April 1973, box 82, "Newsletters, 1973–1974," HP.

74. "Senator Fritz Hollings Reports to South Carolina," August 1972, box 82, "Newsletters, 1971–1972," HP.

75. "Foreign Policy and Foreign Aid," November 1971, box 82, "Press, Newsletters, 1971–1972," HP.

76. "The Fritz Hollings Report," October 1973, box 82, "Newsletters, 1973–1974," HP.

77. "Senator Fritz Hollings Reports to South Carolina," August 1972.

78. "Fritz Hollings Report," October 1973.

79. Kotlowski, *Nixon's Civil Rights*, 33.

80. Bullock and Lamb, *Implementation*, 59.

81. Kotlowski, *Nixon's Civil Rights*, 42.

82. Bullock and Lamb, *Implementation*, 60, 89.

83. Carter, *Politics of Rage*, 398. See also "Nixon's Plan Splits Rivals; Ervin Leads Busing Attack," *New York Times*, March 18, 1972.

84. Carter, *Politics of Rage*, 425, 445.

85. Ferillo, interview with the author, April 17, 2012.

86. Sanders, *Mighty Peculiar Elections*, 19–20.

87. See, for instance, Crespino, "Best Defense," 310–11.

88. Wilkinson, *From Brown to Bakke*, 110.

89. David S. Seeley to Hollings, January 20, 1967, box 99, "Topical, 90th, Education, Public School, Desegregation/Civil Rights Compliance, General (1 of 2)," HP.

90. Sanders, *Mighty Peculiar Elections*, 20.

91. Harvey, *Question of Justice*, 126.

92. Ferillo, interview with the author, April 17, 2012.

93. Byrnes, *One Lifetime*, 408.

94. The case was *Levi Pearson v. Clarendon County and School District No. 26*.

95. "Memorandum from Douglas F. Dent, to Senator Ernest F. Hollings, Re: School Desegregation," January 23, 1970, box 117, "Desegregation, General (2 of 2)," HP.

96. Lassiter, *Silent Majority*, 258.

97. "Bussing Votes" [1973], box 170, "Desegregation, Busing," HP.

98. The brief is printed in the *Congressional Record*. See *Congressional Record—Senate*, October 6, 1970, 35139–47. The proposed constitutional amendment was S.J. Res 112.

99. *Congressional Record—Senate*, February 2, 1970, 2075.

100. Hollings to Mrs. Robert R. Bell, December 13, 1967, box 99, "Public School Desegregation/Civil Rights Compliance, General (1 of 2)," HP.

101. "Obey the Law," August 28, 1970, box 82, "Newsletters, 1967–1970," HP.

102. Campbell, *Senator Sam Ervin*, 159–60.

103. Jackson, Markoe, and Markoe, *Scribner Encyclopedia*, 263.

104. Hollings opinion for the Senate floor, "Not Given—Written," October 9, 1970, box 117, "Desegregation, Busing," HP.

105. Speaking of the peaceful desegregation of Clemson in 1963, state senator Edgar Brown recalled that "many of us had determined to do the right thing for law and order," although such peaceful compliance was "contingent upon using up all the courts." See Grose, *South Carolina*, 112.

106. Sanders, *Mighty Peculiar Elections*, 114.

107. Hollings to Mrs. Eleanor C Pope, July 11, 1971, box 117, "'Desegregation, General (1 of 2)," HP.

108. Ferillo, interview with the author, April 17, 2012. After Ferillo challenged the "freedom of choice" wording, Congressman James Mann provided him with a substitute motion to modify the platform's language.

109. "Blacks, Liberals Win Concession," *Charlotte Observer*, March 26, 1970.

110. Sanders, *Mighty Peculiar Elections*, 121.

111. Emily M. deQuincey-Newman, interview with the author, April 17, 2012.

112. Sanders, *Mighty Peculiar Elections*, 129. Here West mirrored Hollings's complaints about HEW as he approached his reelection contest in 1968.

113. Harvey, *Question of Justice*, 127.

114. Sanders, *Mighty Peculiar Elections*, 138.

115. Crespino, *Strom Thurmond's America*, 244. Both Watts and Washington, D.C., were sites of serious urban rioting in 1965 and 1968, respectively.

116. Sanders, *Mighty Peculiar Elections*, 122–23.

117. Harvey, *Question of Justice*, 123.

118. Sanders, *Mighty Peculiar Elections*, 123, 126.

119. "First Negro Vice Chairman Elected by State Democrats," *Greenville (S.C.) News*, March 26, 1970.

120. Crespino, *Strom Thurmond's America*, 238–39.

121. Strom Thurmond to Harry B. Farr, June 5, 1970, box 117, "Desegregation, General (2 of 2)," HP.

122. Hollings to W. F. Poole, September 12, 1971, box 144, "Busing (1 of 5)," HP. See also Hollings to Isobel S. Lawton, May 10, 1971, ibid.

123. Hollings to Mrs. Robert Moxon, February 29, 1972, box 144, "Busing (3 of 5)," HP.

124. "Text of speech delivered by Senator Fritz Hollings, D-S.C., on Senate floor," February 24, 1972, box 144, "Busing (3 of 5)," HP. See also Hollings to Roy Wilkins, October 9, 1972, box 144, "Busing (5 of 5)," HP.

125. For Hollings's support for educational improvement, see, for instance, "The High Cost of Learning," November 23, 1971, box 82, "Newsletters, 1971–1972," HP.

126. Qtd. in H. Hayes Mizell, remarks presented at the symposium "Implementation of *Brown v. Board:* Confronting Reality," Spartanburg Technical College, Spartanburg, S.C., March 23, 2004.

127. Harvey, *Question of Justice*, 127. With slightly different figures, Neal Peirce observed the same trend. See Peirce, *Deep South States*, 395.

128. "H.R. 514, In the Senate of the United States, January 27, 1970," January 27, 1970, box 117, "Desegregation, General (2 of 2)," HP.

129. Hollings to Robert McNair, January 31, 1970, box 117, "Desegregation, General (2 of 2)," HP.

130. Crespino, "Best Defense," 318.

131. "News from the office of Sen. Ernest F. Hollings," "Statement Relating to Co-Sponsorship of two amendments regarding freedom-of-choice school desegregation," January 27, 1970, box 117, "Desegregation, General (2 of 2)," HP.

132. Crespino, "Best Defense," 312.

133. Bullock and Lamb, *Implementation*, 59.

134. "HEW News," January 14, 1971, box 144, "Busing (1 of 5)," HP.

135. Crespino, "Best Defense," 312–13.

136. *Congressional Record—Senate*, March 9, 1970, 6506.

137. See Senate Voting Record, Senate Democratic Policy Committee, nos. 76–81, 93–95, box 594, "91st Congress, 2nd Session," HP.

138. "5-Year Extension of Voting Rights Passed by Senate," *New York Times*, March 14, 1970.

139. Four other southern senators were paired against the bill.

140. Tennessee Republican Howard Baker voted for the bill, while Texas Democrat Ralph Yarborough was recorded as "announced for."

141. Gore and Spong also voted against the nomination of G. Harrold Carswell to the Supreme Court. See *Congressional Record—Senate*, April 8, 1970, 10769. See also Lassiter, *Silent Majority*, 266, 273.

142. Lamis, *Two-Party South*, 353n13.

143. For Ervin's complaints about Nixon's ambiguity on busing, see Campbell, *Senator Sam Ervin*, 229.

144. "Obey the Law," August 28, 1970, box 82, "Newsletters, 1967–1970," HP. See also edited press release, August 21, 1970, box 117, "Busing," HP.

145. Kotlowski, *Nixon's Civil Rights*, 16, 32.

146. Campbell, *Senator Sam Ervin*, 226–27.

147. Kotlowski, *Nixon's Civil Rights*, 28.

148. Ibid., 18, 32.

149. Kalk, *Origins*, 93.

150. Ibid., 94.

151. This follows Kalk's general argument. See ibid., 104.

152. Hollings and Victor, *Making Government Work*, 143. This version of events agrees with Kotlowksi, "Trial by Error," 86n37. Although Dent claimed he suggested Haynsworth to Mitchell, Kotlowski's research uncovered no documentation to support Dent's assertion. Instead he deferred to John P. Frank's *Clement Haynsworth, the Senate and the Supreme Court*. In Frank's account Hollings recommended Haynsworth. In contrast Kalk recorded Thurmond as the prime mover behind the Haynsworth nomination, with Hollings joining him in support later. See Kalk, *Origins*, 94.

153. Crespino, *Strom Thurmond's America*, 234n26.

154. Kalk, *Origins*, 101.

155. Ibid., 95.

156. Ibid., 102.

157. Ibid., 103.

158. Joseph L. Rauh Jr. to Hollings, September 2, 1969, box 127, "Haynsworth, Clement F. Jr., General, Con (1 of 5)," HP.

159. *Congressional Record—Senate*, November 18, 1969, 34567.

160. Ibid., 34553.

161. For Brooke see Kalk, *Origins*, 107, or Edward W. Brooke to Nixon, October 1, 1969, White House Central Files, Subject Files, FG 51 box 3, "Executive FG 51/A

10/1/69-10/31/69," Nixon Library. For Javits see *Congressional Record—Senate*, November 14, 1969, 34275.

162. Kalk, *Origins*, 104–6.

163. *Congressional Record—Senate*, October 7, 1969, 28878–79.

164. Ibid., 28881.

165. Hollings and Victor, *Making Government Work*, 148.

166. Hollings, interview with Andrea L'Hommedieu.

167. *Congressional Record—Senate*, November 18, 1969, 34554.

168. Ibid., 34555.

169. "Vote of 55 to 45 Gives President 1st Major Rebuff," *Washington Post*, November 22, 1969.

170. Kotlowski, "Trial by Error," 76.

171. "Vote of 55 to 45 Gives President 1st Major Rebuff."

172. Nixon, qtd. in Kalk, *Origins*, 111.

173. Kalk, "Carswell Affair," 262.

174. Kalk, *Origins*, 118.

175. Kalk, "Carswell Affair," 270, 273.

176. "CARSWELL NOMINATION" [1970], form letter, box 127, "Judges, Selection and appointment, Supreme Court, Carswell, George Harrold, 1970 (1 of 3)," HP.

177. Memorandum, William E. Timmons for Nixon, White House Central Files, Subject Files, FG 51 box 4, "Executive, FG 51/A 4/1/70-4/14/70," Nixon Library.

178. "Hollings Hesitates," *Charleston (S.C.) News and Courier*, March 22, 1970.

179. Hollings to Profs. Webster Myers Jr., Douglas Q. Wickham, William S. McAninch, and E. D. Wedlock Jr., April 6, 1970, box 127, "Carswell (3 of 3)," HP.

180. *Congressional Record—Senate*, April 6, 1970, 10391.

181. Hollings to Fulton B. Creech, March 24, 1970, box 127, "Carswell (2 of 3)," HP.

182. "Hollings Charges Nation in 'Limbo,'" *Sumter (S.C.) Daily Item*, October 16, 1971.

183. "Hollings Says Wallace Could Win in Florida," *Hendersonville (N.C.) Times-News*, February 2, 1972.

184. "Wallace Analyzed: Middle Course Is Urged in Democratic Politics," *Charleston (S.C.) News and Courier*, March 16, 1972.

185. "Fritz Strongly Critical of Response by Muskie," *Spartanburg (S.C.) Herald-Journal*, March 16, 1972.

186. "Wallace Analyzed," *Charleston (S.C.) News and Courier*, March 16, 1972.

187. Carter, *Politics of Rage*, 425.

188. On the religious overtones of Wallace's campaigning during the 1972 Florida primary, an Associated Press reporter claimed that a Wallace rally appeared "more like a revival than a political appearance." Ibid., 424.

189. On school prayer see, for instance, *Congressional Record—Senate*, February 6, 1967, 2666; *Congressional Record—Senate*, January 15, 1969, 771; "Classroom Prayer; Supreme Court's Decisions Have Been Much Maligned," *Chicago Tribune*, January 2, 1982; "A Magna Carta for Smut," October 16, 1970, as found in "Fritz Hollings: In His Own Words," HP.

190. Hollings, interview with Terry, December 10, 1990, SCPC.

191. Dyckman, *Reubin O'D. Askew*, 142.

192. "Hollings Candid on Dixie Outlook," *Sumter (S.C.) Daily Item*, August 12, 1972.

193. "Campaign Has Quirks Difficult to Believe," *Charleston (S.C.) News and Courier*, October 8, 1972.

194. Hollings to William R. Watkins Jr., July 20, 1972, box 621, "Campaigns, 1972, Presidential Race, McGovern, George and Sargent Shriver," HP. See also Hollings to Buddy Spivey, July 20, 1972; Hollings to Ruth Watt, August 1, 1972, ibid.

195. For examples of Hollings attacking Nixon over his approach to textiles, see "Here we go again," August 8, 1969; "Foreign Policy—Unemployment in South Carolina," March 1970; "Textile Jobs—What *Can* Be Done," April 8, 1970; "Let's Get a Textile Bill—Now," September 25, 1970; "The Textile Truth," October 8, 1970; "Better Late than Never," October 25, 1971, box 82, "Newsletters, 1971–1972," HP.

196. "Hollings Reports to South Carolina," June 1972, box 82, "Newsletters, 1971–1972," HP.

197. See, for instance, Hollings to Joseph T. Newton III, July 21, 1972; Hollings to Lera Davis, August 1, 1972; Hollings to Burton R. Schools, July 24, 1972, box 621, "McGovern," HP.

198. Robert G. Liming, "Hollings: Nixon Will Win Easily," clipping, November 7, 1972, box 622, "1974, Publicity, Published Materials," HP.

199. Memorandum, June 13, 1973, box 621, "Campaigns, 1974, General," HP; memorandum "To: Senator, From: Mike Copps," January 10, 1974.

200. Herblock, "Anybody in Sight Yet?" *Columbia (S.C.) State*, October 8, 1973.

201. "Memo to Senator from Patty," April 5, 1974, box 622, "Campaigns, 1974, Persons, Bush, Gwen," HP.

202. "Gwen Bush Challenges Hollings 'Labor Stand,'" *Charleston (S.C.) News and Courier*, August 15, 1974.

203. Gwen Bush, speech text, July 8, 1974, box 622, "Bush," HP.

204. "Mrs. Bush Runs Spartan Drive to Oust Hollings from Senate," *Greenwood (S.C.) Index-Journal*, October 26, 1974.

205. Lamis, *Two-Party South*, 352.

206. Memorandum "To: Senator, From: Mike Copps," January 10, 1974.

207. "A study of voter attitudes in South Carolina regarding Senator Fritz Hollings," September–October 1973, box 622, "1974, Voter Research + Polls, Kraft Polls, Hollings, Ernest F., September 1973," HP.

208. Memorandum "To: Senator, From: Mike Copps," January 10, 1974.

Epilogue

1. Cohodas, *Strom Thurmond*, 425–26.

2. Hollings, interview with the author, August 28, 2013.

3. *Congressional Record—Senate*, July 23, 1975, 24336, 24233–34.

4. *Congressional Record—Senate*, July 24, 1975, 24780. Here "southern" describes the eleven former Confederate states.

5. *Congressional Record—Senate*, July 24, 1975, 24770–71.

6. "Dole Compromise Voting Rights Act Signed by President Reagan," press release, June 29, 1982, Robert J. Dole Archive and Special Collections, University of Kansas, http://dolearchive.ku.edu/collections/archives/_files/820629com.pdf (accessed June 25, 2013).

7. Cohodas, *Strom Thurmond*, 475.

8. *Congressional Record—Senate*, June 16, 1982, 13792–93. See also Cohodas, *Strom Thurmond*, 476.

9. Cohodas, *Strom Thurmond*, 480.

10. Ibid., 478.

11. "McGovern Sees Hollings as Presidential Timber," *Charleston (S.C.) News and Courier*, December 6, 1970.

12. Memo to: EFH, RE: Vice Presidency, From: John, January 19, 1971, box 620, "1971, Democratic Party, Democratic National Committee," HP.

13. See box 622, "1975, Hollings' Possible 1976 Presidential Campaign," HP.

14. "Democrat Greeted in Capital; Carter Visits Columbia," *Charleston (S.C.) News and Courier*, October 27, 1976.

15. "Byrd's Rivals Discuss Joint Effort to Bar Him from Leadership Job," *New York Times*, December 10, 1976.

16. "Hollings Quits Senate Leader Race—Byrd Is Favorite over Humphrey," *New York Times*, December 13, 1976.

17. Shapiro, *Last Great Senate*, 6.

18. Ibid., 177, 182.

19. Thomas Terrill, conversation with the author, January 28, 2013.

20. Minchin, "Uphill Fight," 195.

21. Ibid., 202.

22. Cook, interview with the author, April 13, 2012.

23. McLeese, interview with the author, February 21, 2012.

24. Cook, interview with the author, April 13, 2012.

25. Minchin, "Uphill Fight," 200–204.

26. "U.S. Senator Fritz Hollings South Carolina Democrat," folder 1, HCP.

27. "Deficit Reduction: A Love Story; I Want a Divorce," *New York Times*, October 25, 1989.

28. Statement of Candidacy, Senator Fritz Hollings, Midlands Technical College, Columbia, S.C, April 18, 1983, folder 3, HCP.

29. "Reagan Policy Taking Food from Hungry, Hollings Says," *Charleston (S.C.) News and Courier*, August 5, 1983.

30. Hollings, interview, *MacNeil-Lehrer Report*, June 1983, folder 4, HCP.

31. "And Now There Are Six," *Time*, May 2, 1983; "Political Discussion," C-Span video.

32. "The Insider's Candidate: He May Think Better than Mondale or Glenn, and He's a Very Good Senator, but Who's Going to Vote for Him?" *Washingtonian*, December 1983, Folder 7, HCP.

33. See "Reject Polls, Elect Hollings," *Manchester (N.H.) Journal*, February 8, 1984, Folder 7, HCP; "Our Choice Is Hollings," *Claremont (N.H.) Eagle Times*, February 5, 1984, ibid.

34. For instance in 1958 Gore proposed a "full employment bill." See Longley, *Senator Albert Gore*, 141. For Gore's and Johnson's belief in New Deal–style measures, see also Badger, *New Deal/New South*, 182–83.

35. "Stability of State Government" [1956], speech, box 686, "Topical, Hoover Commission, 1955–56," HP.

36. *Congressional Record—Senate*, December 20, 2004, 12093.

37. Novak, "Myth," 753.

38. Copps, interview with Hartsook, August 22, 1996.

39. John Seigenthaler, interview with Tony Badger, February 6, 2003.

40. Historians Lacy K. Ford and Richard Phillip Stone II argued that "the Palmetto State needs to refashion the state development strategy in a manner similar to the remodelling done by the Hollings administration over forty-odd years ago, a refashioning that involved improving the quality of the state as a development 'product' and not simply efforts to package more attractively the same old flawed product." "Economic Development," 44.

41. On the exodus of "low-wage, labor-intensive industries" from the South in the late twentieth century, see Cobb, *South and America*, 209–10.

42. Ford and Stone, "Economic Development," 19, 34, 39.

43. Minchin, "Uphill Fight," 188–89.

44. Minchin, *Hiring the Black Worker*, 48; Ford and Stone, "Economic Development," 28.

45. Cobb, *South and America*, 210.

46. *Census of Population: 1970*, 127; *Census of Population: 1980*, 817–19.

47. During Hollings's brief presidential campaign in 1984, Peatsy declared her opposition to a tax exemption for private schools and asserted that "public schools should be the main concern of this nation because they teach different types of people how to live with each other." "Peatsy Hollings, Wife of Former Sen. Fritz Hollings, Dies at 77," *Charleston (S.C.) Post and Courier*, October 15, 2012.

48. Ford and Stone, "Economic Development," 40.

49. "S.C. Supreme Court Finds for Poor Districts in 20-Year-Old School Equity Suit," *Columbia (S.C.) State*, November 12, 2014.

50. *Abbeville County School District, et al., v. The State of South Carolina, et al.*, South Carolina Supreme Court, Opinion no. 27466, November 12, 2014.

51. "Hollings Makes a Grand Gesture to Charleston—and American—History," *Charleston (S.C.) Post and Courier*, March 15, 2015.

Bibliography

Archival Sources

South Carolina Political Collections, University of South Carolina, Columbia

Ernest F. "Fritz" Hollings Papers

Robert E. McNair Papers

George Bell Timmerman Jr. Papers

William D. Workman Jr. Papers

South Carolina Department of Archives and History, Columbia

Ernest F. "Fritz" Hollings Gubernatorial Records

George Bell Timmerman Jr. Gubernatorial Records

South Caroliniana Library, University of South Carolina, Columbia

South Carolina Council on Human Relations Records

South Carolina State Library, Columbia

South Carolina State Development Board, Annual Reports, 1955–63

1961 Report of Committee Studying the Needs of the State Development Board on the Subject of Vocational and Technical Training

Report of Joint Committee Surveying the Needs of the South Carolina State Development Board, 1959

Citadel Archives, Charleston, South Carolina

Ernest Hollings Papers, 1983–1984

Lyndon Baines Johnson Presidential Library and Museum, Austin, Texas

White House Central Files, Lyndon B. Johnson Papers

White House Central Files Name File, Lyndon B. Johnson Papers

John F. Kennedy Presidential Library and Museum, Boston, Massachusetts

White House Central Name File, John F. Kennedy Papers

Richard Nixon Presidential Library and Museum, Yorba Linda California

White House Central Files

White House Special Files

Online Material

Bass, Jack. Paper presented at the "Art of Political Biography" panel, University of South Carolina, January 22, 2013. http://www.youtube.com/watch?v=JDWMSf_W150 (accessed February 1, 2013).

Coles, Robert and Harry Huge. "Strom Thurmond Country." *New Republic*, November 30, 1968. https://newrepublic.com/article/99653/strom-thurmond-south-carolina-poverty (accessed June 27, 2016).

Edelman, Peter B. Oral history interview with Larry Hackman, March 13, 1974, Robert F. Kennedy Library Oral History Program. http://www.jfklibrary.org/Asset-Viewer/Archives/RFKOH-PBE-08.aspx (accessed September 17, 2013).

Freeman, Orville. Oral History Interview IV, November 17, 1988, by Michael L. Gillette, Internet Copy, LBJ Library. http://www.lbjlib.utexas.edu/johnson/archives.hom/oralhistory.hom/freeman/freeman%20web%204.pdf (accessed June 15, 2013).

"Fritz Hollings: In His Own Words." Documents from the papers of Ernest F. "Fritz" Hollings at the South Carolina Political Collections, University of South Carolina, Columbia. http://library.sc.edu/digital/collections/hollings.html (accessed September 17, 2013).

Hollings, Ernest F. Interview with Andrea L'Hommedieu, June 20, 2012. George J. Mitchell Oral History Project. http://digitalcommons.bowdoin.edu/mitchelloralhistory/200/ (accessed June 17, 2013).

Kestenbaum, Lawrence. "U.S. District Attorneys in South Carolina." http://politicalgraveyard.com/geo/S.C./ofc/usatty.html (accessed February 12, 2013).

"Modjeska Monteith Simkins: In Her Own Words." Documents from the papers of Modjeska Monteith Simkins at the South Carolina Political Collections, University of South Carolina, Columbia. http://library.sc.edu/digital/collections/simkins.html (accessed November 10, 2015).

"Political Discussion." C-Span, February 23, 1984. http://www.c-spanvideo.org/program/PoliticalDiscussion127 (accessed April 15, 2013).

Ph.D. Dissertations

Brown, Millicent Ellison. "Civil Rights Activism in Charleston, South Carolina, 1940–1970." Florida State University, 1997.

Cox, Maxie Myron. "1963—The Year of Decision: Desegregation in South Carolina." University of South Carolina, 1996.

Stone, Richard Phillip, II. "Making a Modern State: The Politics of Economic Development in South Carolina, 1938–1962." University of South Carolina, 2003.

White, John. "Managed Compliance: White Resistance and Desegregation in South Carolina, 1950–1970." University of Florida, 2006.

Published Sources

Arsenault, Raymond. *Freedom Riders: 1961 and the Struggle for Racial Justice.* Oxford and New York: Oxford University Press, 2006.

Badger, Tony. "From Defiance to Moderation: South Carolina Governors and Racial Change." In *Toward the Meeting of the Waters: Currents in the Civil Rights Movement of South Carolina during the Twentieth Century,* edited by Winfred B. Moore Jr. and Orville Vernon Burton, 3–21. Columbia: University of South Carolina Press, 2008.

———. *New Deal/New South: An Anthony J. Badger Reader.* Fayetteville: University of Arkansas Press, 2007.

Barone, Michael, and Richard E. Cohen. *Almanac of American Politics, 2004: The Senators, the Representatives, and the Governors: Their Records and Election Results, Their States and Districts.* Washington, D.C.: National Journal, 2003.

Bartley, Numan V. *The Rise of Massive Resistance: Race and Politics in the South during the 1950's.* Baton Rouge: Louisiana State University Press, 1969.

———. *The New South, 1945–1980.* Baton Rouge: Louisiana State University Press, 1995.

Bass, Jack. "Hunger? Let Them Eat Magnolias." In *You Can't Eat Magnolias,* edited by H. Brandt Ayers and Thomas H. Naylor, 273–83. New York: McGraw-Hill, 1972.

Bass, Jack, and Marilyn W. Thompson. *Ol' Strom: An Unauthorized Biography of Strom Thurmond.* Atlanta: Longstreet, 1998.

———. *Strom: The Complicated Personal and Political Life of Strom Thurmond.* New York: Public Affairs, 2005.

Bass, Jack, and W. Scott Poole. *The Palmetto State: The Making of Modern South Carolina.* Columbia: University of South Carolina Press, 2009.

Bass, Jack, and Walter De Vries. *The Transformation of Southern Politics: Social Change and Political Consequence since 1945.* New York: Basic Books, 1976.

Bast, Kirk K. "'As Different as Heaven and Hell': The Desegregation of Clemson College." *Proceedings of the South Carolina Historical Association* (1994): 38–44.

Bedingfield, Sid. "Partisan Journalism and the Rise of the Republican Party in South Carolina, 1959–1962." *Journalism and Mass Communication Quarterly* 20 (10), published online January 10, 2013: 1–18. http://jmq.sagepub.com/content/early/2013/01/10/1077699012468697.

Berry, Jeffrey M. *Feeding Hungry People: Rulemaking in the Food Stamp Program.* New Brunswick: Rutgers University Press, 1984.

Black, Earl, and Merle Black. *Politics and Society in the South.* Cambridge, Mass.: Harvard University Press, 1987.

———. *Southern Governors and Civil Rights: Racial Segregation as a Campaign Issue in the Second Reconstruction.* Cambridge, Mass.: Harvard University Press, 1976.

Brooks, Jennifer E. "Winning the Peace: Georgia Veterans and the Struggle to Define the Political Legacy of World War II." *Journal of Southern History* 66, no. 3 (2000): 563–604.

Bullock, Charles S., III, and Charles M. Lamb. *Implementation of Civil Rights Policy.* Monterey: Brooks/Cole, 1984.

Burton, Orville Vernon. "'The Black Squint of the Law': Racism in South Carolina." In *The Meaning of South Carolina History: Essays in Honor of George C. Rogers, Jr.*, edited by David R. Chesnutt, and Clyde Norman Wilson, 161–85. Columbia: University of South Carolina Press, 1991.

———. "Dining with Harvey Gantt: Myth and Realities of 'Integration with Dignity.'" In *Matthew J. Perry: The Man, His Times, and His Legacy,* edited by W. Lewis Burke and Belinda F. Gergel, 183–220. Columbia: University of South Carolina Press, 2004.

Burton, Orville Vernon, Beatrice Burton, and Simon Appleford. "Seeds in Unlikely Soil: The *Briggs v. Elliott* School Segregation Case." In *Toward the Meeting of the Waters: Currents in the Civil Rights Movement of South Carolina during the Twentieth Century,* edited by Winfred B. Moore Jr. and Orville Vernon Burton, 176–200. Columbia: University of South Carolina Press, 2008.

Burton, Orville Vernon, Terence R. Finnegan, Peyton McCrary, and James W. Loewen. "South Carolina." In *Quiet Revolution in the South: The Impact of the Voting Rights Act, 1965–1990,* edited by Chandler Davidson, and Bernard Grofman, 191–232. Princeton: Princeton University Press, 1994.

Byrnes, James F. *All in One Lifetime.* New York: Harper, 1958.

Campbell, Karl E. *Senator Sam Ervin, Last of the Founding Fathers.* Chapel Hill: University of North Carolina Press, 2007.

Canup, Claude R., and William D. Workman, Jr. *Charles E. Daniel, His Philosophy and Legacy.* Columbia: Bryan, 1981.

Carter, Dan T. *From George Wallace to Newt Gingrich: Race in the Conservative Counterrevolution, 1963–1994.* Baton Rouge: Louisiana State University Press, 1996.

———. *The Politics of Rage: George Wallace, the Origins of the New Conservatism, and the Transformation of American Politics.* New York: Simon & Schuster, 1995.

Catsam, Derek Charles. "Into the Maw of Dixie: The Freedom Rides, the Civil Rights Movement, and the Politics of Race in South Carolina." *Proceedings of the South Carolina Historical Association* (2005): 1–20.

Cauthen, John K. *Speaker Blatt, His Challenges Were Greater.* 2nd ed. Columbia: University of South Carolina Press, 1978.

Cobb, James C. *Industrialization and Southern Society, 1877–1984.* Lexington: University Press of Kentucky, 1984.

———. *The Selling of the South: The Southern Crusade for Industrial Development, 1936–1980.* Baton Rouge: Louisiana State University Press, 1982.

———. *The South and America since World War II.* New York: Oxford University Press, 2011.

Cohodas, Nadine. *Strom Thurmond and the Politics of Southern Change.* Macon, Ga.: Mercer University Press, 1994.

Cox, Maxie Myron. "'Integration with [Relative] Dignity': The Desegregation of Clemson College and George McMillan's Article at Forty." In *Toward the Meeting of the Waters: Currents in the Civil Rights Movement of South Carolina during the Twentieth Century,* edited by Winfred B. Moore Jr. and Orville Vernon Burton, 274–85. Columbia: University of South Carolina Press, 2008.

Cramer, M. Richard. "School Desegregation and New Industry: The Southern Community Leaders' Viewpoint." *Social Forces* 41, no. 4 (1963): 384–89.

Crespino, Joseph. "The Best Defense Is a Good Offense: The Stennis Amendment and the Fracturing of Liberal School Desegregation Policy, 1964–1972." *Journal of Policy History* 18, no. 3 (2006): 304–25.

———. *In Search of Another Country: Mississippi and the Conservative Counterrevolution.* Princeton: Princeton University Press, 2007.

———. *Strom Thurmond's America.* New York: Hill & Wang, 2012.

Cunningham, David. *Klansville, U.S.A.: The Rise and Fall of the Civil Rights–Era Ku Klux Klan.* Oxford and New York: Oxford University Press, 2013.

Davies, Gareth. *From Opportunity to Entitlement: The Transformation and Decline of Great Society Liberalism.* Lawrence: University Press of Kansas, 1996.

Davis, Michael D., and Hunter R. Clark. *Thurgood Marshall: Warrior at the Bar, Rebel on the Bench.* New York: Carol, 1992.

Dyckman, Martin A. *Reubin O'D. Askew and the Golden Age of Florida Politics.* Gainesville: University Press of Florida, 2011.

Edgar, Walter B. *South Carolina: A History.* Columbia: University of South Carolina Press, 1998.

Ehrenhalt, Alan, and Robert Healy. *Politics in America: Members of Congress in Washington and at Home.* Washington, D.C.: Congressional Quarterly Press, 1982.

Eisinger, Peter K. *Toward an End to Hunger in America.* Washington, D.C.: Brookings Institution Press, 1998.

Felder, James L. *Civil Rights in South Carolina: From Peaceful Protests to Groundbreaking Rulings.* Charleston: History Press, 2012.

Finegold, Kenneth. "Agriculture and the Politics of U.S. Social Provision: Social Insurance and Food Stamps." In *The Politics of Social Policy in the United States,* edited by Margaret Weir, Ann Shola Orloff, et al., 199–234. Princeton: Princeton University Press, 1988.

Fink, Leon. "Union Power, Soul Power: The Story of 1199B and Labor's Search for A Southern Strategy." *Southern Changes* 5, no. 2 (1983): 9–20.

Foley, Michael. *The New Senate: Liberal Influence on a Conservative Institution, 1959–1972.* New Haven: Yale University Press, 1980.

Folwell, Emma. "The Legacy of the Child Development Group of Mississippi: White Opposition to Head Start in Mississippi, 1965–1972." *Journal of Mississippi History* (forthcoming).

Ford, Lacy K., and Richard Phillip Stone II. "Economic Development and Globalization in South Carolina." *Southern Cultures* 13, no. 1 (2007): 18–50.

Frederickson, Kari A. *Cold War Dixie: Militarization and Modernization in the American South.* Athens: University of Georgia Press, 2013.

———. *The Dixiecrat Revolt and the End of the Solid South, 1932–1968.* Chapel Hill: University of North Carolina Press, 2001.

Fry, Joseph A., *Debating Vietnam: Fulbright, Stennis, and their Senate Hearings.* Lanham, Md.: Rowman & Littlefield, 2006.

———. *Dixie Looks Abroad: The South and U.S. Foreign Relations, 1789–1973.* Baton Rouge: Louisiana State University Press, 2002.

Green, Laurie B. "Saving Babies in Memphis: The Politics of Race, Health, and Hunger during the War on Poverty." In *The War on Poverty: A New Grassroots History, 1964–1980,* edited by Annelise Orleck and Lisa Gayle Hazirjian, 133–58. Athens: University of Georgia Press, 2011.

Goldfield, David R. *Cotton Fields and Skyscrapers: Southern City and Region, 1607–1980.* Baton Rouge: Louisiana State University Press, 1982.

Gould, Lewis L. *The Most Exclusive Club: A History of the Modern United States Senate.* New York: Basic Books, 2005.

Grose, Philip G. *Looking for Utopia: The Life and Times of John C. West.* Columbia: University of South Carolina Press, 2011.

———. *South Carolina at the Brink: Robert McNair and the Politics of Civil Rights.* Columbia: University of South Carolina Press, 2006.

Harvey, Gordon E. *A Question of Justice: New South Governors and Education, 1968–1976.* Tuscaloosa: University of Alabama Press, 2002.

Hayes, J. I. *South Carolina and the New Deal.* Columbia: University of South Carolina Press, 2001.

Hays, Samuel P., and Barbara D. Hays. *Beauty, Health, and Permanence: Environmental Politics in the United States, 1955–1985.* Cambridge and New York: Cambridge University Press, 1987.

Hearings before the Select Committee on Nutrition and Human Needs of the United States Senate, Ninetieth Congress, Second Session and Ninety-first Congress, First Session on Nutrition and Human Needs, Part 4—South Carolina. Washington, D.C.: U.S. Government Printing Office, 1969.

Hine, William C. "Civil Rights and Campus Wrongs: South Carolina State College Students Protest, 1955–1968," *South Carolina Historical Magazine* 97, no. 4 (1996): 310–31.

Hollings, Ernest F. *The Case against Hunger: A Demand for a National Policy*. New York: Cowles, 1970.

Hollings, Ernest F., and Kirk Victor. *Making Government Work*. Columbia: University of South Carolina Press, 2008.

Jackson, Kenneth T., Arnie Markoe, and Karen Markoe, eds. *The Scribner Encyclopedia of American Lives Vol. 1, 1981–1985*. New York: Scribner, 1998.

Johnson, Robert David. *Congress and the Cold War*. New York: Cambridge University Press, 2006.

Johnston, Joyce. "Communism vs. Segregation: Evolution of the Committee to Investigate Communist Activities in South Carolina." *Proceedings of the South Carolina Historical Association* (1993): 19–29.

Kalk, Bruce H. "The Carswell Affair: The Politics of a Supreme Court Nomination in the Nixon Administration." *American Journal of Legal History* 42, no. 3 (1998): 261–87.

———. *The Origins of the Southern Strategy: Two-Party Competition in South Carolina, 1950–1972*. Lanham, Md.: Lexington Books, 2001.

Kalman, Laura. *Abe Fortas: A Biography*. New Haven: Yale University Press, 1990.

Katz, Michael B. *The Undeserving Poor: From the War on Poverty to the War on Welfare*. New York: Pantheon Books, 1989.

Katznelson, Ira. *When Affirmative Action Was White: An Untold History of Racial Inequality in Twentieth-Century America*. New York: Norton, 2005.

Key, Vladimir O., Jr. *Southern Politics in State and Nation*. New York: Knopf, 1949.

King, Ronald Frederick. *Budgeting Entitlements: The Politics of Food Stamps*. Washington, D.C.: Georgetown University Press, 2000.

Kornbluh, Felicia. "Food as a Civil Right: Hunger, Work, and Welfare in the South after the Civil Rights Act." *Labor: Studies in Working-Class History of the Americas* 12, no. 1–2 (2015): 135–58. doi:10.1215/15476715-2837640.

———. "Who Shot FAP? The Nixon Welfare Plan and the Transformation of American Politics." *The Sixties: A Journal of History, Politics and Culture* 1, no. 2 (2008): 125–50.

Kotlowski, Dean J. *Nixon's Civil Rights: Politics, Principle, and Policy*. Cambridge, Mass.: Harvard University Press, 2001.

———. "Trial by Error: Nixon, the Senate, and the Haynsworth Nomination." *Presidential Studies Quarterly* 26, no. 1 (1996): 71–91.

Kotz, Nick. *Let Them Eat Promises: The Politics of Hunger in America*. Englewood Cliffs, N.J.: Prentice-Hall, 1969.

Kruse, Kevin Michael. *White Flight: Atlanta and the Making of Modern Conservatism*. Princeton: Princeton University Press, 2005.

Kuzenski, John C. "South Carolina: The Heart of GOP Realignment in the South." In *The New Politics of the Old South*, edited by Charles S. Bullock III and Mark J. Rozell, 25–47. Lanham, Md.: Rowman & Littlefield, 1998.

Lamis, Alexander P. "The Future of Southern Politics: New Directions for Dixie." In *The Future South: A Historical Perspective for the Twenty-First Century*, edited by Joe P. Dunn and Howard L. Preston, 49–80. Urbana and Chicago: University of Illinois Press, 1991.

———. *The Two-Party South*. 2nd ed. New York: Oxford University Press, 1990.

Lassiter, Matthew D. *The Silent Majority: Suburban Politics in the Sunbelt South.* Princeton: Princeton University Press, 2007.

Lawson, Steven F. *Black Ballots: Voting Rights in the South, 1944–1969.* New York: Columbia University Press, 1976.

Lau, Peter F. *Democracy Rising: South Carolina and the Fight for Black Equality since 1865.* Lexington: University Press of Kentucky, 2006.

Levine, Susan. *School Lunch Politics: The Surprising History of America's Favorite Welfare Program.* Princeton and Oxford: Princeton University Press, 2008.

Longley, Kyle. *Senator Albert Gore, Sr.: Tennessee Maverick.* Baton Rouge: Louisiana State University Press, 2004.

Lowe, Stephen. "Grass Roots and Marble Columns: Civil Rights, Public Accommodations and South Carolina Federal Courts, 1955–1966." *Proceedings of the South Carolina Historical Association* (2000): 27–42.

Luebke, Paul. *Tar Heel Politics 2000.* Chapel Hill: University of North Carolina Press, 1998.

MacDonald, Maurice. *Food, Stamps, and Income Maintenance.* New York: Academic Press, 1977.

Maunula, Marko. *Guten Tag, Y'all: Globalization and the South Carolina Piedmont, 1950–2000.* Athens: University of Georgia Press, 2009.

McGovern, George. "The Politics of Hunger." In *Congress and Conscience*, edited by John B. Anderson, 55–72. Philadelphia and New York: Lippincott, 1970.

McMillen, Neil R. *The Citizens' Council: Organized Resistance to the Second Reconstruction, 1954–64.* 2nd ed. Urbana: University of Illinois Press, 1994.

Meier, August, and Mark Fox, eds. *Papers of the NAACP* Frederick, Md.: University Publications of America, 1982.

Merchant, Carolyn. *American Environmental History: An Introduction.* New York: Columbia University Press, 2007.

Merritt, Russell. "The Senatorial Election of 1962 and the Rise of Two-Party Politics in South Carolina." *South Carolina Historical Magazine* 98, no. 3 (1997): 281–301.

Minchin, Timothy J. *Hiring the Black Worker: The Racial Integration of the Southern Textile Industry, 1960–1980.* Chapel Hill: University of North Carolina Press, 1999.

———. "An Uphill Fight: Ernest F. Hollings and the Struggle to Protect the South Carolina Textile Industry, 1959–2005." *South Carolina Historical Magazine* 109, no. 3 (2008): 187–211.

Moore, Robert J. "The Civil Rights Advocate." In *Matthew J. Perry: The Man, His Times, and His Legacy*, edited by W. Lewis Burke and Belinda F. Gergel, 155–82. Columbia: University of South Carolina Press, 2004.

Moynihan, Daniel P. *The Politics of a Guaranteed Income: The Nixon Administration and the Family Assistance Plan.* New York: Vintage Books, 1973.

Newby, Idus A. *Black Carolinians: A History of Blacks in South Carolina from 1895 to 1968.* Columbia: University of South Carolina Press, 1973.

Nominations of Abe Fortas and Homer Thornberry, Hearings before the Committee on the Judiciary United States Senate Ninetieth Congress, Second session . . . July 11, 12, 16, 17, 18, 19, 20, 22, and 23, 1968. Washington, D.C.: U.S. Government Printing Office, 1968.

Novak, William J. "The Myth of the 'Weak' American State." *American Historical Review* 113, no. 3 (2008): 752–72.

Patterson, James T. *America's Struggle against Poverty in the Twentieth Century.* Cambridge, Mass.: Harvard University Press, 2003.

———. *Grand Expectations: The United States, 1945–1974.* New York and Oxford: Oxford University Press, 1996.

Peirce, Neal R. *The Deep South States of America: People, Politics, and Power in the Seven Deep South States.* New York: Norton, 1974.

Quint, Howard H. *Profile in Black and White: A Frank Portrait of South Carolina.* Washington, D.C.: Public Affairs Press, 1958.

Rae, Nicol C. *Southern Democrats.* New York: Oxford University Press, 1994.

Renick, Timothy D. "Solomon Blatt: 'A Segregationist in Moderation'?" *Proceedings of the South Carolina Historical Association* (1991): 61–68.

Robertson, David. *Sly and Able: A Political Biography of James F. Byrnes.* New York: Norton, 1994.

Sanders, Donald Randy. *Mighty Peculiar Elections: The New South Gubernatorial Campaigns of 1970 and the Changing Politics of Race.* Gainesville: University Press of Florida, 2002.

Schulman, Bruce J. *From Cotton Belt to Sunbelt: Federal Policy, Economic Development, and the Transformation of the South, 1938–1980.* Durham, N.C.: Duke University Press, 1994.

Shapiro, Ira S. *The Last Great Senate: Courage and Statesmanship in Times of Crisis.* New York: Public Affairs, 2012.

Shermer, Elizabeth Tandy. "'Take Government out of Business by Putting Business into Government': Local Boosters, National CEOs, Experts, and the Politics of Midcentury Capital Mobility." In *What's Good for Business: Business and American Politics since World War II,* edited by Kim Phillips-Fein and Julian E. Zelizer, 91–106. New York: Oxford University Press, 2012.

Simon, Bryant. *A Fabric of Defeat: The Politics of South Carolina Millhands, 1910–1948.* Chapel Hill: University of North Carolina Press, 1998.

———. "Race Reactions: African American Organizing, Liberalism, and White Working-Class Politics in Postwar South Carolina." In *Jumpin' Jim Crow: Southern Politics from Civil War to Civil Rights,* edited by Jane Elizabeth Daily, Glenda Elizabeth Gilmore, and Bryant Simon, 239–59. Princeton: Princeton University Press, 2000.

Sproat, John G. "'Firm Flexibility': Perspectives on Desegregation in South Carolina." In *New Perspectives on Race and Slavery in America: Essays in Honor of Kenneth M. Stampp,* edited by Kenneth M. Stampp, Robert H. Abzug, et al., 164–84. Lexington: University Press of Kentucky, 1986.

Suggs, Lewis H. "Harvey Gantt and the Desegregation of Clemson University, 1960–1963." In *Integration with Dignity: A Celebration of Harvey Gantt's Admission to Clemson,* edited by Skip Eisiminger, 15–42. Clemson, S.C.: Clemson University Digital Press, 2003.

Synnott, Marcia G. "Crusaders and Clubwomen: Alice Norwood Spearman Wright and Her Women's Network." In *Throwing Off the Cloak of Privilege: White Southern Women Activists in the Civil Rights Era,* edited by Gail S. Murray, 49–76. Gainesville: University Press of Florida, 2004.

———. "Desegregation in South Carolina, 1950–1963: Sometime 'Between "Now" and "Never."'" In *Looking South: Chapters in the Story of an American Region,* edited by Winfred B. Moore Jr. and Joseph F. Tripp, 51–64. New York: Greenwood, 1989.

———. "Federalism Vindicated: University Desegregation in South Carolina and Alabama, 1962–1963." *Journal of Policy History* 1, no. 3 (1989): 292–318.

Tyson, Timothy B. "Dynamite and 'The Silent South': A Story from the Second Reconstruction in South Carolina." In *Jumpin' Jim Crow: Southern Politics from Civil War to Civil Rights*, edited by Jane Elizabeth Dailey, Glenda Elizabeth Gilmore, and Bryant Simon, 275–97. Princeton: Princeton University Press, 2000.

Walker, Anders. *The Ghost of Jim Crow: How Southern Moderates Used Brown v. Board of Education to Stall Civil Rights*. Oxford and New York: Oxford University Press, 2009.

West, John Carl. "Comments." In *Toward the Meeting of the Waters: Currents in the Civil Rights Movement of South Carolina during the Twentieth Century*, edited by Winfred B. Moore Jr. and Orville Vernon Burton, 27–28. Columbia: University of South Carolina Press, 2008.

White, John W. "Race, Grassroots Activism, and the Evolution of the Republican Right in South Carolina, 1952–1974." In *Painting Dixie Red: When, Where, Why, and How the South Became Republican*, edited by Glenn Feldman, 138–71. Gainesville: University Press of Florida, 2011.

Wilkinson, J. Harvie. *From Brown to Bakke: The Supreme Court and School Integration, 1954–1978*. New York: Oxford University Press, 1979.

Woods, Barbara A. "Modjeska Simkins and the South Carolina Conference of the NAACP, 1939–1957." In *Women in the Civil Rights Movement: Trailblazers and Torchbearers, 1941–1965*, edited by Vicki L. Crawford, Jacqueline Anne Rouse, and Barbara Woods, 99–120. Bloomington and Indianapolis: Indiana University Press, 1993.

Woods, Jeff. *Richard B. Russell: Southern Nationalism and American Foreign Policy*. Lanham, Md.: Rowman & Littlefield, 2007.

Workman, William D., Jr. *The Case for the South*. New York: Devin-Adair, 1960.

Zeigler, Eugene N. *When Conscience and Power Meet: A Memoir*. Columbia: University of South Carolina Press, 2008.

Index

About the Author

DAVID T. BALLANTYNE is a lecturer in American history at Keele University in the United Kingdom. He holds Ph.D., M.Phil., and M.A. degrees from the University of Cambridge and has previously worked as a postdoctoral researcher at Leiden University in the Netherlands.